John Russell Bartlett

Bibliography of Rhode Island

John Russell Bartlett

Bibliography of Rhode Island

ISBN/EAN: 9783337379094

Printed in Europe, USA, Canada, Australia, Japan

Cover: Foto ©ninafisch / pixelio.de

More available books at **www.hansebooks.com**

BIBLIOGRAPHY OF RHODE ISLAND.

A CATALOGUE

OF

BOOKS AND OTHER PUBLICATIONS

RELATING TO THE

STATE OF RHODE ISLAND,

WITH NOTES,

HISTORICAL, BIOGRAPHICAL AND CRITICAL.

BY JOHN RUSSELL BARTLETT.

PROVIDENCE:
ALFRED ANTHONY, PRINTER TO THE STATE.
1864.

ONE HUNDRED AND FIFTY COPIES PRINTED.

THE plan of this Bibliography, is to give the title of every printed book and pamphlet that relates, in any way, to the State of Rhode Island. Among these are classes of books that may not directly relate to its history, yet relate to men who have been prominent in its annals, who have rendered distinguished service in public life, or who, by their virtuous and good deeds, deserve to be remembered. Thus Funeral Sermons, as they generally relate to men who have left an impress upon society, are mentioned. Discourses at the Ordination of Ministers, and those at the Consecration of Churches. Addresses before Literary, Scientific, Religious, Agricultural, Mechanical and Temperance Societies, Fourth of July Orations, Political Addresses; all these relate, more or less, to persons or things in the State, or to its Institutions, and hence deserve to be mentioned in a list of books appertaining to the State. Then our venerable institution of learning, Brown University, now in the hundredth year of its existence, deserves as full mention as we can give it. Every book and pamphlet, therefore, relating to the Institution is mentioned. This list includes every Oration, Address, and Poem before it, or any of its Societies; together with Catalogues of Students and of Books from its foundation, thus forming a key to its literary history. The subjects of Education and Public Schools, have also had attention. The publications of our various religious sects are also noted. Those of the Baptists, the largest and oldest sect in the State, are very full and complete. To Mr. R. A. Guild, the accomplished Librarian of Brown University, I am indebted for the completeness of the bibliography of Brown University and of the Baptists. On the long-disputed Boundary Questions, thirty-two works are named, with an analysis, or list of the important papers which the large volumes contain. But, perhaps the most important class of books mentioned is that which relates to the Constitution of 1842, adopted by Rhode Island. This includes one hundred and four separate titles, and refers to 385 documents and State papers, the titles of which are given.

The titles of Books in this catalogue are given under the authors' names, alphabetically arranged, except in cases where they come under a particular head. The titles arranged in classes are as follows:

Almanacs.
Anti-Masonry.
Avery Case.
Baptists.
Boundary Line.
Brown University.
Constitution of 1842.
Fourth of July Orations.
Friends, Publications of the Society of.
Ives and Hazard Case.
Law Cases, or Celebrated Trials.
Schools.
Temperance.
State Papers.
State Debt of Rhode Island.

Books relating to either of the above-named subjects, will be found under those heads, alphabetically arranged. The titles of many will, likewise, be found repeated under the authors' names in their alphabetical places.

A few books relating to New England in general, are mentioned. This list might have been greatly extended. In a bibliography of Massachusetts, this class of books, might, with more propriety, be included.

The earliest book, whose title is given in the bibliography is, Hakluyt's "Divers Voyages," printed in London, in 1582, which contains the voyage of Verrazzano to the coast of America, in 1524, when he entered Narragansett Bay, which he describes.

It is proper to state that every book and pamphlet mentioned in this Catalogue is in the State, either in public or private libraries, and hence accessible. Those printed before the year 1800, including those of great rarity, by Roger Williams, Gorton, Coddington, Winslow, Mather, and others of the 17th and 18th centuries, are in the library of our townsman, John Carter Brown, Esq. All the books relating to the "Baptists," and to "Brown University," with many others named in this catalogue, are in the Library of that Institution. Of the more modern books, or those printed during the present century and a portion of the last, the greater number are in the library of our townsman, the Hon. Albert G. Greene. In political pamphlets, the collection of the Hon. Elisha R. Potter, of Kingston, R. I., is very large, perhaps not surpassed by any in the State. The Hon. William R. Staples, of Providence, and Dr. David King, of Newport, have also very considerable collections of pamphlets relating to the State. To all these gentlemen, I take this occasion to return my sincere thanks for the facilities afforded me in the examination of their libraries; for, with the exception of a few titles furnished me, I have examined and collated every book mentioned in this Catalogue.

Providence, April, 1864.

J. R. B.

BIBLIOGRAPHY.

ACTS AND RESOLVES of the General Assembly of the Governor and Company of the English Colony of Rhode Island, and Providence Plantations, in New England, in America. 67 vols. folio. *Providence and Newport*, 1747 to 1815.

The earliest printed volume of the Acts and Resolves, or, as they are more frequently called, the "Schedules" of the General Assembly, bears the date of 1747, though the earliest publication in the State Library is 1758, from which period, the State series is complete to the present time. Mr. John Carter Brown, whose unrivalled collection of books is well known, is so fortunate as to possess a sett which goes back to the year 1747. There are also tolerably perfect setts in the Library of the Rhode Island Historical Society, in that of the Hon. Albert G. Greene, of Providence, and in the possession of the City of Providence. How complete the setts are in the other towns in the State, I am not aware.

In the Schedule for July, 1776, the title of "Colony" is changed to that of the "STATE of Rhode Island and Providence Plantations." The folio series terminates with the February session, 1817, since which time the publication has been continued in the octavo form. The separate title of "Acts and Resolves of the General Assembly," etc., was first prefixed to the publication of the January session, 1850, and has been since so continued. Each session is separately printed, with an Index. A complete Index to all the printed Acts, Resolves, Reports, etc., was compiled by John R. Bartlett, Secretary of State, which extends to the close of the year 1850, and printed by order of the General Assembly, (see Bartlett.) This Index was continued by the same to the end of the year 1862, and printed in the year 1863.

The Acts and Resolves of the General Assembly, previous to 1747, as well as the Records and Proceedings of the four earliest settled towns of the Colony, beginning in the year 1636, will be found at length in the "Colonial Records," which see under its title for particulars.

ACTS AND RESOLVES of the General Assembly, from 1815 to the present time.
8vo.   *Providence. Various Printers.*

THE ACTS OF THE ELDERS, commonly called the Book of Abraham; containing a revelation made to him at a protracted meeting, to which is appended a chapter from the Book of Religious Errors, with notes of explanation and commentation, from commencement to termination. Calculated for the meridian of Rhode Island; but will answer for the New England States. Written by Himself.
Square 12mo. pp. 160.   *Prov. Printed for the purchaser.* 1842.

This curious book relates to the dissensions among various religious denominations in Rhode Island. It is written in scriptural language and divided into chapters and verses.

AN ACCOUNT of the Massachusetts Society for promoting Christian Knowledge.
12mo. pp. 81.   *Andover. For the use of the Society.* 1815.

In this pamphlet is the report of two missionaries who were sent to Rhode Island to examine its religious condition. Their report exhibits a sad condition of the people. After relating accounts of their visits to various parts of the State, they add, "From the mass of materials, contained in the journals, it would be easy to multiply facts in proof of the deplorable condition of Rhode Island, with regard to learning, religion and morals. Those given, it is presumed, will suffice to excite the compassion of every man, who has a heart to feel for the complicated wretchedness of so many thousands of his fellow men in a neighboring sister State," etc. p. 40.

AN ACCOUNT OF THE PIRATES, with divers of their Speeches, Letters, &c. And a Poem made by one of them: *Who were executed at Newport, on Rhode Island, July 19th,* 1723.
12mo. pp. 16.   *Re-printed in the year* 1769.

Extract from the introduction. "A number of Men, gathered, by the wonderful Providence of God, from several Parts of the British World; from England, from *Wales,* from *Scotland, Ireland, Isle of Man,* the *Massachusetts,* (in New-England) from *New-York,* from *Pennsylvania,* from *Virginia,* from *Barbados,* taken by a Man of War, on June 10th; were brought into this Harbor June 11th, and were confined in Prison June 12th. (Seven more on July 11th.) One of these died, (on July 15th) all the rest were tried on July 11 and 12. Eight were cleared, twenty-eight were found guilty of Piracy, and were condemned to die; two of them were reprieved, twenty-six were executed July 19, 1723."

ACTS OF THE COMMISSIONERS of the United Colonies of New England. [Printed with the Records of the Colony of New Plymouth.] Printed by order of the Legislature of the Commonwealth of Massachusetts. Edited by David Pulsifer.
2 vols. small folio. Vol. 1, 1643 to 1651, pp. xvi. and 237, vol. 2. pp. 492. *From the Press of William White, Printer to the Commonwealth.* Boston. 1859.

——— For the same, see *Hazard's State Papers*.

ADAMS, JOHN G. REV. Our Country, and its claims upon us. An oration delivered before the municipal authorities and citizens of Providence, July 4, 1863.
8vo. pp. 30. *Providence. Knowles, Anthony & Co.* 1863.

ADAMS, SAMUEL SMITH. Eulogy on. See *Isaac Fisk*.

AN ADDRESS to the citizens of Rhode Island on the choice of Electors of President and Vice President of the United States.
8vo. pp. 15. *November.* 1808.
The persons recommended for electors were Thomas P. Ives, of Providence, Christopher Fowler, of Newport, James Rhodes, of Warwick, and Thomas Noyes, of Westerly.

ADDRESS to the Freemen of the State of Rhode Island. By a citizen. Dated at Warwick, March 6, 1817.
8vo. pp. 14. *No place.* [1817.]
Relates to the State Election, in which William Jones and Nehemiah R. Knight were candidates for the office of Governor.

ADDRESS to the Freemen of Rhode Island, by a Freeman, [relative to the election of Representatives to Congress, Tristam Burges and William Sprague being candidates.]
8vo. pp. 12. *No place or date.*

ADDRESS to the Freemen of Rhode Island, on the annual election of State Officers, to take place April 16, 1828.
8vo. pp. 16. [*Providence.* 1828.]

ADDRESS to the Farmers of Rhode Island, on the subject of the General Election of Officers, in April, 1828. By a Farmer.
12mo. pp. 12. *Providence. H. H. Brown.* 1828.

AN ADDRESS to the People of Rhode Island; proving that more than eight millions of public money has been wasted by the present administration. By a Landholder.
8vo. pp. 28. *Providence. John S. Green.* 1828.
Ascribed to Wilkins Updike, Esq., of Kingston.

ADDRESS to the Freemen of the Agricultural and Manufacturing interests of Rhode Island.
8vo. pp. 24. *Providence. Herald Office.* 1829.

AN ADDRESS to the Freemen of Rhode Island, by a Republican Farmer.
8vo. pp. 20. [*Providence.* 1828 or 1829.]
Relates to the election of Representatives to Congress. Tristam Burges and Dutee J. Pearce on the one hand, and Samuel Eddy and Job Durfee on the other.

ADDRESS. Slanders Refuted, being a reply to the foul and abusive attacks made on Dutee J. Pearce, and Tristam Burges.
8vo. pp. 18. *No Place or date.*

ADDRESS to the Freemen of Rhode Island. By a Landholder. [E. R. Potter.]
8vo. pp. 16. *Providence. Herald Office.* 1831.

AN ADDRESS to the Freemen of Rhode Island on the subject of the Spring Elections, 1832. By a Republican Farmer.
8vo. pp. 16. *April.* 1832.

[ADDRESS] To the Farmers of Rhode Island! By a Farmer.
8vo. pp. 7. 1835.
Written when Mr. Knight was a candidate for Governor in 1834 or 1835.

AN ADDRESS to the Whigs of Rhode Island, with political portraits. The Scourge No. 1.
8vo. pp. 8 *No date.*
Relative to the contest between Gov. Fenner and the Hon. Charles Jackson, signed "Terry Durham"

ADDRESS of the Whig State Convention to the People of Rhode Island. [Signed by W. R. Watson and Charles Randall.]
8vo. pp. 24. 1848.

ADDRESS of the Rhode Island State Republican Committee to the electors of Rhode Island.
8vo. pp. 7. *Providence. Knowles, Anthony & Co.* 1859.

ADDRESS of the Republican State Central Committee to the Electors of Rhode Island.
8vo. pp. 8. *Providence. Knowles, Anthony & Co.* 1860.

[ADDRESS] To the Freemen of Rhode Island! From a Rhode Island Freeman.
8vo. pp. 12. *No date.*
Urges the election of Messrs. Burges and Cranston to Congress.

[ADDRESS] To the Democratic Party of Rhode Island.
8vo. pp. 10. [*April.* 1836.]

THE ADDRESS of a Farmer to the Honest Men of all parties in the State of Rhode Island and Providence Plantations. [By Tristam Burges.]
8vo. pp. 16. *No date.*

ADDRESS of John Whipple, to the people of Rhode Island, on the approaching election.
8vo. pp. 16. *Providence. Knowles & Vose.* 1843.

AN ADDRESS to the people of Rhode Island, published in the Providence Journal, in a series of articles, during the months of September and October, 1844. By Hamilton.
8vo. pp. 44. *Providence. Knowles & Vose.* 1844.
"The Whig Party; its objects—its principles—its candidates—its duties and its prospects."

AN ADDRESS to the people of Rhode Island, upon the course of the Hon. Elisha R. Potter, in the House of Representatives of the United States, upon the question of the annexation of Texas; with an outline of the proceedings of the Convention at which he was nominated for re-election. (By Young Narragansett.)
8vo. pp. 8. [1845.]

An Address to the people of Rhode Island, upon the claims of Wilkins Updike to a seat in the Congress of the United States. By a true Whig.
8vo. pp. 8. [1847.]

Adlam, S. The First Church in Providence, not the oldest of the Baptists in America, attempted to be shewn. By S. Adlam, Pastor of the First Church in Newport, R. I.
8vo. pp. 28. *Newport. Cranston & Norman.* 1850.

A Few Observations on the government of the State of Rhode Island. By a citizen.
8vo. pp. 18. *Providence. John Carter.* 1809.

Affaires De L'Angleterre et l'Amerique.
17 vols. 8vo. *A Anvers.* 1776.

This remarkable collection is so little known, (from its great scarcity,) that no satisfactory account of it exists. It has been supposed that it was a translation or imitation of the "American Remembrancer;" but a slight examination will show that the contents are quite different. In the preface it is styled "a chonological collection of acts and discussions to serve as a political history of England and the Colonies." It was issued in "Cahiers" or parts, and appears to have been printed in one year; and though it bears the name of "Anvers," was probably printed in Paris. Among the editors (according to Barbier) were Franklin, Cour de Gebelin, Robinet, etc. It relates to the Revolutionary war, and contains much about the operations in Rhode Island. Copies of this scarce work are in the Library of Hartford College, of Mr. J. Carter Brown, in Providence, and of Dr. King, in Newport.

African Church. A short history of the African Union Meeting House, erected in Providence, R. I., in the years 1819–20–21, with notes for its future Government.
8vo. pp. 32. *Providence. Brown & Danforth.* 1821.

Agricultural Reports. See *Rhode Island Agricultural Society for the Encouragement of Domestic Industry.*

A Letter to a Member of Congress on the subject of a British War, dated Providence, February 2, 1812.
8vo. pp. 32. *Providence. John Carter.* 1812.

Angell, Joseph K. An Essay upon the right of a State to tax a body corporate, considered in relation to the present Bank Tax in Rhode Island.
8vo. pp. 44. *Boston. Hilliard, Gray, Little & Wilkins.* 1857.

ANGELL WILL CASE. The Angell Will Case, recently adjudicated, in Providence, R. I. By I. Ray, M. D. From the American Journal of Insanity, for October, 1863.
8vo. pp. 43. *Utica, N. Y.* 1863.

ANSWER to the White-Washing Committee. Broadside. 1831.

Relates to the pamphlet entitled "Examination of certain charges against Lemuel H. Arnold."

ANTHONY, SUSANNA. The Life and Character of Susanna Anthony, who died in Newport, R. I., June 23, 1791, in the 65th year of her age. Consisting chiefly in extracts from her writings, with some brief observations on them. By Samuel Hopkins, D. D., Pastor of the First Congregational Church in Newport.
12mo. pp. 168. *Hartford. Hudson & Goodwin.* 1799.

First edition printed in Worcester, Mass.

ANTOINE, JOS. Examination of Joseph Antoine, John Fransoeis Wohlfahrt, and Joanna Susan Wohlfahrt, suspected of the murder of Samuel Field and Francis C. Jenkerson; before Justices Aplin, Staples and Patten.
8vo. pp. 32. *Providence H. H. Brown.* 1828.

ALLEN, PAUL. Oration at the election of the officers of the Independent Companies of the town of Providence, April 29, 1799. Published at the request of the Independent Co. Cadets.
8vo. pp. 14. *Providence. John Carter. Jan.* 1799.

ALLEN, CAPT. WM. H., U. S. N.. See notice of, in American Naval Biography. By Isaac Bailey. 1815.
——— Sketch of, in R. I. Literary Repository, with a portrait. *Providence.* 1814.

ALLEN, ZACHARIAH. Memorial of Roger Williams. A paper read before the Rhode Island Historical Society, May 18, 1860.
12mo. pp. 10. *Providence.* 1860.

ALLYN, ROBERT. A Special Report of the Commissioner of

Public Schools, on Truancy and Absenteeism in Rhode Island, made by order of the General Assembly, at its May session, 1856.
8vo. pp. 35 and xxviii.
     Providence. A. Crawford Greene & Bro. 1856.
ALMANACS. Printed in Rhode Island.

—— POOR JOB. An Almanack, &c., 1751 to 1755, (by Job Shepherd, Philom.)
12mo.   *Newport. Printed by James Franklin.*

—— THE RHODE ISLAND ALMANAC, 1772, (by John Anderson, Philmath.)
12mo.   *Newport. Printed by Solomon Southwick.*

—— THE NEW ENGLAND ALMANACK, 1772, by Benjamin Wirt, A. M.
12mo.   *Newport. Printed by Ebenezer Campbell.*

—— THE NORTH AMERICAN CALENDAR, 1784, by Benjamin West, A. M., A. A. S.
12mo.   *Newport. Printed by Bennett Wheeler.*

—— AN ALMANACK, 1788, 1789, by Elisha Thornton, of Smithfield.
12mo.   *Newport. Printed by Peter Edes.*

—— THE RHODE ISLAND ALMANAC, 1791, 1792. The Astronomical calculations by E. Thornton.
12mo.   *Newport. Printed by Peter Edes.*

—— THE NEWPORT ALMANAC, 1800.
12mo. *Newport. Printed by Oliver Farnsworth, Printer to the State of Rhode Island.*

—— THE NEW ENGLAND CALENDAR and Ephemeris, 1800. The Astronomical Calculations by Eliab Wilkinson, of Smithfield, Philom.
12mo. *Newport. Printed for Jacob Richardson, of Newport.*

—— THE RHODE ISLAND ALMANAC, 1804 to 1806. The Astronomical Calculations by Benjamin West, L. L. D.
12mo.   *Newport. Printed by Oliver Farnsworth.*

—— THE COLUMBIAN CALENDAR, an Almanac, 1806. By

Remington Southwick, Teacher of Mathematics in Washington Academy.
12mo. *Newport. Printed for the Author.*

——— THE NEWPORT TIDE ALMANAC, 1861.
12mo. *Published by Charles E. Hammett, Esq.*

——— THE RHODE ISLAND ALMANAC, with an Ephemeris for the year 1794. The Astronomical Calculations by Elisha Thornton.
12mo. *Printed at Warren, R. I., by Nathaniel Phillips, for Jacob Richardson, Esq. Newport.*

——— PHILLIPS'S UNITED STATES DIARY, or an Almanac, 1798. *Printed at Warren, R. I., by Nathaniel Phillips.*

——— THE ALMANAC, 1763, by Benjamin West, Philomath.
12mo. *Printed and sold by William Goddard.*

——— THE NEW ENGLAND ALMANAC, 1764, 1765, by Benjamin West, Philomath.
12mo. *Printed and sold by William Goddard.*

——— Do. Do. 1766, by Benjamin West, Philomath.
12mo. *Providence, in New England. Printed and sold by Sarah and William Goddard, at the Post Office.*

——— Do. Do. 1767, by Benjamin West, Philomath.
12mo. *Providence, in New England. Printed and sold by Sarah Goddard and Company.*

——— Do. Do. 1768. By Benjamin West, Philomath.
12mo. *Providence, New England. Printed and sold by Sarah Goddard and John Carter, at Shakspeare's Head.*

——— Do. Do. 1769. By Benjamin West, Philomath.
12mo. *Boston. Printed by Mein & Fleming, at the New Printing Office in Newbury Street, and to be sold by Mein, at the London Book Store, North side of King Street, and by Benjamin West (the Author), in Providence. Price, two pistareens by the Dozen, and six coppers single.*

——— Do. Do. 1770 to 1778, by Benjamin West, A. M.
12mo. *Providence. Printed and sold by John Carter, at his Printing Office, the sign of Shakspeare's Head.*

—— Do. Do. 1774 to 1780, by Benjamin West, A. M. 12mo. *Providence. Printed and sold by John Carter, at Shakspeare's Head, in Meeting Street.*

—— Do. Do. 1781 to 1790. ("By Isaac Bickerstaff, Esq., Philom.") 12mo. *Providence. Printed and sold by John Carter, at the Post Office, at Shakspeare's Head.*

—— Do. Do. 1791, 1792. ("By Isaac Bickerstaff, Esq.) 12mo. *Providence. Printed and sold by John Carter, at the Post Office.*

—— Do. Do. 1793. ("By Isaac Bickerstaff, Esq., Philom.") 12mo. *Providence. Printed and sold by John Carter.*

—— Do. Do. 1794. ("By Isaac Bickerstaff, Esq., Philom.") 12mo. *Providence. Printed and sold by Carter & Wilkinson.*

—— Do. Do. 1795, 1796. The Astronomical Calculations by Elisha Thornton, Philom. 12mo. *Providence. Printed and sold by Carter and Wilkinson.*

—— Do. Do. 1797. The Astronomical Calculations by Elisha Thornton and Eliab Wilkinson. Philom. 12mo. *Providence. Printed by Carter & Wilkinson, and sold at their Book and Stationery Store.*

—— Do. Do. 1798, 1799. ("By Isaac Bickerstaff, Esq.) 12mo. *Providence. Printed by Carter & Wilkinson, and sold at their Book and Stationery Store.*

—— Do. Do. 1800 to 1814. ("By Isaac Bickerstaff.") 12mo. *Providence, R. I. Printed by John Carter.*

—— Do. Do. 1815, 1816. ("By Isaac Bickerstaff, Esq.") 12mo. *Providence. Printed by Brown & Wilson, near the South-east corner of the Market House.*

—— Do. Do. 1817 to 1820. ("By Isaac Bickerstaff.") 12mo. *Providence. Printed and sold by Hugh H. Brown.*

—— Do. Do. 1821 to 1825. ("By Isaac Bickerstaff.")
12mo. *Providence. Printed and sold by Brown & Danforth.*
—— Do. Do. 1826, 1827. ("By Isaac Bickerstaff, Esq.")
12mo. *Providence. Printed and sold by Carlile & Brown.*
—— Do. Do. 1828 to 1861. ("By Isaac Bickerstaff, Esq.")
12mo. *Providence. Printed and sold by H. H. Brown.*
—— Do. Do. 1862 to 1864. ("By Isaac Bickerstaff, Esq.")
12mo. *Published and sold by A. Crawford Greene.*

—— THE NEW ENGLAND TOWN AND COUNTY ALMANAC, 1769. ("By Abraham Weatherwise, Gent."
12mo. *Providence. Printed and sold by Josiah Goddard & John Carter, at Shakspeare's Head, (with Portrait, &c., of John Wilkes, Esq.)*

—— THE NORTH AMERICAN CALENDAR, or An Almanac, 1780. ("By John Anderson, A. M.")
12mo. *Providence. Printed and sold by Bennett Wheeler, at the New Printing Office in the Main Street.*

—— THE NORTH AMERICAN CALENDAR, &c., 1782 to 1785, by Benjamin West, A. A. S.
12mo. *Providence. Printed by Bennett Wheeler.*

—— Do. Do. 1786. ("By Copernicius Partridge, A. M.")
12mo. *Providence. Printed by Bennett Wheeler.*

—— Do. Do. 1787 to 1798. By Benjamin West, Professor of Mathematics and Astronomy in the College of R. I.
12mo. *Providence. Printed by Bennett Wheeler.*

—— WHEELER'S NORTH AMERICAN CALENDAR, &c., 1789 to 1803.
12mo. *Providence. Printed by Bennett Wheeler.*

—— PROVIDENCE ALMANAC AND BUSINESS DIRECTORY, 1843 to 1845, by Benjamin Fillmore.
18mo. *Providence. Printed by B. F. Moore.*

—— Do. Do. 1846 to 1850, by John F. Moore.
18mo. *Providence. Printed by J. F. Moore.*

—— PROVIDENCE ALMANAC AND BUSINESS DIRECTORY, containing also a Business Directory for the City of Newport;

also for the Towns of Bristol, Warren, Westerly, Woonsocket and Pawtucket, 1855, 1856.
12mo.　　Providence. H. H. Brown, 3 South Main Street.

ANDROSSE, SIR EDMUND. Narrative of the Proceedings of Sir Edmond Androsse and his Complices, who acted by an illegal and arbitrary Commission from the late King James, during his Government in New England.
4to. pp. 　　　　　　　　　　　　　　　London. 1691.

———— A narrative of the miseries of New England, by reason of the arbitrary government erected there. Printed in the tyrannic reign of Sir Edmund Andross.
8vo. pp. 8.　　　　　　　　　　　　　　Boston. 1775.

———— Commission to Sir Edmund Andross, from King James the Second. 1686.

———— Papers relative to the period of the usurpation of Sir Edmund Andros in New England, 1686-87. See *Mass. Hist. Coll. 3d Series, vol. vii.*

———— Commission, Instructions and other papers relating to Sir Edmund Andros. *Rhode Island Colonial Records.* Vol. 3, p. 210 and 248, and *New York Docs.* Vol. 3, p. 543.

Sir Edmund Andros figures largely in the History of Rhode Island. In 1686 he was commissioned, among other colonies, as Governor of the Narragansett country. Arriving in Rhode Island, agreeably to orders, he dissolved the government, broke the seal of the charter, and reduced the colony to a single county. In 1688 he received a second commission from James the 2d, which extended his government over the province of New York, Connecticut, Rhode Island, and other British colonies. From this period the government of Rhode Island was completely subverted by Andros. The revolution in England soon after, put an end to his power. He was seized by the people of Boston, and thrown into prison. In 1689 the colony re-organized under its former charter. The records and papers connected with the administration of Andros will be found in the 3d vol. of R. I. Colonial Records.

ANTI-MASONRY. Books relating to.

———— Declaration of the Freemasons of Rhode Island.
12 mo. pp. 12.　　　　　　　　　　　　　No date.

———— Letters, addressed to Joel Mann, Pliny Merrick, Thomas H. Smith, Augustus B. Read, Seceding Masons. By Samuel M. Fowler, editor of the Pawtucket Chronicle.

To which is added Mr. Mann's reply, and a rejoinder to the same.
12 mo. pp. 34.　　　　　*Pawtucket. Chronicle Office.* 1830.

―――― Proceedings of the Rhode Island Anti-masonic Convention, September 14th, 1831.
12 mo. pp. 28 and 3. *Providence. Daily Advertiser Office.* 1831.

―――― Strictures on Seceding Masons, with reviews of the Anti-Masonic characters of Pliny Merrick, Esq., of Worcester, Mass.—Rev. Joel Mann, of Suffield, Conn.—Rev. Thomas M. Smith, of Troy, Mass.—and Elder David Bernard, of Freedonia, New York. From the Boston Masonic Mirror.
12 mo. pp. 32.　　　　　*Boston. Carr and Page.* 1830.

―――― Address of the Grand Lodge of the State of Rhode Island and Providence Plantations, to the people of said State.
8vo. pp. 16.　　　　　*Providence. B. Cranston.* 1831.

―――― The same.
8vo. pp. 14.　　　　　*Pawtucket. S. M. Fowler.* 1831.

―――― Address of the Committee of the Grand Lodge, to the people of Rhode Island.
8vo. pp. 8.　　　　　*Providence.* 1831.

―――― Report of the Committee appointed by the General Assembly of the State of Rhode Island and Providence Plantations, to investigate the charges in circulation against Freemasonry and Masons in said State; together with all the official documents and testimony relating to the subject.
8vo. pp. 149.　　　*Providence. William Marshall.* 1832.
Published by order of the General Assembly, superintended by the Committee.

―――― An official report by William Sprague, Jun., one of the Committee of the House of Representatives of Rhode Island upon the subject of Masonry.
8vo. pp. 23.　　　*Providence. Daily Advertiser.* 1832.

―――― Legislative investigation into Masonry; being a correct history of the investigation of more than fifty adhering and seceding Masons, before a committee of the General

Assembly of Rhode Island, held at Providence and Newport, between December 7, 1831, and January 7, 1832. Reported from minutes taken at the time. By Benj. F. Hallett, George Turner and others, and carefully compared.
8vo. pp. 85, and index. *Boston. Daily Advocate.* 1832.

——— An Address delivered before the Grand Lodge of Rhode Island, at their Anniversary Festival of St. John the Baptist, at East Greenwich, R. I., Friday, June 24, 1831. By Robert Frieze, G. Chaplain.
8vo. pp. 24. *Providence. B. Cranston,* 1831.

——— A portrait of Masonry and Anti-masonry as drawn by Richard Rush, John Quincy Adams, William Wirt, &c.
12mo. pp. 60. *Providence. Daily Advertiser.* 1832.

——— Proceedings of the Grand Lodge of the State of Rhode Island and Providence Plantations, at their annual meeting, holden at Masons' Hall, in Pawtucket, June 24th, A. L. 5833.
12mo. pp. 12. *Providence. Cranston & Hammond.* 1833.

——— Letters addressed to William L. Stone, Esq., of New York, and to Benjamin Cowell, Esq., of Rhode Island, upon the subject of Masonry and Anti-Masonry. By John Quincy Adams. To which is added a portrait of Masonry, by John C. Spencer.
12mo. pp. 24. *Providence. Edw'd & J. W. Cory.* 1833.

——— Letters addressed to the Hon. John Quincy Adams, in refutation of charges made by that gentleman against a committee of the Legislature of Rhode Island and against the Legislature itself. By B. Hazard, Esq., Chairman of that committee.
12mo. pp. 46. *Providence. Marshall, Brown & Co.* 1834.

——— Proceedings of the Anti-masonic Convention held January 16, 1835. And the proceedings of their nominating committee held at the State House in Providence, Feb. 20, 1835.
8vo. pp. 8. *Providence. W. Simons, Jun.* 1835.

——— Reply to the summons of the Rhode Island Royal

Arch Chapter, March 22d, 1832. By the Rev. Henry Tatem. 3d edition.
8vo. pp. [*Providence*. 1832.]

ANTIQUITATES AMERICANÆ sive scriptores septentrionales rerum ante-columbianarum in America Edidit societas regia antiquariorum septentrionalium.
Royal 4to. pp. xl and 479. *Hafniæ*. 1837.
This work is edited by Prof. C. C. Rafn, and was published under the auspices of the Royal Society of Northern Antiquaries at Copenhagen, in Denmark. It contains a reprint of the ancient Icelandic Sagas, which relate to the discovery of America by the Scandinavians in the tenth century. The text embraces, first, the Sagas in the *Icelandic*; second, a version in *Danish*; and third, a translation in *Latin*, accompanied by notes and commentaries. These are followed by the correspondence in English with the Rhode Island Historical Society relative to the famous sculptured rock on the banks of Taunton river near Dighton, the characters upon which have been attributed to the Northmen, and to other evidences of an early intercourse between that people and Rhode Island; the Vineland of the ancient sagas being located in this State. Preceding the Sagas is an abstract in English of the historical evidence contained in the work. The volume also contains 17 plates of facsimilies of the Sagas, of ancient monuments, maps, etc. A few copies are printed in a superior style upon large paper, in Imperial quarto.

The Historical Essay alluded to, has been separately printed in English, French, German, Danish, Swedish, Spanish, Italian and Dutch.

APES REV. WILLIAM, an Indian. Eulogy on King Philip, as pronounced at the Odeon, in Federal Street, Boston.
8vo. pp. 60. *Boston*. 1836.

APPEAL to the Senate of Rhode Island.
8vo. pp. 11. *Providence*. 1829.
Relates to taxing the property of churches, buildings for schools, academies, colleges, etc.

ARNOLD, L. H. Examination of certain charges against Lemuel H. Arnold, Esq., the National Republican candidate for Governor, being a Report of a Committee appointed April 12, 1821.
8vo. pp. 28. *Providence*. 1831.

ARNOLD, HON. SAMUEL GREENE. The Spirit of Rhode Island History. A Discourse delivered before the Rhode Island Historical Society, on the evening of Monday, January 17, 1853.
8vo. pp. 32. *Providence. George H. Whitney*. 1853.

———— History of the State of Rhode Island and Providence
Plantations, 1636—1700.
Vol. 1. pp. xii and 574.   *New York. D. Appleton & Co.*
Vol. 2.   1700 to 1790.   pp. 592.   1860.

ARNOLD, WELCOME. Sermon on the death of, see *Marcy*.

ARTICLES OF FAITH and Covenant of the First Baptist Church
in South Kingstown, R. I.
12mo. pp. 8.   *Wakefield. D. Gillis*. 1859.

ASPINWALL, THOMAS. Remarks on the Narragansett Patent.
Read before the Massachusetts Historical Society, June,
1862.
8vo. pp. 44.   *Boston. John Wilson & Son*. 1863.

ATHERTON, HUMPHREY. Act of the Assembly of Rhode Island
in favor of Humphrey Atherton.   Oct. 30, 1672.
                       Mass. Hist. Coll. First Series, Vol. 5.

ATHENÆUM. See *Providence Athenæum*.

ATTEMPTED SPECULATION. Lemuel H. Arnold and James
F. Simmons, upon the funds of the State, while they were
members of the General Assembly.
8vo. pp. 23.   *Providence. Herald Office*. 1831.
This pamphlet relates to the proposition to unite the two Pawtucket Turnpikes.
See "Examination of certain charges against Lemuel H. Arnold," for a
reply to the above.

AUSTIN, SAMUEL. An oration pronounced at Newport, R. I.,
July 4, 1822. The 46th anniversary of the Independence
of the United States of America.
8vo. pp. 16.   *Newport. W. Simons*. 1822.

AVERY CASE. Books relating to.

———— AVERY. Report of the examination of the Rev.
Ephraim K. Avery, for the murder of Sarah Maria Cornell. By Luke Drury.
8vo. pp. 64.   (*Rhode Island.*) 1833.

———— A full report of the Trial of Ephraim K. Avery,
charged with the murder of Sarah Maria Cornell, before
the Supreme Court of Rhode Island, at a special Term in
Newport, held in May, 1833; with all the incidental ques-

tions raised in the Trial carefully preserved, the testimony of the witnesses, and a correct map and references of all the Localities described in the Testimony, prepared expressly for this report alone. Reported by Benjamin F. Hallett.
8vo. pp. 207 and 40. 2 editions. *Boston. Daily Advocate.* 1833.

―――― The arguments of counsel in the close of the trial of Rev. E. K. Avery, for the murder of Sarah M. Cornell, &c. Hon. Jeremiah Mason, of Boston, for the prisoner, Albert C. Greene, Attorney General for the prosecution. Reported without abridgment, by Benj. F. Hallett. Also a literal report of the Medical testimony of Prof. Walter Channing and Dr. William Turner, revised by the witnesses, and not before published.
8vo. pp. 94. *Boston. Daily Advocate.* 1833.

―――― Strictures on the case of Ephraim K. Avery, originally published in the Republican Herald, Providence, R. I., with corrections, revisions and additions. By Aristides.
12mo. vo. pp. 100. *Providence. William Simons, Jr.* 1833.

―――― A Vindication of the result of the trial of the Rev. Ephraim K. Avery; to which is prefixed his statement of facts relative to the circumstances by which he became involved in the prosecution. With a map.
8vo. pp. 74. *Boston. Russell, Odiorne & Co.* 1834.

―――― Narrative of the apprehension in Ridge, N. H., of the Rev. E. K. Avery, charged with the murder of Sarah M. Cornell: together with the proceedings of the inhabitants of Fall River. By Harvey Harnden.
8vo. pp. 36. *Providence. W. Marshall & Co.* 1833.

―――― A correct, full and impartial report of the trial of Rev. Ephraim K. Avery, before the Supreme Judicial Court of the State of Rhode Island, at Newport, May 6, 1833, for the murder of Sarah M. Cornell.
12mo. pp. 174. *Providence. Marshall & Brown.* [1833.]

BACKUS, ISAAC. A History of New England, with particular reference to the denomination of Christians called Baptists. Containing the principles and settlements of the country; the rise and increase of the Baptist churches therein, the intrusion of arbitrary power under the cloak of religion; the Christian testimonies of the Baptists and others against the same, with their sufferings under it, from the beginning to the present time. Collected from the most authentic records and writings, both ancient and modern. By Isaac Backus, Pastor of the first Baptist church in Middleborough. 3 vols. 8vo.

Vol. 1. pp. 563.   Boston. *Edward Draper.* 1777.
Vol. 2. pp. 448.   Providence. *John Carter.* 1784.
Vol. 3. pp. 334.   Boston. *Manning & Loring.* 1796.

An abridgment of this work was published in 1804, when the author was eighty years of age. The Rev. Dr. Allen says that the original "contains many facts, for which the public are indebted to the patient industry of the writer, and it must be a very valuable work to the Baptists, as it presents a minute account of almost every church of that denomination in New England." The work is now exceedingly rare, and commands a high price. Bancroft the historian, bears honorable testimony to the author's fidelity, considering his history, as to its facts, "more to be depended on, than any of the early histories of New England."

The author, who was a distinguished Baptist minister, was born at Norwich, Conn., in 1724, and commenced preaching in 1746. He was ordained as a Congregationalist in 1748; but in 1751, was baptized by immersion. To his exertions the Baptist denomination in America, is much indebted for its prosperity. He died Nov. 28, 1806, aged 82 years. He was the author of many works besides that under notice.

———— Memoir of the Life and Times of, see *Hovey*.

BACON, REV. HENRY. Sermon on the installation of, see *E. H. Chapin.*

BAKER, LUTHER. An address delivered to the Philanthrophic Society, at their request, on its twelfth anniversary, Feb. 22, 1806.
12mo. pp. 16.   *Warren, R. I. N. Phillips.* 1806.

BALCH, WM. S. Oration before the R. I. Suffrage Association. See *Suffrage*.

BANK RETURNS. Abstract exhibiting the condition of the Banks in Rhode Island; also, abstract exhibiting the condition of the Institutions for Savings in Rhode Island. 1819 to 1857.   *Providence.*

Annual Returns exhibiting the condition of the Banks and Institutions for Savings in Rhode Island have been printed since the year 1819. Until the year 1849 they were printed on a large sheet and appended to the schedules. Since that period they have been printed in a pamphlet form.

BANKS. Report of the committee appointed by the House of Representatives of the State of Rhode Island, &c., to inquire into the expediency of increasing the Banking Capital within the State; made at June session, 1826.
8vo. pp. 40.   *Providence. Smith & Parmenter.* 1826.

This report, which was written by Benjamin Hazard, is one of the most able papers on Banking which has ever been written in the State.

———— PROVIDENCE BANK, VS. THOMAS G. PITMAN, General Treasurer of the State of Rhode Island, et. al. Argument of the counsel [Benjamin Hazard] on the part of the State. Supreme Court of the United States, January Term, 1830.
8vo. pp. 22.

———— Argument of the opening counsel in the same case.
8vo. pp. 32.   *January*, 1830.

———— Report of the Committee appointed by the General Assembly of the State of Rhode Island to visit the Banks in the State; made at the June session, Newport, 1836.
8vo. pp. 34.   *Providence. W. Simons, Jr.* 1836.

This committee consisted of S. Y. Atwell, Thomas W. Dorr, and Geo. Curtis.

BANVARD, JOSEPH. A guide to Providence River and Narragansett Bay, from Providence to Newport.
12mo. pp. vi and 66.   *Providence. Coggeshall & Stewart.*

BAPTISTS. Books relating to.

———— The Sentiments and Plan of the Warren Association. 4to. pp. 4. *Germantown. Printed by Christopher Sower.* 1769.

NOTE.—This venerable body held its first meeting at Warren, R. I., in the year 1767. It originated with the Rev. Dr. Manning, at that time Pastor of the Baptist Church in Warren, and also President of Rhode Island College, now Brown University. But four churches were then incorporated, by the name of the Warren (Baptist) Association, viz. Warren, Haverhill, Bellingham, and Middleborough. The next year four more churches joined them, viz. Boston, Sutton, Leicester, and Ware. In 1769 the foregoing "Sentiments and Plan," drawn up and presented by the Rev. Dr. Manning, were formally adopted as the platform, so to speak, of the Association.

———— Minutes of the Philadelphian Association in MDCCLXIX. 4to. pp. 7. *Germantown. Printed by Christopher Sower.* 1769.

This body was organized in the year 1707, and is the oldest Baptist Association in the United States. To it Brown University owes its origin, and to its fostering care the Warren Association is greatly indebted. The Minutes for this year contain many allusions to Rhode Island, and pleasing accounts of Rhode Island College.

———— Minutes of the Warren Association, held at Sutton, in the Province of Massachusetts-Bay, September, 1771. 4mo. pp. 7. *Boston. Printed by John Boyles.* 1771.

———— Ibid. At Middleborough, Sept. 8 and 9, 1772.
12mo. pp. 8. *Boston. Printed by J. J. Kneeland.* 1772.

———— Ibid. At Medfield, Sept. 7, 8, and 9, 1773.
12mo. pp. 8. *Boston. Isaiah Thomas.* 1773.

———— Ibid. At Medfield, Sept. 13 and 14, 1774.
12mo. pp. 8. *Boston. John Kneeland.* 1774.

———— Ibid. At Warren, Sept. 12 and 13, 1775.
12mo. pp. 8. *Norwich. Robertsons & Trumbull.* 1775.

———— Ibid. At Grafton, Sept. 10 and 11, 1776.
12mo. pp. 8. *Boston. T. & J. Fleet.* 1776.

———— Ibid. At Middleborough, Sept. 9 and 10, 1777.
12mo. pp. 7. *Boston. E. Draper.* 1777.

———— Ibid. At Leicester, Sept. 8th and 9th, 1778.
12mo. pp. 4. (*Place and printer not given.*) 1778.

———— Ibid. At Attleborough, Sept. 7 and 8, 1779.
8vo. pp. 7. (*Place and printer not given.*) 1779.

——— Ibid. At Royalstone, Sept. 12 and 13, 1780.
12mo. pp. 7. (*Place and printer not given.*) 1780.
——— Ibid. At South Brimfield, Sept. 11 and 12, 1781.
12mo. pp. 8. *Providence. John Carter.* 1781.
——— Ibid. At Providence, Sept. 10, 1782.
12mo. pp. 8. *Providence. John Carter.* 1782.

At this meeting the Providence Church was received into the Association. The delegates upon the occasion were James Manning, Ephraim Wheaton, Samuel Whitman, John Jenckes, and Aaron Mason. The views entertained by many members of this church in regard to the doctrine of "Laying on of Hands," and also in regard to Singing in public worship, prevented, perhaps, its being received into the fellowship of the Association at an earlier day.

From this date the proceedings of the annual meetings were regularly printed from year to year. Sometimes [at Boston, but mostly at Providence, especially after the year 1800.

The Minutes for the first four meetings were never printed. They exist in manuscript, and may be found among the papers of the Rev. Isaac Backus, who was the first Clerk of the Association. The printed Minutes for the year 1771 are in the possession of the Rev. Dr. Benedict, of Pawtucket. The Minutes from 1772 to 1825 inclusive, with the "Sentiments and Plan," and the Minutes of the Philadelphia Association for 1769, bound together in a single octavo volume, are in the possession of Mr. John Carter Brown. They were collected by his father, the Hon. Nicholas Brown, and constitute the only complete set in existence. The Minutes from 1825 to the present time are in the Library of Brown University, together with a set of the earlier printed minutes, and the manuscript minutes of Backus.

In regard to the character and influence of this Body we quote from Arnold's History of Rhode Island, as follows: "The Warren Association originated with the Warren Church, and had for its object to secure for the denomination in the neighboring Colonies those civil and religious rights hitherto enjoyed solely by the established church." * * * * "In a few years the Association extended over New England, and held its meetings at various places. It became an active body in the cause of civil and religious liberty, presenting many able addresses upon this subject to the government of Massachusetts, and to the Continental Congress through the whole period of the Revolution. Although the Association has no longer that intimate connection with the University which at first existed, and the growth of Baptist Churches in New England has given rise to many other similar associations, the parent body still continues to exert a wide-spread and beneficent influence over the objects of its charge."

——— Minutes of the First Annual Meeting of the Narragansett Association, held with the Second Baptist Church in Hopkinton, R. I., Oct. 2 and 3, 1860.
8vo. pp. 22. *Westerly. Starr & Farnham, Printers.* 1860.

―――― The same. Second third and fourth annual meetings for 1861, 1862 and 1863.

―――― Minutes of the First Anniversary of the Providence Baptist Association, held with the Baptist Church in Woonsocket, Sept. 18 and 19, 1844.
8vo. pp. 19. *Providence. H. H. Brown.* 1844.

These Minutes have been printed regularly from year to year until the present time. A complete set is in the Library of the University.

―――― Act of Incorporation and Minutes of the Baptist Convention of the State of Rhode Island and vicinity, held at Newport, April 8, 1826.
12mo. pp. 12. *Providence. H. H. Brown.* 1829.

The act of incorporation was passed by the General Assembly, at their October session, 1826. The Minutes for 1829, 1830, 1832, and from 1835 inclusive to the present time, are in the Library of Brown University. The first Anniversary of the Convention was held in 1826. The Minutes for 1840 contain an account of the organization of the Rhode Island Baptist Sabbath School Association, Sept. 11, 1839. This Association in 1854 was reorganized and called the "Rhode Island Baptist Sunday School Convention." In 1841 the "Proceedings of the Baptist Education Society of the Warren Association, Auxiliary to the Northern Baptist Education Society," were first published in the Minutes of the Baptist Convention. This practice has been continued to the present time, under the name, since 1847, of the "Rhode Island Baptist Education Society."

―――― Minutes of the Fourteenth Anniversary of the Rhode Island Baptist Sunday School Convention; held in the Meeting House of the First Baptist Church, Providence, June 14, 1854.
12mo. pp. 57. *Providence. Knowles, Anthony & Co.* 1854.

In 1839 the "Rhode Island Baptist Sabbath School Association" was organized, under the auspices of the Baptist State Convention. The large number of Schools connected with the Baptist denomination throughout the State, and the increasing interest felt in the cause, led eventually to a distinct and separate organization. At a meeting of the State Convention in April, 1854, the old Association was merged into the present Sunday School Convention. Prof. S. S. Green, of Brown University, was elected President, A. M. Gammell, of Warren, Vice President, and Reuben A. Guild, of Brown University, Secretary. These gentlemen were successively re-elected to their respective offices from year to year, until 1860 and 1862, when they declined serving in order that the system of rotation in office might be introduced.

―――― Fifteenth Anniversary, held with the Stewart Street Church, Providence, June 13, 1855.
12mo. pp. 49.   *Providence. Knowles, Anthony & Co.* 1855.

―――― Sixteenth Anniversary, held with the Church in Warren, June 4, 1856.
12mo. pp. 42.   *Providence. Knowles, Anthony & Co.* 1856.

―――― Seventeenth Anniversary, held with the Central Church, Providence, June 3, 1857.
12mo. pp. 40.   *Providence. Knowles, Anthony & Co.* 1857.

―――― Eighteenth Anniversary, held with the Second Church, Newport, June 2, 1858.
12mo. pp. 24.   *Providence. Knowles, Anthony & Co.* 1858.

―――― Nineteenth Anniversary, held with the Friendship Street Church, Providence, June 1, 1859.
12mo. pp. 30.   *Providence. Knowles, Anthony & Co.* 1859.

―――― Twentieth Anniversary, held with the Church in Woonsocket, June 6, 1860.
12mo. pp. 38.   *Providence. Knowles, Anthony & Co.* 1860.

―――― Twenty-first Anniversary, held with the Brown Street Church, Providence, June 4, 1862.
12mo. pp. 36.   *Providence. Knowles, Anthony & Co.* 1862.

―――― Annals of the American Pulpit; or Commemorative Notices of distinguished American Clergymen of various denominations from the early settlement of the country to the close of the year 1855. By William B. Sprague, D. D. Vol. VI.
8vo. pp. 883.   *New York. R. Carter & Brother.* 1860.

This volume contains biographical sketches of Roger Williams, John Clarke, Comer, Upham, Thurston, Manning, Thompson, Gano, Maxcy, Messer, Knowles, and other Baptist worthies.

―――― Minutes of the Philadelphia Baptist Association, from 1707 to 1807; being the first one hundred years of its existence. Edited by Rev. A. D. Gillette, A. M.
8vo. pp. 476.   *Philadelphia. American Bap. Pub. Soc.* 1851.

This volume is a most important contribution to the Baptist History of Rhode Island.

―――― The First Church in Providence, not the Oldest of the Baptists in America, attempted to be shown by S. Adlam, Pastor of the First Church in Newport, R. I.
8vo. pp. 28.   Newport. Cranston & Norman. 1850.

―――― Minutes of the Baptist Yearly Meeting of the ancient order of Six Principles of the doctrine of Christ, held at Coventry, R. I., 11th, 12th, and 13th days of September, 1812.
8vo. pp. 8.   Providence. 1812.

―――― A review of a report, presented to the Warren Baptist Association, at its meeting in 1849, on the subject of the true date of the First Baptist Church in Newport, R. I. Prepared by a Committee of the First Baptist Church in Providence, and read at the Warren Baptist Association, September 12, 1850.
8vo. pp. 26.   Providence. H. H. Brown. 1850.

The Committee which prepared this report consisted of the Rev. James N. Granger, D. D., Rev. Alexis Caswell, D. D., and Prof. William Gammell.

―――― An Historical Discourse delivered at the Celebration of the Second Centennial Anniversary of the First Baptist Church, in Providence, November 7, 1839. By William Hague, Pastor of the Church.
12mo. pp. 192.   Providence. B. Cranston & Co. 1839.

―――― Historical Sketch with the Confession and Covenant of the Warwick and Coventry Baptist Church, Crompton, R. I.
12mo. pp. 8.   Providence. Knowles, Anthony & Co.

―――― An Historical Discourse, delivered in the Central Baptist Meeting House, Newport, R. I., January 8, 1854. By the Pastor, Henry Jackson. Published by order of the Church.
8vo. pp. 45.   Newport. Cranston & Norman. 1853.

―――― Charter and By-Laws of the Charitable Baptist Society, in Providence, with the amendments.
8vo. pp. 12.   Providence. Knowles, Anthony & Co. 1855.

―――― A list of members of the First Baptist Church, in Providence, with Biographical Sketches of the Pastor.
12mo. pp. 48. . *Providence. H. H. Brown.* 1832.

―――― A list of members, with the general rules and regulations of the First Baptist Church, in Providence, R. I.
8vo. pp. 27. *Providence. H. H. Brown.* 1855.

For History of the Baptists in Rhode Island, see *Backus, Benedict, Knowles' Memoirs of Roger Williams, Gammell's ditto, Elton's ditto, Hague's Historical Discourse, Tustin's ditto, Jackson's Churches in Rhode Island, Francis Smith's Discourse, ditto Historical Discourse.*

BARNARD, HENRY. Report on the Condition and Improvement of the Public Schools of Rhode Island, submitted November 1, 1854.
8vo. pp. 255. *Providence.* 1854.

―――― Journal of the Rhode Island Institute of Instruction. 3 vols. 8vo. 1845 to 1848.

BARRATT, B. F. The Holy City New Jerusalem, or Doctrine of the New Church. A Sermon preached at the Dedication of the New Church Temple, in Providence R. I., Oct. 14, 1843.
12mo. pp. 47. *New York. John Allen.* 1843.

BARTLETT, CHARLES R., M. D. An account of the rise and progress of the Malignant Fever, commonly called the Yellow Fever! which lately appeared in Newport;—and an account of the treatment that proved most successful in it. Also a note of advice, regarding the preventive means, most likely to have effect, against the return of this dreadful malady the ensuing warm season. To which is added some remarks on the conduct of the author, and others immediately concerned in this first transaction of this unfortunate affair.
8vo. pp. 48. *Newport. Dion Farnsworth.* 1801.
At the end is Moses Brown's account of those who died in Providence of the disease.

BARTLETT, JOHN RUSSELL. Records of the Colony of Rhode Island and Providence Plantations in New England. Printed by order of the General Assembly. Edited by John Russell Bartlett, Secretary of State. 10 vols. 8vo.

Volume 1. 1636 to 1663.
pp. 549. *Providence. A. Crawford Greene & Bro.* 1856.
Volume 2. 1664 to 1667.
pp. 609. *Providence. A. Crawford Greene & Bro.* 1857.
Volume 3. 1668 to 1706.
pp. 595. *Providence. Knowles, Anthony & Co.* 1858.
Volume 4. 1707 to 1740.
pp. 622. *Providence. Knowles, Anthony & Co.* 1859.
Volume 5. 1741 to 1756.
pp. 594. *Providence. Knowles, Anthony & Co.* 1860.
Volume 6. 1757 to 1769.
pp. 629. *Providence. Knowles, Anthony & Co.* 1861.
Volume 7. 1770 to 1776.
pp. 643. *Providence. A. Crawford Greene.* 1862.
Volume 8. 1776 to 1779.
pp. 661. *Providence. Cooke & Danielson.* 1863.
Volume 9. 1780 to 1783.
pp. 763. *Providence. Alfred Anthony.* 1864.
Volume 10. 1784 to 1790.
pp. *Providence. Alfred Anthony.*

Now in the course of publication, nine volumes have been published. A tenth will probably complete the work, to which will be added a volume of State Papers illustrative of the Records.

—— A History of the Destruction of His Britannic Majesty's Schooner Gaspee, in Narragansett Bay, on the 9th of June, 1772; accompanied by the correspondence connected therewith: the action of the General Assembly of the Colony of Rhode Island thereon, and the Official journal of the proceedings of the Commissioners of Enquiry appointed by King George the Third on the same.
8vo. pp. 140. *Providence. A. Crawford Greene.* 1861.

—— The same, imperial 8vo. same. 1861.

This History may also be found in the 7th volume of the Rhode Island Colonial Records.

—— Index to the printed Acts and Resolves, and of the Petitions and Reports to the General Assembly of the State of Rhode Island and Providence Plantations from

the year 1858 to 1860. Printed by order of the General Assembly.
8vo. pp. 104.   *Providence. Knowles, Anthony & Co.* 1856.

———— Index to the printed Acts, Resolves, and of Petitions and Reports, from 1850 to 1862.
8vo. pp. xxxiv. and 103. *Providence. Alfred Anthony.* 1863.

———— Census of the Inhabitants of the Colony of Rhode Island and Providence Plantations, taken by order of the General Assembly, in the year 1774; and by the General Assembly of the State ordered to be printed.
8vo. pp. 239.   *Providence. Knowles, Anthony & Co.* 1858.

———— History of Lotteries in Rhode Island. Published in six numbers of the Providence Journal.

———— The Naval History of Rhode Island. Published in the Providence Journal in the years 1860-61-62. Numbers 1 to 26. To be continued.

———— Report on the State Beneficiaries; including the Deaf and Dumb, the Blind and Insane. Presented to the General Assembly, January, 1863.
8vo. pp. 15.   *Providence. Alfred Anthony.* 1863.

BARTON, GEN. WILLIAM. Life of. See *Catherine Williams.*

BEAMISH, NORTH LUDLOW. The Discovery of America by the Northmen, in the tenth century, with notices of the early settlements of the Irish in the Western Hemisphere.
8vo. pp. xliii. and 239. 2 maps and plate of the inscription on Dighton Rock.   *London. T. & W. Boone.* 1841.

This volume contains an English version of the Icelandic Sagas contained in the "Antiquitates Americanæ," with an introduction giving a sketch of the rise, eminence and extinction of Icelandic Historical Literature.

BENEDICT, REV. DAVID, A. M. A General History of the Baptist Denomination in America, and other parts of the world.
2 vols. 8vo. pp. 606 and 503, and subscribers' names.
        Boston. Lincoln & Edmands. 1813.

———— D. D. the same. Portrait of the author. Royal 8vo. pp. viii. and 970. *New York. Lewis Colby & Co.* 1848.

―――― Fifty Years Among the Baptists.
12mo. pp. 437.   *New York. Sheldon & Co.* 1860.

―――― The Watery War; a poetical description of the existing controversy between the Pedobaptists and Baptists on the subjects and mode of Baptism. By John of Enon.
12mo. pp. 34.   *Boston. Manning & Loring.* 1808.

Although it does not bear his name, this work is known to have been written by Dr. Benedict, when a student in Brown University.

BENEVOLENT CONGREGATIONAL SOCIETY, Act of Incorporation of, in the town of Providence, in the Colony of Rhode Island, &c. Together with the rules of said Society. To which is prefixed a short account of the Congregational Society in said town, under the pastoral care of the Rev. M. Rowland.
8vo. pp. 15.   *Providence. John Carter.* 1771.

―――― The same work. To which is prefixed a short account of the First Congregational Society under the pastoral care of the Rev. Dr. Hitchcock.
8vo. pp. 19.   *Providence. John Carter.* 1802.

―――― Annual Report of, presented November, 1832, to which is added the articles of faith and covenant, and a list of the officers and members.
8vo. pp. 60.   *Providence. Edward & J. W. Cory.* 1833.

BESSE, JOSEPH. A collection of the sufferings of the people called Quakers, for the testimony of a good conscience, from the time of their being first distinguished by that name in the year 1650, to the time of the act, commonly called the *Act of Toleration*, granted to the Protestant dissenters in the first year of the reign of King William the Third and Queen Mary, in the year 1689. Taken from original records and other authentic documents. 2 vols. folio. Vol. 1. pp. iv. and 767. Vol. 2. 638.
London. Luke Hyde. 1753.

The second volume of this work contains a chapter relating to the Quakers in New England, in which are embraced letters from prominent members of the fraternity in Rhode Island. Among them are letters from Governor William Coddington, Anne Coddington, and Mary Dyer.

BIBLE SOCIETY. A statement respecting the Bible Society of the State of Rhode Island and Providence Plantations; with an appendix addressed to the public by the Board of Trustees.
8vo pp. 28. *Providence. Miller, Goddard & Mann.* 1814.

———— Report of the Board of Trustees of, presented at their annual meeting, September 7, 1829.
8vo. pp. 24. *Providence. Miller & Mathews,* 1820.

BINNEY, BARNABAS, M. D. See note to *Goddard's Memoir of Manning,* p. 20.

BISBEE, NOAH, JUN. An oration delivered in Newport on the Fourth of July, 1805.
8vo. pp. 52. *Newport. Asa Barber.* 1805.

BISSETT, GEORGE, M. A. A sermon preached in Trinity Church, Newport, Rhode Island, June 3, 1771, at the funeral of Mrs. Abigail Wanton, late consort of the Hon. Joseph Wanton, Jun., Esq., who died May 31, 1771, in the 36th year of her age.
Small 4to. pp. 20. *Newport. S. Southwick.* 1771.

BLACKSTONE CANAL. Account of the proposed canal from Worcester to Providence, containing the report of the engineer; together with some remarks upon Inland navigation. Published by order of the Committee for the County of Worcester.
8vo. pp. 18. *Worcester. Wm. Manning.* 1822.

———— The same work.
8vo. pp. 16. *Providence. John Miller.* 1825.

———— Charter, by-laws, &c., of the Blackstone Canal Corporation.
8vo pp. 39. *Providence. Cranston & Hammond.* 1835.

BLACKSTONE, WILLIAM, an early planter of Boston. Memoir of. See *Massachusetts Historical Coll.* 2d series, *Vol. x.*

BLACKSTONE MONUMENT ASSOCIATION. An address delivered at the formation of the Blackstone Monument Association, together with the preliminaries and proceedings at Study Hill, July 4, 1855. Prepared for the press by the Secretary, and published by order of the Board of Directors of the Association.

8vo. pp. 39. *Pawtucket, R. I. James L. Estey.* 1855.

BOUNDARY LINE BETWEEN RHODE ISLAND AND MASSACHUSETTS. Books relating to.

────── Records of the Court of Commissioners for settling and determining the boundaries of the Colony of Rhode Island in America, eastwards towards the Province of Massachusetts-Bay, held at the town of Providence in the said Colony, Tuesday, the 7th day of April, 1741, in the fourteenth year of the reign of His Majesty King George the Second. *Manuscript.*

Royal folio. pages 420. Dated Providence, September, 1741.

The Royal Commissioners on the Boundary were Cadwallader Colden, Abraham Vanhorn, Philip Livingston, Archibald Kennedy and James Delancey of the Province of New York; John Hamilton, John Wells, John Reading, Cornelius Vanhorn and William Provost of the Province of New Jersey; and William Skene, William Sheriff, Henry Cope, Erasmus James Phillips and Otho Hamilton, of the Province of Nova Scotia. The records and papers of the Commissioners were ordered to be kept in the office of the Secretary of New York, where they still remain. The volume from which this title is taken is in the collection of our townsman, Mr. John Carter Brown, for whom it was copied from the original in the British State Paper Office, London. It is attested by Robert Lemon, Chief Clerk of the State Paper Office, and also by His Excellency, Louis M'Lane, the American Minister at the Court of St. James. Another copy is among the State Archives, furnished under a resolution of the Legislature of the State of New York, March, 1849. The latter copy fills 251 folio pages.

────── . Massachusetts-Bay and Rhode Island. The case of His Majesty's Province of the Massachusetts-Bay, upon two appeals relating to the Boundaries between that Province and the Colony of Rhode Island and Providence Plantations. To be heard before the Right Honorable the Lords of the Committee of His Majesty's most Honorable the Privy Council, at the Council Chamber at the Cockpit, Whitehall, 1743.

Folio. pp. 9. *London.* 1743.

BOUNDARY LINE. Books relating to.

——— Letters, Reports and other papers in manuscript, relating to the Boundary Line between Rhode Island and Massachusetts from 1694 to 1753, in the office of the Secretary of the State of Rhode Island.
2 vols. folio.

——— Report of the Committee of both Houses to whom was referred the Message of the Governor, communicating certain resolutions of the General Assembly of the State of Rhode Island, relating to the Southern Boundary of Massachusetts. Senate Document. No. 34.
8vo. pp. 15. *Boston.* 1832.

——— Supreme Court of the United States. Rhode Island *vs.* Massachusetts. Papers put into the case of Rhode Island *vs.* Massachusetts, as evidence on the part of Rhode Island.
8vo. pp. 120. [*Washington.*] *J. & G. S. Gideon.*

CLASS FIRST.

Various charters and acts recited in the bill, and admitted, or not denied in the answer.

CLASS SECOND.

No. 1.	Bounds of the Plantation at the Ponds. 1661.	Page	1
" 2.	Grants of the town of Medfield. 1659.	"	3
" 3.	Wrentham, bounded on Charles River north:—extracts from the records of the town of Dedham. 1660.	"	4
" 4.	Wrentham. Proprietor's Records. 1698.	"	5
" 5.	Act incorporating the town of Wrentham. 1673.	"	10
" 6.	Deed—John Ware to Peter Adams, of land bounded on Jacks' Pasture Brook. 1708.		10
" 7.	Deed—Farrington to Kingsbury, of lands on both sides of Jacks' Pasture Brook. 1711.		11
" 8.	Deed—Fisher to Barbour. 1715.	"	13
" 9.	Ancient papers, from A to M, inclusive.	"	15
" 9.	A. Extracts from the Mendon records, five papers.	"	34
" 10.	Deed—Partridge to Partridge. 1719.	"	36
" 11.	Deed—Samuel Harden to Joseph Whiting, Jun. 1754.	"	38
" 12.	Act incorporating the town of Franklin. 1768.	"	41

CLASS THIRD.

" 1.	Running of Commissioners of Massachusetts and Plymouth, in 1664, of their dividing line. 1664.	"	42
" 2.	Copy of letter from Massachusetts. 1709.	"	44

BOUNDARY LINE. Books relating to.

No. 3. Law of Connecticut establishing a ferry in Windsor. 1642. Page 44
" 4. Commission from Charles 2d to settle disputes about boundaries. 1664. " 45
" 5. Deposition of Richard Callicott, taken in 1672; also of James Taylor, taken in 1711. " 47

CLASS FOURTH.

" 1. Report of Commissioners that run the North lines in 1750. " 48
" 2. Claim of Cumberland to a part of Wrentham in 1794. " 52
" 3. Acts of the General Assembly of R. I., from 1705 to 1825. " 52

CLASS FIFTH.

" 1. Act of Massachusetts relative to the Boundary Line. " 80

CLASS SIXTH.

" 1. Act of Connecticut, appointing Roger Wolcott and Phineas Lyman to concur with ours respecting northern line, 1751. " 88
" 2. Acts and Agreements of 1713. " 88
" 3. Copies of papers from Connecticut, 1750 to 1752 inclusive. " 92
" 4. Copy of the Connecticut case in 1703. " 103

———— Deposition of Simeon Borden, 1843.
8vo. pp. 54. [*Washington.*] *J. & G. S. Gideon.* 1844.

———— Supreme Court of the United States. Rhode Island *vs.* Massachusetts. Papers put into the case by Massachusetts.
8vo. pp. 54. [*Washington.*] *J. & G. S. Gideon.*

Nos. 1 to 9. Deeds and notes of land surveyors, 1711 to 1765. Page 1
No. 10. Copy of Wrentham and Bellingham line, 1735. " 16
" 11. Report about Wrentham and Bellingham line, April 1735. " 17
" 12. Petition, grant and plat of Bellingham town, 1719. " 19
" 13. Report of the Committee for running the south line, 1709. " 22
" 14. Various deeds, letters, surveys, records and reports. 24 to 54

———— Argument in the case Rhode Island against Massachusetts, Supreme Court of the United States, January term, 1838. [By Benjamin Hazard.] Printed by order of the General Assembly.
8vo. pp. 60. *Providence. Knowles, Vose & Co.* 1838.

———— Resolve concerning the Boundary Line between the States of Massachusetts and Rhode Island, 1843. With the petition of Church Gray and 79 others.
8vo. pp. 8. *Senate Doc. of Massachusetts.* 1844.

———— Abstract of Historical events relating to the North and South lines of Massachusetts, prepared by the Counsel for Rhode Island in the case Rhode Island *vs.* Massachu-

setts, pending in the Supreme Court of the United States. January Term, 1845.
8vo. pp. 42.   1845.

——— Report of the Massachusetts Commissioners appointed under a resolve of the Legislature of Massachusetts, (of Feb. 2, 1844, on the petition of Church Gray and others,) upon the Boundary Line between Rhode Island and Massachusetts, from Pawtucket Falls to Bullock's Neck, Jan. 23, 1846, together with the report of Simeon Borden.
8vo. pp. 21.   *House Doc. No. 11, of Massachusetts.* 1846.

——— Communication of Gov. Briggs to the House of Representatives of Massachusetts, dated March 23, 1846; and a letter from Daniel Webster, accompanying the opinion of Judge McLean delivered in the Supreme Court of the United States, December Term, 1845, in the case of the State of Rhode Island *vs.* Massachusetts. Also, Resolves concerning the Boundary Line between Massachusetts and Rhode Island.
8vo. pp. 22.   *House Doc. No. 76, of Massachusetts.* 1846.

——— Report of the Commissioners of the State of Massachusetts and Rhode Island, appointed to ascertain, establish and definitely mark the true Boundary Line between said States, from the Atlantic Ocean to the northwest corner of Rhode Island.
8vo. pp. 4.   *House Doc. of Massachusetts, January.* 1847.

——— Resolve concerning the Boundary Line between Massachusetts and Rhode Island.
House Doc. of Massachusetts, No. 116. 1847.

——— Documents relating to the Boundary Line and Disputed Territory between Massachusetts and Rhode Island.
8vo. pp. 64.   *Fall River. Henry Pratt.* 1847.

This pamphlet was printed by order of the town of Fall River, with a view to furnish the citizens and the community with the principal documents and facts relating to the territory in dispute.

No. 1. A brief report made to the town of Fall River at its town meeting in April 10, 1847, by a committee appointed for that purpose.   Page 3

BOUNDARY LINE. Books relating to.

No. 2. Petition of the town of Fall River, through their Committee to the Legislature; in which is given a succinct history of the proceedings of the last hundred years, touching the Boundary Line, March 6, 1847. Page 6
" 3. The award of the Commissioners of George 21, who met at Providence in 1741; which award was confirmed by the King in Council in 1746. " 24
" 4. Report of the Commissioners appointed by Massachusetts in 1781, to meet the Commissioners of Rhode Island. " 27
" 5. Report of the Survey of Simeon Borden to the Commissioners appointed to ascertain and establish the Boundary between the States of Rhode Island and Massachusetts, from the Atlantic Ocean to the Burnt Swamp Corner (so called) in Wrentham. " 31
" 6. Recent agreement between a majority of the Massachusetts and Rhode Island Commissioners, April 28, 1847. " 39
" 7. Call and doings of a Convention held at Fall River, June 23, 1847. " 42
" 8. Resolves passed by the Legislature of Massachusetts in 1844-45, concerning the Boundary Line. " 55
" 9. Decision of the Supreme Court of the United States with the case of Rhode Island vs. Massachusetts, December Term, 1845. " 59

—— Papers on the Boundary Line between Massachusetts and the easterly line of Rhode Island. First published in September and October, 1847, in the Boston Atlas. By Plymouth Colony.

8vo. pp. 19. [*Boston.*] *No date.*

—— Report of the Boundary Commissioners, transmitting Simeon Borden's Survey of the Line from Burnt Swamp corner, in Wrentham, to a monument in Thompson, Connecticut, January, 1847.

Memorial from the town of Fall River to the Commissioners, Sept. 21, 1846.
Memorial from the town of Westport to the Commissioners, Jan, 28, 1847.
Memorial from the town of Fall River to the Legislature of Massachusetts, March 6, 1847.
Memorial from Pawtucket to ditto.
Memorials from Seekonk and Rehoboth, January, 1846, and January, 1847. Massachusetts House Document, No. 57, 1857. 8vo.
The above are Documents of the Massachusetts Legislature. House Nos. 13, 93, 80, 57. 1847.

—— Petition from inhabitants of Fall River, by their Committee, to the Legislature of Massachusetts, relative to the South Boundary of Fall River, March 6, 1847.

8vo. pp. 21. *House Doc. of Mass. No. 93. March. 1847.*

BOUNDARY LINE. Books relating to.

—— Report of Simeon Borden to the Commissioners of the States of Massachusetts and Rhode Island, for determining the Boundary Line between said States. 8vo. pp. *House Document of Massachusetts. No.* 14. 1847.

—— Report of the Joint Special Committee, appointed under a Resolve of the General Court of Massachusetts, of March 18, 1844, [on the Eastern Boundary,] made in April, 1848. [With an Appendix of Documents.] 8vo. pp. 140. *Senate Document, No.* 128. *April.* 1848.

The following documents comprise the Appendix:

A. Letter from Rhode Island to the Earl of Clarendon, with "some reasons for settling the eastern line, according to the meaning and letter of the Charter." Page 72
B. Extract from the Speech of Gov. Shirley, Dec. 30, 1746, etc. " 76
Report of Rhode Island Ex-parte Commissioners in 1715. " 78
C. Act of Rhode Island, appointing Boundary Commissioners, 1791. " 81
D. Report of Rhode Island Commissioners, 1792. " 81
Report of Massachusetts Commissioners, 1792. " 83
E. Testimony taken before the Joint Special Committee of the Legislature of Massachusetts, on the Boundary Line, March 2, 1848. T. Wentworth, Chairman. " 87
F. 1. Letters and memorials from inhabitants of the town of Fall River.
2. Protest of qualified voters in the town of Pawtucket.
3. Remonstrance from citizens of the town of Seekonk.
4. Remonstrance from inhabitants of the town of Attleborough.
5. Remonstrance from inhabitants of the town of Westport.
6. Petitions from inhabitants of the town of Swanzey.

—— Report of the Commissioners appointed Feb. 27, 1844, to ascertain and establish the true Boundary Line between Massachusetts and Rhode Island, from Pawtucket Falls to Bullock's Neck; and a minority report on the same subject: with an appendix of twenty-four documents, and the decision of the Supreme Court of the United States, December Term, 1845. Folding Map. 8vo. pp. 132. *Mass. Senate Doc. No.* 14. *January.* 1848.

—— Report of the Joint Committee upon the Boundary Line between the States of Rhode Island and Massachusetts; made to the Legislature of Rhode Island, January

BOUNDARY LINE. Books relating to.

Session, A. D., 1848. Printed by order of the Legislature.
8vo. pp. 58. *Providence. Joseph Knowles.* 1849.
The Commissioners were E. R. Potter, Stephen Branch, Wm. D. Brayton, Alfred Bosworth, Fenner Brown and Nathan F. Dixon.

——— Report of the Joint Committee upon the Boundary Line between the States of Rhode Island and Massachusetts ; made to the Legislature of Rhode Island, January Session, A. D., 1849. Printed by order of the Legislature.
8vo. pp. 58. *Providence. Joseph Knowles.* 1849.

——— Message of Gov. Boutwell to the Legislature of Massachusetts, accompanying the Report of the Massachusetts Commissioners on the Boundary Line between the States of Rhode Island and Massachusetts, March 15, 1851.
8vo. pp. 14. *House Document, No. 120.* 1851.

——— Report of the Joint Special Committee, to the Legislature of Massachusetts on the Boundary question, (upon the petitions from Pawtucket, Seekonk, Rehoboth and Fall River,) with accompanying resolves. April, 1852.
8vo. pp. 15. *Senate Document, No. 106.* 1852.

——— Supreme Court of the United States, September Term, 1852. [Bill of Complaint.] The Commonwealth of Massachusetts *vs.* The State of Rhode Island and Providence Plantations.
4to. pp. 200. With maps and plans.
Boston. White & Potter. 1852.

——— Supreme Court of the United States, at its December Term, at Washington, A. D., 1855. (In Equity.) [Answer to the State of Rhode Island.] The Commonwealth of Massachusetts *vs.* The State of Rhode Island and Providence Plantations.
Folio. pp. 37 and 40. Appendix of doc. *Providence.* 1855

——— Majority report of the Joint Committee of the General Assembly on the disputed Boundary between Rhode Island and Massachusetts.
8vo. pp. 12. *Providence. Knowles, Anthony & Co.* 1860.

BOUNDARY LINE. Books relating to.

―――― Some Considerations touching the proposed change of Boundary between the States of Massachusetts and Rhode Island. By a Rhode Islander.
8vo. pp. 8.   *Providence.* 1861.

―――― Supplementary Bill in Equity, the Commonwealth of Massachusetts *vs.* The State of Rhode Island, December Term, 1860. Certified by Oliver Warner, Secretary of the Commonwealth.
8vo. pp. 11.   *Boston. January.* 1861.

―――― Answer to the Supplementary Bill in Equity, the Commonwealth of Massachusetts *vs.* the State of Rhode Island, December Term, 1860. Certified by John R. Bartlett, Secretary of State.
8vo. pp. 9.   *Providence. January* 23. 1861.

―――― Supreme Court of the United States, No. 3. The Commonwealth of Massachusetts, complainant, *vs.* The State of Rhode Island. Bill in Chancery.
8vo. pp. 261.   *Gov. Printing Office.* [*Washington.*] 1862.

The following are the contents of the volume:
Bill. Massachusetts *vs.* Rhode Island.	Page 1
Agreement of parties, December Term, 1854.	" 122
Answer of the State of Rhode Island to the Bill of Complaint of the State of Massachusetts.	" 123
Replicatson of Massachusetts to the answer of Rhode Island.	" 228
Stipulation of Counsel and order of Court.	" 229
Agreement to extend time.	" 229
Motion for leave to file Supplementary Bill.	" 237
Motion for United States to intervene.	" 243
Assent of United States to interlocutory order.	" 243
Interlocutory order and report.	" 244
Motion for leave to file 2d Supplementary Bill.	" 248
Motion for leave to file 2d Supplementary Bill and answer.	" 248
Order granting leave to file 2d Supplementary Bill and answer.	" 248
Second Supplementary Bill.	" 249
Answer to Ditto.	" 254
Final Decree. Filed December 16, 1861.	" 257

The following are the titles of the Public Laws which appertain to the Boundary question recently enacted by the General Assembly of Rhode Island, all of which will be found in the Supplements to the Revised Statutes:

BOUNDARY LINE. Books relating to.

An act in amendment of act an passed at the January Session, A. D., 1860, entitled "an act for the adjustment of the Eastern Boundary of this State, and for a boundary of agreement." Chapter 357, January Session, 1861.

An act in addition to an act providing for an adjustment of the Eastern Boundary of this State, and for a boundary by agreement, and to the act in amendment thereof. Chapter 379, May Session, 1861.

An act regulating suits at law, and granting possessions, and establishing titles of land and property, affected by the establishment of the Boundary Line between the States of Rhode Island and Massachusett, and for other purposes. Chapter 391. Passed in January Session, 1862.

An act in addition to, and in amendment of, "an act in addition to an act, providing for an adjustment of the Eastern Boundary of this State, and for a boundary by agreement, and to the act in amendment thereof." Passed at the May Session, A. D., 1851. Chapter 892.

An act in amendment of an act entitled "an act regulating suits at law, and of uniting possessions; and establishing titles of land and property affected by the establishment of the Boundary Line between the States of Rhode Island and Massachusetts, and for other purposes." Passed at the May Session, A. D., 1862. Chapter 415.

An act to provide for the valuation of the property within the territory over which the State of Massachusetts, prior to the first day of March last exercised jurisdiction, for taxation and other purposes. Passed at the May Session, A. D., 1862. Chapter 417.

BOWEN, HENRY L. Memoir of Tristam Burges, with selections from his speeches and occasional writings.

8vo. pp. xii. and 404. Portrait.

Providence. Marshall, Brown & Co. 1855.

BOURS, JOHN. An appeal to the Public, in which the misrepresentations and calumnies, contained in a pamphlet, entited a Narrative of certain matters relative to Trinity Church, in Newport, in the State of Rhode Island, by a very *extraordinary* man, the Rev. Jamey Sayere, A. M., late Minister of said Church, are pointed out, and his very strange conduct during the time of his ministration at Newport, faithfully related. By John Bours, Merchant, and one of the vestry of said Church.

8vo. pp. 39. Appendix v. *Newport. Peter Edes.* 1789.

BLOCK ISLAND. Memoir of Block Island, or Manisses. A. D., 1762. By Dr. Stiles.

Mass. Hist. Coll. 1st series. Vol. 7.

BLOCK ISLAND. The History of. By Henry T. Beckwith. Read before the Rhode Island Historical Society, Nov. 1856. 4to. pp. 8. *Historical Magazine. April.* 1858.

——— A paper on the early history of. Read before the Rhode Island Historical Society, and published in the Providence Journal, 1859. By Hon. William P. Sheffield.

BRADFORD, REV. ZABDIEL. Sermon on. See *J. N. Granger.*

BRENTON, WILLIAM. Letter to John Endicott, dated Newport, November 9, 1861.
Mass. Historical Collection. 2d series, vol. 1.

BRIDGHAM, SAMUEL W. An oration delivered at the Benevolent Congregational Meeting House, Providence, on the 4th of July, 1798.
8vo. pp. 12. *Providence. Carter & Wilkinson.* 1798.

BRISTOL. An account of the settlement of the Town of Bristol, in the State of Rhode Island; and of the Congregational Church therein, with the succession of Pastors from its origin to the present time; together with the act of incorporation of the Catholic Congregational Society, and the rules established in said Society.
8vo. pp. 16. *Providence. Printed by Bennett Wheeler.* 1785.

BRIGGS, JOHN, A. B. An oration delivered at the North Meeting House, in Tiverton, on the 11th February, 1800, on the death of General George Washington. By the request of the Honorable Town Council of Tiverton.
8vo. pp. 10. *Newport. Henry Barber.* 1800.

BRISTED, REV. JOHN. Funeral discourse on. See *Eastburn.*

BRITISH EMPIRE IN AMERICA. A new and complete History of the British Empire in America.
3 vols. 8vo. [*London.*] 1756.

The first volume of this work contains an introduction of fifty-two pages, and an account of Hudson's Bay, Newfoundland, Nova Scotia and New England, in 402 pages. The second continues the history of New England, and gives that of New York, New Jersey and Pennsylvania, 498 pages. The third contains Maryland, Virginia and North Carolina, ending abruptly at page 272. It contains well executed maps and plates.

BROAD RIMMED WHEELS.   See *Hints to Farmers of R. I.*

BROOKS, REV. CHARLES T. Sermon on the death of Dr. Channing. Preached in the Union Meeting House. Portsmouth, R. I., Oct. 10, 1842.
<small>Printed in the Boston Evening Gazette, early in 1843.</small>

———— Aquidneck. A Poem. Pronounced on the 100th Anniversary of the Incorporation of the Redwood Library, Newport, R. I., Aug. 24. 1847; with other commemorative pieces.
12mo. pp. 63.   *Providence. C. Burnett, Jun.* 1848.

———— The controversy touching the Old Stone Mill, in the town of Newport, Rhode Island, with remarks introductory and conclusive. With three wood cuts.
12mo. pp. 91.   *Newport. C. E. Hammett, Jun.* 1851.

———— Songs of Field and Flood. Printed for the Ladies' Fair at the Ocean House, Newport, August, 1853.
8vo. pp. 47.   *Boston. John Wilson & Son.* 1853.
<small>Contains "Lines on leaving Mount Hope Bay."—"Sabbath Morning at Pettaquamscutt."—"Indian Summer Noon at Rhode Island," etc.</small>

———— The old Rhode Island Question. Review of Arnold's History of Rhode Island. In Christian Examiner, for March, 1859.

———— The Soldier's Welcome Home! Spoken by Master Fred. P. Sayer, at the reception of the Newport Artillery, Colonel Tew and General Burnside. Aug. 6, 1861.
          Broadside. Newport Advertiser Office. 1861.

<small>Mr. Brooks is the writer of twenty-six different New Year's addresses, written and printed as Broadside's, between the years 1839 and 1863, which, more or less, relate to the history of the State.</small>

BROWN, MOSES. From the meeting for sufferings for New England, to the several Quarterly and Monthly meetings belonging to the Yearly Meeting. Eleventh of the 11th month, 1782.
4to. pp. 19.   *Providence. John Carter.* [1782.]

Brown, Nicholas. A sermon preached May 31, 1791, in Providence, State of Rhode Island, on the death of Nicholas Brown, Esq., who died the 29th preceeding, Æt. 62. Published at the desire of the bereaved family. By Samuel Stillman, D. D., Pastor of the First Church in Boston, and Fellow of Rhode Island College.
8vo. pp. 24 and iv.   *Providence. J. Carter.* [1791.]

———— Brief Notices of the Life and Character of. Reprinted from the Providence Journal of October 4, 1841. 12mo. pp. 15.   *Providence.* 1841.

———— A discourse on the Life and Character of, delivered in the chapel of Brown University, November, 3, 1841. By Francis Wayland, D. D., President of the University. 8vo. pp. 30.   *Boston. Gould, Kendall & Lincoln.* 1841.

———— Notice of, in Teasdale's Hist. Discourse before the First Baptist Church in New Haven. p. 36. 1842.

Brown, Hon. Nicholas. Sketch of the educational and other benefactions of. By Prof. Wm. Gammell. Reprinted from Barnard's American Journal of Education, June, 1857. 8vo. pp. 26.

Brown Family. Genealogy of a portion of, principally from the Moses Brown papers and from other authentic sources. 12mo. pp. 16.   *Providence. H. H. Brown.* 1851.

Brown, Col. William W, of the Providence First Light Infantry Company, on charges preferred by Gen. Joseph S. Pitman, Brigadier General, Second Brigade, Rhode Island Militia ; at Providence, August, 1856.
8vo. pp. 23.   *Providence. A. Crawford Greene.* 1856.

———— Statement respecting the Court Martial ordered by General Burnside for the trial of Col. W. W. Brown, on charges preferred by General Pitman.
8vo. pp. 11.   *Providence.* 1856.

BROWN UNIVERSITY. Books relating to.

Addresses, Orations, *Sermons and Poems, delivered before Brown University and its Literary Societies, or otherwise connected with it* ; also Catalogues of Books and Students.

BROWN UNIVERSITY. Books relating to.

——— Addeman and Colby. Class of 1862. An Oration and a Poem delivered in the chapel of Brown University, on Class Day, June 12, 1862. Printed at the request of the class. Oration by Joshua M. Addeman, of Providence, R. I. Poem by Henry F. Colby, of Newton Centre, Mass.

8vo. pp. 43. *Providence. Cooke & Danielson.* 1862.

——— Account of the First Commencement of Rhode Island College, celebrated at Warren, Thursday, September 7, 1769.

Small 4to. *Newport. Printed by Solomon Southwick.* 1769.

ALLEN, BENJAMIN, A. B. An oration in defence of Divine Revelation; together with the Valedictory Address; delivered at the Baptist Meeting House, in Providence, at the Commencement of Rhode Island College, September 6, 1797. Published by request.

8vo. pp. 16. *Providence. Carter & Wilkinson.* 1797.

ALLEN, PAUL, JUN., A. B. An oration on the necessity of Political Union at the present day; delivered at the Baptist Meeting House, in Providence, at the Commencement of Rhode Island College, A. D., 1797.

8vo. pp. 8. *Providence. Carter & Wilkinson.* 1797.

——— A. M. An Oration, delivered at the Benevolent Congregational Meeting House, in Providence, before the Corporation of the Federal Adelphi, at their Anniversary meeting, on the 4th day of September, 1798.

8vo. pp. 19. *Providence. Bennett Wheeler.* 1798.

——— An Oration on the principles of Taste, delivered before the Federal Adelphi, September 4, 1800, at the Baptist Meeting House, in Providence.

8vo. pp. 14. *Providence. Bennett Wheeler.* 1800.

ALLEN, PAUL, JUN. An Oration on the death of Roger Williams Howell, a member of the Senior Class of Rhode Island College, who died Oct. 7, 1792, æt at 20. Pronounced in College Chapel, Nov. 22, 1792.

8vo. pp. 11. *Providence. Printed by J. Carter.* 1792.

BROWN UNIVERSITY. Books relating to.

ALLEN, BENJAMIN F. An Oration pronounced before the Students of Brown University, in the College Chapel, July 4, 1817, in commemoration of the anniversary of American Independence.
8vo. pp. 16. *Providence. Jones & Wheeler.* 1817.

BINNEY, BARNABAS, A. B. An Oration delivered at the late Public Commencement at Rhode Island College, in Providence, Sept. 17, 1774. Being a plea for the right of private judgment in religious matters; or, for the liberty of choosing our own religion, corroborated by the well known consequences of priestly power. To which are annexed the valedictions of the class then first graduated.
Small 4to. pp. 44. *Boston. John Kneeland.* 1774.

BRIDGHAM, SAMUEL W. An Oration delivered at the Commencement of R. I. College, in Providence, Sept. 6, 1797.
8vo. pp. 7. *Providence. Carter & Wilkinson.* 1797.

BURGES, TRISTAM, A. M. The Art of Excelling; an oration delivered in the Benevolent Congregational Meeting House, at Providence, before the Society of Federal Adelphi, on their Anniversary, September 5, 1798.
8vo. pp. 22. *Providence. John Carter, Jun.* 1799.

—— An Oration delivered before the R. I. Federal Adelphi, September 8, 1831.
8vo. pp. 36. *Providence. Weeden & Knowles.* 1831.

—— The Cause of Man; an oration, together with Valedictory Addresses, pronounced at the Commencement of Rhode Island College, Sept. 7, A. D., 1796. " Say rather man's as perfect as he ought."—*Pope.*
8vo. pp. 17. *Providence. Carter & Wilkinson.* 1796.

BURGESS, GEORGE, A. M. Minister of Christ's Church, Hartford, Conn. The Martyrdom of St. Peter and St. Paul; a Poem recited before the Rhode Island Alpha of the Phi Beta Kappa Society of Brown University, Sept. 3, 1834.
12mo. pp. 48. *Providence. Marshall, Brown & Co.* 1834.
Ths author is now Bishop of Maine.

BROWN UNIVERSITY. Books relating to.

BAILY, ISAAC. A Poem delivered before the Philermenian Society of *Brown University*, on their Anniversary, Sept., 1812. Published at the request of the Society.
8vo. pp. 15.   *Providence. David Hawkins, Jun.* 1812.

BURRAGE, HENRY S. A Poem by. See *Shearman*.

BARTON, IRA. Eulogy delivered in the Chapel of Brown University, on Mr. Ezra Bailey, member of the Sophomore Class, who died Oct. 7, 1818. By Ira Barton, member of the Senior Class.
8vo. pp. 16.   *Providence. Miller & Hutchens.* 1817.

CASWELL, ALEXIS. A Discourse delivered before the Phi Beta Kappa Society of Rhode Island, Sept. 2, 1835.
8vo. pp. 18.   *Printed in the Biblical Repository.* 1836.

CUSHING, CALEB. A Discourse on the Social Influence of Christianity, delivered at Providence, R. I., Sept. 1835, at the instance of the Phi Beta Kappa Society of Brown University.
8vo. pp. 28.   *Andover. Gould & Newman.* 1839.

DEANE, REV. SAMUEL, of Scituate, Mass. The Populous Village; a Poem, recited before the Philermenian Society of Providence, Sept., 1826. Published by the Society.
8vo. pp. 18.   *Providence. Miller & Grattan.* 1826.

DEXTER, ANDREW, JUN., A. B. An Oration on the importance of Science and Religion, particularly to American Youth. Pronounced at the Commencement of Rhode Island College, Sept. 5, 1798. Published at the request of the Students.
8vo. pp. 8.   *Providence. Carter & Wilkinson.* 1798.

DODGE, PAUL, A. B. A Poem; delivered at the Commencement of Rhode Island College, Sept. 6, A. D., 1797. Published by request.
8vo. pp. 8.   *Providence. Carter & Wilkinson.* 1797.

DURFEE, JOB. The influence of scientific discovery and invention on Social and Political progress. Oration delivered

BROWN UNIVERSITY. Books relating to.

before the Phi Beta Kappa Society of Brown University, of Providence, R. I., on Commencement day Sept. 6, 1843.
8vo. pp. 52. *Providence. Cranston & Hammond.* 1843.

EMMONS, WILLIAMS. Senior Sophister. An oration on the death of Mr. Levi Hoppin, a member of the Sophomore Class of Brown University, pronounced March 27th, 1805, in the University Chapel.
8vo. pp. 12. *Providence. J. Carter.* 1805.

EVERETT, ALEXANDER H. An Address to the Philermenian Society of Brown University, on the moral character of the Literature of the last and present century. Delivered at Providence, R. I., September 4, 1837. Published by request.
8vo. pp. 54. *Providence.* 1837.

FISK, AMASA. An Oration delivered September 3, 1841, before the Philermenian Society, at Providence.
12mo. pp. 12. *Providence. Jones & Wheeler.* 1841.

FISK, ISAAC. An Eulogy on Mr. Samuel Smith Adams, member of the Senior Class of Brown University, who died Feb. 6, 1812, Aetat 22 years. Pronounced in the University Chapel, April 18, 1812. By Isaac Fisk, classmate of the deceased.
8vo. pp. 16. *Providence. Jones & Wheeler.* 1812.

To this Eulogy is appended an Elegiac Stanzas, published in the Rhode Island American, March 6, 1812.

GRAY, FRANCIS C. Oration before the Phi Beta Kappa Society of Brown University, Providence, R. I., on Commencement day, September 7, 1842.
8vo. pp. 40. *Providence. B. Cranston & Co.* 1842.

GREENE, ALBERT G. Anniversary Poem, pronounced before the Philermenian Society, at their 34th celebration, September 2d, 1828.
8vo. pp. 8. *Providence. Smith & Parmenter.* 1829.

GODDARD, WILLIAM G. An Address to the Phi Beta Kappa Society, of Rhode Island, delivered September 7, 1836.
8vo. pp. 30. *Boston. John H. Eastburn.* 1837.

BROWN UNIVERSITY. Books relating to.

MAXCY, REV. JONATHAN, A. M. Proposals for printing by subscription a Poem, on the "Prospects of America," with the Valedictory Addresses subjoined. Spoken at the public Commencement, in Providence, September 5, 1787. By the author, Jonathan Maxcy. Lately appointed one of the Trustees of Rhode Island College. To which is added, Notes and Observations, with an appendix by another hand, containing a short typographical and historical account of the State of Rhode Island, but more particularly of the Town of Providence—of the College, its Regulations and the Studies pursued there, etc., etc.

This work was printed in accordance with the proposals, and sold for 12s. It is, however, so exceeding rare that no complete copy has ever come to our knowledge. Signatures C and E, pp. 17—40, containing the latter part of the Poem, and the first part of the typographical and historical portion, are in the Brown University Collection. It is not certain that the entire work was ever printed.

——— President of Rhode Island College. An Address delivered by, to the Graduates at the Commencement, Sept. 8, 1794. "Hence appears the necessity of cultivating our reason, and subjecting our passions to its control."

8vo. pp. 8.   *Providence. Bennett Wheeler.* 1794.

——— An Address delivered to the Graduates of Rhode Island College, at the Anniversary Commencement, September 5, 1798.

8vo. pp. 12.   *Providence. Carter & Wilkinson.* 1798.

Dedicated to the Honorable John Brown, Esq., for his public generosity, eminent patriotism and liberal patronage of Rhode Island College.

——— An Address delivered to the Candidates for the Baccalaureate in Rhode Island College, at the Anniversary Commencement, September 2, 1801.

8vo. pp. 15.   *Wrentham, Mass. Nath'l. Heaton, Jun.* 1801.

——— President of Rhode Island College. A sermon delivered in the Chapel of Rhode Island College, to the Senior Class. Commencement, September 3, 1800.

8vo. pp. 15.   *Providence. Bennett Wheeler.* 1801.

The last page contains a catalogue of the Baccalaureate of Rhode Island College, 1800.

BROWN UNIVERSITY. Books relating to.

——— An Address delivered to the Graduates of Rhode Island College, at the public Commencement, September 1, 1802. Published by request.
8vo. pp. 15.   *Wrentham, Mass. Nath'l. Heaton, Jun.* 1802.
The last page contains a catalogue of the Graduates of Rhode Island College, September 1, 1802.

MAXCY, VIRGIL. A Discourse before the Phi Beta Kappa Society of Brown University, September 4, 1833.
8vo. pp. 31.   *Boston. Lilly, Wait, Colman & Holden.* 1833.

MESSER, ASA, A. M. A Discourse delivered in the Chapel of Rhode Island College, to the Senior Class, on the Sunday preceding their Commencement, 1799. By A. M. Professor of the Learned Languages.
8vo. pp. 16.   *Providence. John Carter, Jun.* 1799.
Dedicated to the young gentlemen of the Senior Class.

——— President of Rhode Island College. An Address delivered to the Graduates of Rhode Island College, at their public Commencement, Sept. 7, 1803.
8vo. pp. 12.   *Providence. Nath'l. Heaton, Jun.* 1803.

——— D. D., the President. An Address delivered to the Graduates of Brown University, at the Commencement, September 5, 1810. Published by request of the Class.
8vo. pp. 12.   *Providence. Dunham & Hawkins.* 1810.

METCALF, THERON. An Address to the Phi Beta Kappa Society of Brown University. Delivered Sept. 5, 1832.
8vo. pp. 28.   *Boston. Lilly, Wait, Coleman & Holden.* 1833.

NEAL, JOHN. Man: A Discourse before the United Brothers' Society of Brown University, Sept. 5, 1838.
8vo. pp. 25.   *Providence. Knowles, Vose & Co.* 1838.

PARK, THOMAS. An Oration; delivered in the College Hall, at Providence, Aug. 13, 1798, on the death of Mr. Nathan Merrick. By Thomas Park, member of the Junior Class.
" Quis desiderio set pudor, aut modus tam chari caputis ?"
8vo. pp. 16.   *Providence. Bennett Wheeler.* 1788.

PEABODY, ANDREW F. The Immutable Right; an Oration

BROWN UNIVERSITY. Books relating to.
——— delivered before the Phi Beta Kappa Society of Brown University, Aug. 31, 1858. Published by request.
8vo. pp. 25.   Boston. Crosby, Nichols & Co. 1858.
PAINE, EMERSON. (Of the Senior Class.) An Oration pronounced before the Students of Brown University, at the First Congregational Meeting House, in Providence, July 5, 1813, in commemoration of the Anniversary of American Independence.
8vo. pp. 30.   Providence. H. Mason & Co. 1813.
PITMAN, JOHN, JUN., A. M. An Oration pronounced before the Corporation of the Federal Adelphi Society, on their Anniversary, September 5, 1805, in the First Congregational Meeting House, Providence. Published by request.
8vo. pp. 20.   Providence. Heaton & Williams. 1805.
——— A Poem, on the Social State and its future progress; delivered before the Philermenian Society of Brown University, at its Anniversary, Sept. 3, 1811.
12mo. pp. 14.   Providence. Jones & Wheeler. 1811.
——— Address to the Alumni Association of Brown University, delivered in Providence, at their first anniversary, Sept. 5, 1843. Published by request.
8vo. pp. 64.   Providence. B. Cranston. 1843.
This address is mostly biographical and historical. The appendix gives accounts of early Commencements of Brown University, down to 1786.
PHILERMENIAN SOCIETY. April, 1821.
16mo. pp. 32.   Providence. Miller & Hutchens. 1821.
ROBBINS, ASHER. A Discourse before the Phi Beta Kappa Society of Brown University. Delivered Sept. 3, 1834.
8vo. pp. 28.   Boston. Lilly, Wait, Coleman & Holden. 1834.
RICHMOND, WILLIAM E. Mount Hope, an Evening Excurcursion. (Read before the Federal Adelphi of Brown University, Sept., 1816.)
12mo. pp. 69..   Providence. Miller & Hutchens. 1818.
RUSSELL, GEORGE. The Merchant. An Oration before the Rhode Island Alpha of the Phi Beta Kappa Society, at Providence, R. I., Sept. 4, 1849.
8vo. pp. 60.   Boston. Ticknor & Fields. 1849.

BROWN UNIVERSITY. Books relating to.

RUSSELL, GEORGE R. Eulogy delivered in the Chapel of Brown University, on Mr. Henry Smith, member of the Senior Class, who died Dec. 28, 1820. By George R. Russell, classmate of the deceased.
8vo. pp. 16.   *Providence. Miller & Hutchens.* 1821.

REED, JOHN, JUN. An Oration, delivered on Commencement at Brown University, Sept. 3, 1806. Published by request.
4to. pp. 11.   *Providence. John Carter.* 1806.

SPRAGUE, DANIEL S. Eulogy, delivered in the Chapel of Brown University, on Mr. Isaac Fuller, member of the Freshman Class, who died May 20, 1819.
8vo. pp. 16.   *Providence. Office of the American.* 1819.

SHEARMAN, SUMNER U. Oration delivered at Brown University, on Class Day, June 13, 1861.
8vo. pp. 28.   *Providence. Miller & Simons.* 1861.

THAYER, THATCHER, D. D. The State. An Oration before the Rhode Island Alpha of the Phi Beta Kappa Society, at Brown University, Sept. 27, 1862.
8vo. pp. 30.   *Providence. Sidney S. Rider.* 1862.

THOMSON, OTIS. A funeral oration, delivered in the Chapel of Rhode Island College, on Wednesday, March 29, 1797, occasioned by the death of Mr. Eliab Kingman, a member of the Junior Class. By Otis Thomson, classmate of the deceased.
8vo. pp. 8.   *Providence. Carter & Wilkinson.* 1797.

THOMPSON, OTIS, A. B. An Oration urging the necessity of Religion, as the only permanent basis of civil government. Pronounced at the Commencement of Rhode Island College, September 5, 1798. Published at the request of the Students.
8vo. pp. 8.   *Providence. Carter & Wilkinson.* 1798.

TOWNSEND, SHEARJASHAB B. Pastor of the Church in Sherburne, Mass. An Oration on the Aids of Genius;

BROWN UNIVERSITY. Books relating to.

—— delivered at Providence, Sept. 3, 1822, before the United Brothers' Society of Brown University.
8vo. pp. 21. *Providence. Brown & Danforth.* 1822.

WAYLAND, FRANCIS, D. D. President of Brown University. A Discourse on the Philosophy of Analogy, delivered before the Phi Beta Kappa Society, of Rhode Island, September 7, 1831.
8vo. pp. 32. *Boston. Hilliard, Gray & Co.* 1831.

WEBB, CONRAD, A. B. Union considered as the only safety of the United States. An Oration, together with the valedictory address, pronounced at the Commencement of Rhode Island College, September 5, 1798. Published by request.
8vo. pp. 16. *Providence. Bennett Wheeler.* 1798.

WHEATON, HENRY. The Progress and Prospects of Germany; a Discourse before the Phi Beta Kappa Society of Brown University, at Providence, R. I., Sept. 1, 1847.
8vo. pp. 54. *Boston. Little & Brown.* 1847.

WINSOR, WILLIAM, A. B. The Poetic Art; a Poem delivered before the United Brothers' Society, of Brown University, on their Anniversary, Sept. 3, 1811.
8vo. pp. 12. *Providence. Jones & Wheeler.* 1812.

WHITMAN, BENJAMIN, JUN. The Heroes of the North; or the Battles of Lake Erie and Champlain. Two Poems.
8vo. pp. 24. *Boston.* 1816.
With two engravings representing the Battles. These Poems were delivered at Anniversaries of Brown University.

—— Benevolentissimo ac eximia virtute, doctrinaque utilissima praedito, viro, Stephano Hopkins, Armigero, Collegii hujusce, intra Coloniae Insulae Rhodiensis Fines, Cancellario; Admodum Reverendo aeque ac Honorando Jacobo Manning, Praesidi, omnibus Artibus liberalibus, Scientiisque, et Pietate Praesigni induto, cujus sub moderamine sequentia philosophemata sunt defendenda; Totis Curatoribus et Sociis eruditissimis, hujusce Academiae Observantissimus; Doctissimo pariterque dignissimo Davidi Hoell, ejusdem Seminarii

BROWN UNIVERSITY. Books relating to.

Tutori; Denique, omnibus desiderio Scientiæ afflatis ubicunque in Terrarum Orbe, tam Ecclesiarum Pastoribus quam Reipublicæ bene meritis, præcipue nostro Collegio Faventibus;

Theses hasce (Numine fausto) Juvenes, in Artibas initiati, defensuri, Josephus Belton, Carolus Thompson, Josephus Eaton, Jacobus Mitchel Varnum, Gulielmus Rogers, Gulielmus Williams, Richardus Stites.. *Summa Observantia.* Apud Novum—Portum, ex Typis Solomonis Southwick. 1769.

The above, with Latin Theses on Grammar, Rhetoric, Logic, Mathematic, Physics, Theology, Ethics, Political Economy, &c., was published in a large sheet form, for the first commencement of the College held at Warren, Sept. 7, 1769. This practice was continued from year to year, until 1812, when the pamphlet took the place of the sheet form. After 1817, the publication of the Latin Theses for Commencement occasions, was discontinued altogether.

BROWN UNIVERSITY. Order of Exercises and Theses for Commencement, September 2, 1812.
8vo. pp. 16. *Providence. Jones & Wheeler.* 1812.
Ibid. September 1, 1813.
8vo. pp. 20. *Providence. Mann & Co.* 1813.
Ibid. September 7, 1814.
8vo. pp. 29. *Providence. Miller, Goddard & Mann.* 1814.
Ibid. September 6, 1815.
8vo. pp. 23. *Providence. Brown & Wilson.* 1815.
Ibid. September, 1816. (Order of exercises wanting.)
8vo. pp. 20. [*Providence.*] 1816.
Ibid. September 3, 1817.
8vo. pp. 20. *Providence. Wm. G. Goddard.* 1817.
The publication of these Theses for Commencement was discontinued from this time.

———— A Letter to the Corporation of Brown University, suggesting certain improvements in its Academical System. "Quod opus sit benigne præbeatur. *Ter.*"
8vo. pp. 20. 1815.
Signed Alumnus Brunensis, and dated August 18, 1815.

BROWN UNIVERSITY. Books relating to.

AN EXPOSITOR of certain newspaper publications relative to the affairs of Brown University, August, 1826.
8vo. pp. 15. *Providence.* 1826.
An anonymous publication, signed X Y Z.

——— A true and candid statement of facts, relative to the late affairs and proceedings of the government of Brown University. "Stat nominis umbra."
8vo. pp. 15. *New Haven, Conn. January.* 1826.
An anonymous publication, written, it is said, by the Rev. John Holroyd, of the Class of 1802. This pamphlet had much to do with the removal of President Messer.

——— Sketch of the History of Brown University. Published in the 7th number of the Brunonian, 1830.
8vo. pp. 8. *Providence.* 1830.

——— Annual Report of the Faculty of Brown University to the Corporation of that Institution, made Sept. 3, 1829. Signed F. Wayland, Jun., President. Published by order of the Corporation.
8vo. pp. 15. *Providence. H. H. Brown.* 1829.

——— Annual Exhibition of the University Grammar School, at Manning Hall. July 15, 1853, commencing at 10 o'clock, A. M.
12mo. pp. 4. *Providence. J. Albro's Print.* 1853.

——— Dedication of the New Chapel of Brown University, Wednesday, February 4th, 1835. Being the Order of Exercises, with an original Ode by Albert G. Greene, Esq.

THE BRUNONIAN. Edited by Students of Brown University. "Haec olim meminisse juvabit."
8vo. pp. 368. *Providence. H. H. Brown.* 1831.
Only 12 numbers of this periodical were published. The first is dated July 1829, and the last March, 1831.

THE BROWN PAPER. Brown University. Vol. 1. Nos. 1–7.
Folio. 1857–63.
This paper is published from year to year during the month of November. It gives a list of members of the secret literary and religious societies in the College, together with spicy editorials, and information pertaining to the general condition of the University.

Brown University. Books relating to.

Burges and Wayland. Article from the Providence Journal of September 10, 1830, in reference to the resignation of Tristam Burges as Professor of Oratory and Belles Lettres in Brown University.

Brown University. Historical Sketch of. Reprinted from the Rhode Island Schoolmaster for March, 1858. 8vo. pp. 8.

——— Its Origin, Progress and present condition. Published in Providence Journal, September 2, 1857.

——— Historical Sketch of the Library of Brown University, with regulations. (From the University Quarterly, April, 1861.) 8vo. pp. 20. *New Haven. Tuttle, Moorehouse & Taylor.* 1861.

——— A Sketch of the History and present organization of. Published by the Executive Board. (With a fine steel engraving of the University.) 8vo. pp. 15. *Providence. Knowles, Anthony & Co.* 1861.

——— List of contributors to the Funds collected in England and Ireland in 1767–69, by Rev. Morgan Edwards, A. M., "for founding and endowing a College in the Colony of Rhode Island." Small 4to.

The preliminary matter printed. The signatures are all original. The total amount subscribed was £891,11, 53-4 sterling.

——— An exact list of Benefactions, etc., to Rhode Island College, collected and got subscribed in North Carolina and Georgia, by the Rev. Hezekiah Smith, 1769–70.

The list is in Mr. Smith's hand writing. The total amount of subscriptions is given as £3,710,17,6, South Carolina currency.

——— Report to the Corporation of Brown University on changes in the system of Collegiate Education. Read March 28, 1850. 8vo. pp. 76. *Providence. George H. Whitney.* 1850.

The Committee which made this report consisted of the following: Francis Wayland, D. D., President; Robert E. Pattison, D. D.; Barnas Sears, D. D.; Zachariah Allen; Rufus Babcock; Samuel Boyd Tobey, M. D.; William Hague, D. D.; Nathan Bishop; Alva Woods, D. D.; John Kingsbury and Samuel G. Arnold.

BROWN UNIVERSITY. Books relating to.

—— Report of the Committee of the Corporation of Brown University, appointed to raise a fund of one hundred and twenty-five thousand dollars.
8vo. pp. 16.   *Providence. Knowles, Anthony & Co.* 1851.

—— Right of a Legislature to grant a perpetual exemption from taxation. A Report presented in the Rhode Island Senate, August 26, 1862. By the Hon. Elisha R. Potter, of South Kingstown, recommending the Legislature to amend the charter of Brown University by repealing so much thereof as exempts the professors from taxation.
8vo. pp. 16.   *Providence. Alfred Anthony.* 1862.

—— Act of Congress granting lands for the establishing of Agricultural Colleges; with the Resolutions passed by the General Assembly of the State of Rhode Island accepting these lands, and assigning the same to Brown University; also a resolution providing for State Scholarships in that University.
8vo. pp. 12.   *Providence. Alfred Anthony.* 1863.

—— Circular of Horace T. Love, Agent of Brown University, in regard to the disposal of the Lands in Kansas granted to that Institution. Dated April 1, 1863. Certified to Barnes Sears, President, Samuel Boyd Tobey, Chancellor of the University.
Quarto. pp. 2.

JEWETT, PROFESSOR CHARLES C. Preface to the Catalogue of the Library of Brown University, with the Laws of the Library.
8vo. pp. 26.   *Providence.* 1843.

—— Facts and Considerations relative to duties on Books; addressed to the Library Committee of Brown University. By C. C. Jewett, Librarian. Printed by order of the Committee.
8vo. pp. 24.   *Providence.* 1843.

—— Proceedings of the Corporation and of the Alumni of Brown University, in reference to the resignation of President Wayland, and the Induction of President Sears.
8vo. pp. 23.   *Providence. Knowles, Anthony & Co.* 1836.

BROWN UNIVERSITY. Books relating to.

——— Extracts from the report of Prof. C. C. Jewett, relative to purchases made by him for the Library of Brown University, during his visit to Europe in 1843–46. Published in the Providence Journal, September 26, 1846.

GUILD, REUBEN A., A. M. Librarian of Brown University. Library of Brown University, with an engraving.
8vo. pp. 12.   *From the Librarian's Manual.* 1858.

——— The Librarian's Manual; a Treatise on Bibliography, to which is added Sketches of Public Libraries.
4to. pp. x. and 304.   *New York. C. B. Norton.* 1858.

The second part contains a history of the Library of Brown University, with an engraving, and a view of Redwood Library, Newport.

NORTON, WILLIAM A. and John A. Porter. Circular of, in reference to their difficulties with President Wayland and the Executive Board of Brown University, dated,
4to. pp. 3.   *Providence. Feb.* 18. 1862.

SONGS OF ALPHA DELTA PHI. Issued on the twenty-seventh year of the Fraternity.
12mo. pp. 36.   *New York.* 1859.

A chapter of this Society is connected with Brown University.

CATALOGUE OF BOOKS belonging to the Library of Rhode Island College.
12mo. pp. 38.   *Providence. J. Carter.* 1793.

CATALOGUE OF BOOKS in Brown University.
8vo. pp. 61.   *Providence. Walter R. Danforth.* 1826.

CATALOGUE OF THE LIBRARY of the Rev. W. Richards, L. L. D., of Lynn, England, bequeathed to Brown University in the year 1818. Manuscript folio.

A CATALOGUE OF THE LIBRARY of Brown University, in Providence, Rhode Island. With an Index of Subjects.
8vo. pp. 586.   *Providence.* 1843.

This excellent Catalogue was prepared by Professor Charles C. Jewett, who was the Librarian of the Institution from 1842 to 1848. It contains a history of the Library to 1843, and the Rules and Regulations of the Library Committee.

BROWN UNIVERSITY. Books relating to.

CATALOGUE OF THE BOOKS in the Library of the Philermenian Society, together with the names of its members; Brown University.
16mo. pp. 16.   *Providence. Jones & Wheeler.* 1810.
Ibid. 12mo. pp. 22.   *Providence. Miller & Hutchens.* 1817.

CATALOGUE OF THE LIBRARY of Members of the Philermenian Society. Founded A. D., 1794.
12mo. pp. 46.   *Boston. W. S. Damrell.* 1838.
Ibid. 12mo. pp. 55.   *Boston. J. Putnam.* 1841.
Ibid. 12mo. pp. 60.   *Boston. S. N. Dickinson.* 1844.

TRIENNIAL CATALOGUE of the Library and the Members of the Philermenian Society in Brown University. Founded A. D., 1794.
8vo. pp. 92.   *Providence.* 1849.

A CATALOGUE OF THE LIBRARY of the United Brothers' Society of Brown University, with the names of members. Founded A. D., 1806.
12mo. pp. 40.   *Providence. Knowles, Vose & Co.* 1837.
Ibid. 12mo. pp. 51.   *Providence. Knowles & Vose.* 1839.
Ibid. 12mo. pp. 59.   *Providence. Knowles & Vose.* 1841.

TRIENNIAL CATALOGUE of the United Brothers' Society of Brown University. Instituted A. D., 1806.
8vo. pp. 64.   *Providence.* 1848.
Ibid. 8vo. pp. 84.   *Providence. A. C. Greene.* 1853.

CATALOGUS eorum qui in Collegio Rhod. Ins. et Prov. Plant. Nov. Anglorum, ab anno 1769 ad annum 1775, alicujus Gradus Laurea donati sunt.
Small folio sheet.   *Providence. Typis Johannis Carter.* 1775.
The first Triennial Catalogue, so-called, published in Rhode Island.
Ibid. ad annum 1786.
Ibid. ad annum 1789.   *Typis Bennett Wheeler.* 1789.
Ibid. ad annum 1795.
Large folio sheet.   *Prov. Typis Carter et Wilkinson* 1795.
This was the last of the sheet Triennials.

BROWN UNIVERSITY. Books relating to.

CATALOGUS eorum qui in Collegio Rhodiæ Insulæ quod est Providentiæ, ab anno MDCCLXIX ad annum MDCC-XCVIII, Alicujus Gradus Laurea donati sunt.

12mo. pp. 22. *Providence. Carter et Wilkinson.* 1798.

Ibid. ad annum MDCCCIV.

12mo, pp. 24. *Providence. Typis Johannis Carter.* 1804.

CATALOGUS eorum qui in Universitate Brownense quæ est Providentiæ, ab anno MDCCLXIX ad annum MDCCCXIII, alicujus Gradus Laurea donati sunt.

12mo. pp. 28. *Providence. Typis Johannis Carter.* 1808.

Ibid. ad annum MDCCCXI.

12mo. pp. 31. *Providence. Printed by John Carter.* 1811.

Ibid. ad annum MDCCCXIV.

12mo. pp. 36. *Providence. Brown & Wilson Printers.* 1814.

CATALOGUS PRÆSIDUM ET SOCIORUM, cum Professoribus, Tutoribus, et Omnibus, qui in Universitate Brunensi, Providentiæ, in Republica Insulæ Rhodiensis, alicujus Gradus Laurea exornati fuerunt.

8vo. pp. 22. *Providence. N. Mann & Co.* 1815.

This catalogue is dedicated to the Rev. Dr. Messer, President of the University, by the editor, J. L. Blake, author of the well known Biographical Dictionary.

CATALOGUS UNIVERSITATIS BROWNENSIS. MDCCCXVII.

8vo. pp. 23. *Providence. Hugh H. Brown.* 1817.

Ibid. MDCCCXX.

8vo. pp. 25. *Providence. Brown & Danforth.* 1820.

Ibid. MDCCCXXII.

8vo. pp. 27. *Providence. Brown & Danforth.* 1823.

CATALOGUS SENATUS ACADEMICI, eorum qui munero et officia gesserunt, quique alicujus gradus laurea donati sunt in Universitate Brownensi, Providentia, in Republica Insulæ Rhodiensis.

8vo. pp. 28. *Providenciæ. Typis H. H. Brown.* 1827.

Ibid. 8vo. pp. 30. *Providentiæ. Typis H. H. Brown.* 1830.

BROWN UNIVERSITY. Books relating to.

CATALOGUS SENATUS ACADEMICI, eorum dui munera et officia gesserunt, quique alicujus gradus laurea donati sunt, in Universitate Brunensi, Providentiæ, in Republica Insulæ Rhodiensis.
8vo. pp. 51. Bostoniæ. Dutton et Wentworth. 1836.

This edition of the triennial catalogue was prepared with great care, by the Hon. Judge Metcalf, of Boston, for many years a member of the Board of Fellows.

Ibid. 8vo. pp. 58. Bostoniæ. Dutton et Wentworth. 1842.
Ibid. 8vo. pp. 63. Bostoniæ. Freeman et Bolles. 1846.
Ibid. 8vo. pp. 74. Prov. Knowles, Anthony et Sociis. 1852.
Ibid. 8vo. pp. 78.. Prov. Knowles, Anthony et Sociis. 1858.
Ibid. 8vo. pp. 81. Prov. Knowles, Anthony et Sociis. 1860.

EXHIBITION of Rhode Island College and Brown University. Sophomore, Junior and Senior. Order of Exercises as follows:

April 21, 1803; Aug. 24, 1803; April 18, 1814; Aug. 22, 1804; Aug. 21, 1805; April 23, 1806; Aug. 20, 1806; Dec. 31, 1806; Aug. 19, 1807; Dec. 30, 1807; April 19, 1808; April 18, 1809; April 16, 1811; Aug. 18, 1813; Dec. 29, 1813; Dec. 28, 1814; April 20, 1815; Dec. 27, 1815; Aug 21, 1816; Aug. 20, 1817; Aug. 19, 1818; Dec. 30, 1818; April 21, 1819; Dec. 29, 1819; April 19, 1820; Dec 21, 1821; Dec. 24, 1822; April 23, 1823; Aug. 20, 1823; Aug. 18, 1824; Dec. 29, 1824; Dec. 28, 1825; April 18, 1826; May 8, 1829; May 8, 1830; Dec. 31, 1830; May 7, 1831; Dec. 5, 1855; July 16, 1836; Dec. 3, 1836; March 25, 1837; Dec. 2, 1837; April 24, 1838; Dec. 1, 1838; June 27, 1840; Nov. 28, 1840; March 20, 1841; March 19, 1842; March 25, 1843; Dec. 2, 1843; March 25, 1845; Nov. 29, 1845; March 21, 1846; March 20, 1847; March 18, 1848; Dec. 2, 1848; March 24, 1849; March 23, 1850; Nov. 28, 1850; May 24, 1851; Nov. 22, 1851; May 22, 1852; Nov. 20, 1852; May 21, 1853; Nov. 19, 1853; May 13, 1854; Nov. 25, 1854; May 12, 1855; Nov. 24, 1855; May 3, 1856; Nov. 22, 1856; May 2, 1857; May 1, 1758; April 30, 1859; April 28, 1860; April 27, 1861; April 26, 1862; April 25, 1863.

BROWN UNIVERSITY. Class of 1858. Exercises of Class Day, June 10, 1858.
Ibid. Class of 1859, June 9, 1859.
Ibid. Class of 1860, June 14, 1860.
Ibid. Class of 1861, June 13, 1861.
Ibid. Class of 1862, June 12, 1862.

BROWN UNIVERSITY. Books relating to.

"Class Day" was introduced into Brown University in 1858, since which time it has been regularly observed.

CATALOGUE OF THE OFFICERS AND STUDENTS of Brown University, Providence, Rhode Island, April 1, 1804.

This is the first annual catalogue of the College ever published. It consists of a single folio sheet, printed on one side. The officers are
The Hon. Jabez Brown, L. L. D., Chancellor.
The Rev. Asa Messer, A. M., President.
The Hon. David Howell, L. L. D , Professor of Law.
Calvin Park, A. M., Professor of the Learned Languages.
Ferdinand Ellis, A. B., John Reed, A. B., Tutors.

CATALOGUE of the Students of Brown University, April 1, 1806.

Folio sheet.   Also the same. April 1, 1807.

These two catalogues omit the names of the officers of the University.

CATALOGUE of the Officers and Students of Brown University. 1808 to 1823 inclusive.

In 1807, and thence onward to 1823, inclusive, the catalogue was published in a larger folio sheet than formerly, and during the month of October instead of April. In 1820 it was also published in its present pamphlet form.

ANNUAL CATALOGUES of the Officers and Students of Brown University, for the years 1820 to 1863.
Octavo, from 1820 to 1835, inclusive.
Duodecimo, from 1835 to 1847, inclusive.
Octavo, from 1848 to 1863, inclusive.

The first annual Catalogue of the College was published in a sheet form in the year 1805. The first in a pamphlet form was published in 1820 as above. The Catalogue for 1821 contains the Order of Exercises for the Senior Exhibition, Monday, Dec. 24.

A CATALOGUE of the Officers and Students in Brown University, 1842–43.
8vo. pp. 32.   *Providence.* 1842.

This edition of the annual catalogue was published by the Students who disliked the cheap looking duodecimo style of the "regular edition."

A CATALOGUE of the Officers and Students of Brown University, 1850–51.
8vo. pp. 40.   *Providence. John F. Moore.* 1850.
Ibid. Second edition.
8vo. pp. 42.   *Providence. John F. Moore.* 1851.

BROWN UNIVERSITY. Books relating to.

A CATALOGUE of the Officers and Students of Brown University, 1852–54. First Term.
12mo. pp. 47.   *Providence. A. C. Greene.* 1852.

Ibid. Second edition.
8vo. pp. 47.   *Providence. Knowles, Anthony & Co.* 1852.

A CATALOGUE of the Officers and Students of the Sophomore Class in Brown University, 1845–46. Second edition.
8vo. pp. 8.   *Providence.* 1845.

The publication of this singular document was the source of much merriment to the Students. The following at the end is a sufficient explanation of the reasons which perhaps led to its preparation: "The catalogue of the remaining classes is confidently expected at some time previous to the next Fourth of July."

CATALOGUE of the Delta Phi Society, [connected with Brown University.] 12mo. pp. 39.   *Providence.* 1845.
——— The same. 8vo. pp. 55.   *New York.* 1851.

CATALOGUE of the Psi Upsilon Society.
12mo. pp. 18.   1842.
——— The same. 12mo. pp. 37.   *New York.* 1844.
——— The same. 12mo. pp. 49.   *New York.* 1847.
——— The same. 8vo. pp. 72.   *New Haven.* 1849.
——— The same. 8vo. pp. 115.   *New York.* 1852.
——— The same. 8vo. pp. 144.   *New York.* 1855.

A chapter of this Society is connected with Brown University.

CATALOGUE of the Alpha Delta Phi Society.
8vo. pp. 44.   *Cambridge.* 1851.
——— The same. 8vo. pp. 126.   *Boston.* 1856.
——— The same. 8vo. pp. 129.   *Providence.* 1857.

A chapter of this Society is connected with Brown University.

CATALOGUE of the Delta Kappa Epsilon Fraternity.
8vo. pp. 36.   *New Haven.* 1851.
——— The same. 8vo pp. 90.   *New Haven.* 1855.

The Upsilon chapter of this Society is connected with Brown University.

CATALOGUE of the Fraternity of Q B K, Alpha of Rhode Island. Brown University. Providence, 1839.
8vo. pp. 15.   *Providence. Knowles & Vose.* 1839.

BROWN UNIVERSITY. Books relating to.
——— The same for the year 1843.
8vo. pp. 16.　　　　Providence. Knowles & Vose. 1843.

——— The same for the year 1850.
8vo. pp. 24.　　　　Providence. John F. Moore. 1850.

——— The same for the year 1862.
8vo. pp. 28.　　　　Providence. Knowles, Anthony & Co. 1862.

COMMENCEMENTS of Rhode Island College and Brown University. Order of Exercises for 1795, and from that year to the present time.

These were at first printed on a single small folio sheet, but in 1822 the present folded octavo sheet was substituted therefor. No order of exercises in a printed form has been found of any earlier date than 1795.

CHARTER. The Charter of Rhode Island College, granted 1764.
8vo. pp. 16.　　　Newport. Printed by Samuel Hall. London. Reprinted for Blythe & Beaver, No. 87 Cornhill.

——— The same. 8vo. pp. 12.　Prov. J. Carter 1803.

——— The same. 8vo. pp. 15.　Prov. H. H. Brown. 1834.

LAWS OF RHODE ISLAND COLLEGE. Copied from the President's copy, by Enoch Pond, of Wrentham, Mass. Dated on the cover March 12, 1774.

Note at the end. "Having perused the above, I find them to correspond to the copy." James Manning, President. Mr. Pond graduated in 1777.

——— The Laws of Rhode Island College, in the original handwriting of James Manning, President.

At the end of these laws is the following: The subscribers having been appointed a Committee to form a digest of Laws for this Institution, have agreed to the foregoing, and do report them accordingly, this 22d day of February, 1783. JAMES MANNING, JABEZ BROWN, NICHOLAS BROWN, DAVID HOWELL.

——— The Laws of Rhode Island College, enacted by the Fellows and Trustees.
12mo. pp. 35.　　　　Providence. J. Carter. 1793.

——— Supplement to the Laws of Rhode Island College.
12mo. pp. 7.　　　　Providence. 1793.

BROWN UNIVERSITY. Books relating to.
────── The Laws of Rhode Island College, enacted by the Fellows and Trustees.
8vo. pp. 20. *Providence. J. Carter.* 1803.
────── Supplement to the Laws of Rhode Island College.
8vo. pp. 7. *Providence. J. Carter.* 1803.
────── The Laws of Brown University, enacted January 23, 1823.
8vo. pp. 16. *Providence. Brown & Danforth.* 1823.
────── The same. Enacted March, 1827.
8vo. pp. 20. *Providence. W. R. Danforth.* 1827.
────── The same. Revised edition, 1835.
8vo. pp. 20. *Providence. H. H. Brown.* 1835.
────── The same. Enacted August 1, 1850.
8vo. pp. 25. *Providence. Joseph Knowles.* 1850.
────── The same. 8vo. pp. 27. *Prov. A. C. Greene.* 1861.
────── The same. 8vo. pp. 24.
Providence. Knowles, Anthony & Co. 1856.

BULKLEY, REV. JOHN, A. M. An impartial account of a late debate at Lyme, in the Colony of Connecticut, &c., with some account of the rise of the Antipedo-Baptist Persuasion. In which is added, a narrative of one lately converted from dreadful errors by another hand.
16mo. pp. 199. *New London. T. Greene.* 1729.
This volume contains some remarks on the Theological tenets of Mrs. Hutchinson, Samuel Gorton, and Roger Williams.

BURGES, TRISTAM, A. M. The Spirit of Independence: An Oration, delivered before the Providence Association of the Mechanics and Manufacturers, at their annual election, April 14, 1800.
8vo. pp. 28. *Providence. B. Wheeler.* 1800.

────── Liberty, Glory, Union; or, American Independence. A Fourth of July Oration.
8vo. pp. 22. *Providence. R. I. American Office.* 1810.
────── Address to the Rhode Island Society for the Encour-

agement of Domestic Industry, delivered at Pawtuxet, October 17, 1821.
8vo pp. 29.　　　　　*Providence. Miller & Hutchens.* 1822.

────── Address to the Landholders and Farmers of Newport County, delivered at a meeting of the friends of Messrs. Pearce and Burges, holden at Howland's Ferry Bridge, August 7, 1829. Third edition.
8vo. pp. 22.　　　　　*Providence. Daily Advertiser.* 1829.

────── Remarks of, at the celebration of the Fourth of July in Clayville, R. I., in reply to a sentiment expressed at the dinner given on that occasion. Furnished at the solicitation of the citizens of Clayville and vicinity, and published at their request.
8vo. pp. 31.　　　*Providence. Daily Advertiser Office.* 1829.

────── An Oration pronounced before the citizens of Providence, on the Fourth of July, 1831.
8vo. pp. 32.　　　　*Providence. W. Marshall & Co.* 1831.

────── A Statement of some leading principles adopted by General Jackson, and of the effects of these principles and measures on the union, prosperity and constitution of the American people. An address to the citizens of Rhode Island, in answer to their call on the delegation of this State in Congress.
8vo. pp. 12.　　　　*Providence. Wm. Marshall & Co.* 1832.

────── A Brief Sketch of the remarks delivered at East Greenwich at a Convention of National Republicans, on the 23d August, 1832.
8vo. pp. 15.　　　　*Providence. Wm. Marshall & Co.* 1832.

────── Reasons why the Hon. Elisha R. Potter should not be a Senator in Congress. By one of the people.
8vo. pp. 12.　　　　　　　　*? Providence.* 1834.
This pamphlet was attributed to Tristam Burges.

────── Address before the Rhode Island Peace Society, June 29, 1819.
8vo. pp. 20.　　　　　*Providence. Joseph Knowles.* 1849.

────── Speech of, delivered at a meeting of his fellow citi-

zens, in the Town House in Providence, on Friday evening, March 3, 1835.
8vo. pp. 16. [*Providence.*] 1835.

———— Remarks sent to the people who celebrated the 4th of July, 1835, at Woonsocket Falls.
8vo. pp. 16. *Woonsocket Falls. Sherman & Wilder.* 1835.

———— A Brief of the remarks made before the Committee on Railways and Canals, on the petition of the Seekonk Branch Railroad Company.
8vo. pp. 7. *No place or date.*

———— Battle of Lake Erie; with notices of Commodore Elliott's conduct in that engagement.
12mo. pp. xv. and 117. *Phila. W. Marshall & Co.* 1839.

———— The same.
12mo. pp. xv. and 132. *Providence. Brown & Cady.* 1839.

———— Report from the Select Committee of the House of Representatives of the U. S., to which was referred the memorial of the officers and soldiers of the Rhode Island Brigade, their heirs and representatives. February 25, 1835. (23d Congress, 2d Session.)
8vo. pp. 40. *Report No. 128. Washington.* 1835.

———— The Plough and the Sickle, or Rhode Island in the war of the revolution of 1776.
8vo. pp. 28. *Prov. B. T. Albro, for the author.* 1846.
This relates to the Old State Debt.

———— Memoir of, with his Speeches. See *Bowen.*
Mr. Burges was born at Rochester, Mass., Feb. 26, 1770, and graduated at Brown University in 1796, receiving the highest honors of his class. In 1799, he was admitted to practice at the bar in Rhode Island, and soon rose to the head of his profession as a scholar and well-read lawyer. In 1811, he was appointed Chief Justice of the Supreme Court of Rhode Island. In 1815, he was appointed Professor of Oratory and Belles Lettres in Brown University. In 1825 he was elected a representative to Congress, and served two subsequent terms in that body. His speeches which have become prominent portions of our literature, show the ability with which he performed his duty, and the success that attended him as a debator in the national councils. He died October 13, 1853, in the 84th year of his age.

BURNYEATT. The truth exalted in the writings of this eminent and faithful servant of Christ, John Burnyeatt: collected into this ensuing volume as a memorial to his faithful labors in and for the truth.

Small 4to. pp. vi and 264. *London. Thomas Northcott.* 1691.

———— New England's Fire Brand Quenched. Being an answer unto a Slanderous Book, entitled George Fox digged out of his Burrowes, etc. etc.

Small 4to. pp. 256. *London. Printed in the year* 1679.

For the full title, which is very long, see GEORGE FOX, whose name precedes that of Burnyeatt as the author.

John Burnyeatt was a distinguished missionary and preacher of the Society of Friends, and spent some time in Rhode Island. George Fox says that Burnyeatt travelled and preached in Rhode Island and other parts of New England, "and had many disputes with priests and professors that opposed the truth."

BURRILL, GEORGE, A. B. An Oration, delivered before the Providence Association of Mechanics and Manufacturers, at their annual election, April 11, 1796.

8vo. pp. 18. *Providence. Bennett Wheeler.* 1796.

———— An Oration, delivered in the Benevolent Congregational Meeting House, on the 4th of July, A. D. 1797, in commemoration of American Independence. Ecce Spectaculum dignum. Published by request. Providence.

8vo. pp. 18. *Providence. Carter & Wilkinson.* 1797.

———— An Oration pronounced in Providence at the Funeral Ceremony on the death of George Washington.

8vo pp. 15. *Providence. John Carter.* 1800.

BURROUGHS, PELEG, V. D. M. An oration with some observations, pronounced at the Congregational Meeting House in Tiverton, on the 22d Feb'y, 1800, at the funeral ceremony on the death of General George Washington. (With a poem.)

8vo pp. 13 and 2. *Newport. Henry Barber.* 1800.

BURT, REV. JOHN, of Bristol. See Shepard's Historical Discourse, p. 17.

BURTON, ASA, D. D. A sermon preached at the ordination of the Rev. Caleb J. Tenney, to the Pastoral care of the First Congregational Church of Christ, in Newport, R. I.,

Sept. 12, 1804. Charge by Rev. Dan'l Hopkins, and Right-hand of Fellowship by Rev. Wm. Patten.
8vo. pp. 24.　　　　　　*Newport Mercury Office.* (1804.)

Butler Hospital for the Insane, Providence, R. I. Description of. By I. Ray, M. D., Superintendent. [Journal of Insanity] with a view and ground plan.
8vo. pp. 20.　　　　　　　　　　　　　　　　1847.

―――― Charter of the Butler Hospital for the Insane: proceedings under the same, Reports of Trustees, &c. &c.
8vo. pp. 36.　　　　　　*Providence. John F. Moore.* 1847.

―――― Design for the Butler Hospital for the Insane at Providence, Rhode Island. By Luther V. Bell.
8vo. pp. 22.　　　　　　　　　　　　　　　　No date.

―――― Report of the Board of Trustees of the Butler Hospital for the Insane, presented to the corporation, at their annual meeting, January, 1848. With view and plan.
8vo. pp. 18.　　　　　　*Providence. Moore & Choate.* 1848.

―――― Reports of the Trustees and Superintendent of the Butler Hospital for the Insane, presented to the corporation, at their annual meeting, Jan. 24, 1849, together with an abstract of the proceedings of the Corporation.
8vo. pp. 32.　　　　　　*Providence. John F. Moore.* 1849.

―――― Annual Reports of the Trustees and Superintendent of the Butler Hospital, January, 1850, to January, 1864.

ALDWELL, SAMUEL L. A sermon preached in the First Baptist Meeting House, in Providence, Sunday morning, June 9, 1861, before the Second Regiment of Rhode Island Volunteers.
8vo. pp. 12.   *Prov. Knowles, Anthony & Co.* 1861.

CALDWELL, SAMUEL L., D. D. Oration before the municipal authorities and citizens of Providence, July 4, 1861.
8vo. pp. 23.   *Providence. Knowles, Anthony & Co.* 1861.

CAHOONE, MISS SARAH. Sketch of Newport and vicinity; with notices respecting the History, Settlement and Geography of Rhode Island. Illustrated with engravings.
12mo. pp. 213.   *New York. John S. Taylor & Co.* 1862.

CALLENDER, JOHN. Historical and Religious Discourse, with affairs of the Colony of Rhode Island and Providence Plantations in New England in America. From the first settlement, 1638, to the end of the first century. By John Callender, A. M. Dedicated to Wm. Coddington.
8vo. pp. 14 and 120.   *Boston. Printed and sold by S. Kneeland and T. Green, in Queen Street.* 1739.

——— The same. With a memoir of the author; Biographical notices of some of his distinguished contemporaries; and annotations and original documents, illustrative of the History of Rhode Island and Providence Plantations, from the first settlement to the end of the first century. By Romeo Elton, D. D.
8vo. pp. 270.   *Knowles, Vose & Company. Providence.* 1838.
This work also forms the fourth volume of the collections of the Rhode Island Historical Society.

———— A Discourse occasioned by the death of the Rev. Mr. Nathaniel Clapp, Pastor of a church in Newport on Rhode Island. On October 30, 1745, in the 78th year of his age.
12mo. pp. 36. *Newport. Printed by the Widow Franklin.* 1746.

John Callender was a Baptist minister in Newport, and was born in Boston in 1706. His father, John Callender, was the son of the Rev. Ellis Callender, minister of the First Baptist Church, in Boston, from 1708 to 1726. He graduated at Harvard College in 1723, and died on the 26th January, 1748, aged 41 years. He was distinguished as a preacher as well as a writer.

CALVERT, GEORGE H. Oration on the occasion of celebrating the Battle of Lake Erie, delivered Sept. 10, 1853, in Newport, R. I.
8vo. pp. 40. *Boston. Metcalf & Co.* 1853.

CAMPBELL. A sermon preached at Tiverton, October 1, 1746, by the Rev. Othniel Campbell, on his installment to the pastoral office in the Church of Christ lately gathered there.
12mo. pp. 29. [*Newport. R. I. Widow Franklin.* 1747.

CAPITAL PUNISHMENT. Report to the General Assembly of Rhode Island, of the Committee on Education, on the subject of Capital Punishment.
8vo. pp. 43. *Providence. Albert C. Greene.* 1852.

CASWELL, ALEXIS. A Discourse delivered before the Phi Beta Kappa Society of Rhode Island, September 2, 1835. Printed in the Biblical Repository.
8vo. pp. 18. *Boston.* 1836.

———— Smithsonian Contributions to Knowledge. Meteorological Observations made at Providence, R. I., extending over a period of twenty-eight years and a half, from December, 1831, to May, 1860. By Alexis Caswell, D. D., Professor of Natural Philosophy and Astronomy in Brown University, Providence, Rhode Island. (Accepted for publication, August, 1859.)
Quarto, pp. 179. *Washington, D. C.*

CASWELL, MRS. ESTHER LOIS. Sermon on the death of. See *F. Wayland.*

CENSUS of the inhabitants of the Colony of Rhode Island, taken
June, 1774. Folio. The original returns.
——— The same arranged by John R. Bartlett, Secretary
of State, and printed by order of the General Assembly.
8vo. pp. 237. *Providence. Knowles, Anthony & Co.* 1858.

CENSUS of the male inhabitants of the State of Rhode Island,
between the ages of 16 and 60 years, taken in April, 1777.
Folio. The original returns on printed forms.
This census was intended to show the number of men capable of bearing arms.

CENSUS of Rhode Island, abstracts taken in 1730, 1748, 1755,
1791. Massachusetts Historical Collections vol. vii.

CHANNING, WILLIAM ELLERY, D. D. A discourse delivered
at the dedication of the Unitarian Congregational Church
in Newport, Rhode Island, July 27, 1836.
8vo. pp. 44. *Boston. S. N. Dickerson.* 1836.

——— A discourse delivered at the ordination of the Rev.
Frederick A. Farley, as Pastor of the Westminster Congregational Society, in Providence, R. I., Sept. 10, 1828.
12mo. pp. 28. *Boston. Bowles & Dearborn.* 1828.

——— Memoir of, with extracts from correspondence and Mss.
3 vols. 12mo. *Boston.* 1848.

——— Essay on the philosophical character of. *See Hazard.*

Dr. Channing was born in Newport, R. I., April 7, 1780. His father, William Channing, was an eminent lawyer of that town, and his mother was the daughter of William Ellery, one of the signers of the Declaration of Independence. He graduated at Harvard University in 1798, where he attained the highest honors. In 1803 he became pastor of the Federal Street Society in Boston. In 1812 he was appointed Dexter lecturer on biblical criticism in Harvard College, but was compelled to resign the place the following year, on account of ill health. His feeble constitution induced him to visit Europe, and subsequently the West Indies, yet he continued to officiate in the pulpit until 1840, when he resigned. He died at Bennington, Vermont, when on a journey, October 2, 1842, aged 62 years. Dr. Channing's published works include a large number of religious discourses; essays on Milton, Bonaparte and Fenelon, and a number of tracts on Slavery, and the condition of the laboring classes. Several editions of his works have been published in Boston, Glasgow and London.

CHANNING, EDWARD T. Life of William Ellery, (vol. 6,
Sparks' Library of American Biography.)
24mo. pp. 85 to 150. *Boston. Hillard, Gray & Co.* 1836.

CHAPIN, REV. E. H. The position and duties of Liberal Christians. A sermon delivered at the installation of the Rev. Henry Bacon, as pastor of the First Universalist Society, Providence, R. I., March 17, 1842.
8vo. pp. *Providence. B. Cranston & Co.* 1842.

CHARTERS. A list of copies of Charters from the commissioners for Trade and Plantations, presented to the Hon. the House of Commons, in pursuance of an address to H. M. of the 25th of April, 1740, viz: Maryland charter, granted by Charles 1, in the 8th year of his reign; Connecticut, Charles 2d, 14th of his reign; Rhode Island, Charles 2d, 15th year of his reign; Pennsylvania, Charles 2d, 33d year of his reign; Massachusetts, William and Mary, 3d year of their reign; Georgia charter, granted by his present Majesty, in the 5th year of his reign.
Folio. *London.* 1741.

THE CHARTERS of the following provinces of North America, viz: Virginia, Maryland, Connecticut, Rhode Island, Pennsylvania, Massachusetts Bay and Georgia. To which is prefixed a faithful narrative of the proceedings of the North American Colonies, in consequence of the late stamp act.
Quarto, pp. 70. *London.* 1766.

CHARTERS AND LEGISLATIVE DOCUMENTS illustrative of Rhode Island History; showing that the people of Rhode Island, from the foundation of the State, until their constitution of 1842, possessed and exercised the rights of self-Government; and in what manner and under what form of government they declared their independence, in 1776, and became a member of the confederation of the United States, in 1778, and adopted the constitution of the United States in 1790.
8vo. pp. 68. *Providence. Knowles and Vose.* 1844.

THE CHARTER, granted by His Majesty King Charles the Second to the Governor and Company of the English Colony of Rhode Island and Providence Plantations in New England, in America.
Folio. Manuscript. *Dated at London.* 1663.

The original charter upon parchment, framed in the office of the Secretary of State. This charter is also printed at the beginning of the second volume of Public Laws of Rhode Island. See also, under *Constitution*, various charters connected with the adoption of that instrument in 1842.

CHASTELLUX, MARQUIS DE. Voyage de Newport a Philadelphie, Albany, etc.
Quarto, pp. 188. *Newport. R. I.* 1761.
" De l'Imprimerie Royale de l'Escadre."
"The Marquis de Chastellux caused twenty-four copies of this journal to be printed at a press on board one of the ships of the French squadron, at Newport. It consists only of that part which forms the first volume of the edition of Paris of 1785, comprising his travels in the winter of 1780-81, and was printed, he says, to avoid the trouble of making ms. copies for his friends in Europe." *Rich.* His travels which exist in French and English, contain many interesting incidents relative to Rhode Island.

CHILD, ANNE P. Whatcheer, a story of olden times. One of sister Rhody's collections of historical facts, for the amusement and instruction of Young People.
18mo. pp. ix and 194. *Prov. Knowles, Anthony & Co.* 1857.

CHILD, MAJOR JOHN. New England's Jonas cast up at London: or A Relation of the proceedings of the Court at Boston in New England, against divers honest and godly persons, for Petitioning for Government in the Commonwealth, according to the laws of England, and for the admittance of themselves and children to the sacraments in their Churches; and in case that should not be granted, for leave to have Ministers and Church government according to the best Reformation of England and Scotland.

Together with a Confutation of some Reports of a fained Miracle upon the foresaid Petition, being thrown overboard at sea; as also a brief answer to some passages in a late Book (entitled " Hypocrisie unmasked") set out by Mr. Winslowe, concerning the independent churches holding communion with the Reformed Churches.
Small 4to. pp. 22. *London. Printed by T. R. and E. M.* 1647.
———— The same, reprinted in *Massachusetts Historical Collections, 2d series, vol. iv.*
The second part or "Postscript," to this pamphlet, relates to Edward Winslow's book against Samuel Gorton, entitled " Hypocrisie Unmasked," which see.

CHENEY, REV. MARTIN. A sermon delivered at the installation of the Rev. Lorenzo D. Johnson, as Pastor of the

Roger Williams Baptist Church Society, in Providence, Oct. 25, 1827.
8vo. pp. 22. *Providence. H. H. Brown.* 1827.

CHILDS, MRS. HANNAH, [of Johnson, Rhode Island.] The Life of, who long in darkness lay, will now be brought to light.
8vo. pp. 27. *Providence.* [1859.]

CHOULES, REV. JOHN OVERTON, of Newport. Funeral Discourse on the Life and Character of. See *Hague.*

CHURCH, THOMAS. The Entertaining History of King Philip's war, which was began in the month of June, 1675. And also of expeditions more lately made against the common enemy, and Indian Rebels, in the Eastern part of New England: With some account of the Divine Providence towards Col. Benjamin Church, by his son *Thomas Church, Esq.*
4to. pp. 120. *Boston.* 1716.

——— The same.
12mo. pp. 199. Second edition. *Newport. Reprinted and sold by Solomon Southwick, in Queen street.* 1772.

The portrait of King Philip, first published in this edition, is fictitious, as well as that of Colonel Church. The latter was evidently copied from the portrait of Charles Churchill, the English poet, with the addition of a powder horn around his neck.

——— The History of Philip's war, commonly called the great Indian war of 1675 and 1676. Also of the French and Indian wars of the Eastward, in 1689, 1690, 1692, 1696 and 1704. By Thomas Church, Esq., with numerous notes to explain the situation of the places of battles, the particular geography of the ravaged country, and the lives of the principal persons engaged in those wars. Also, an appendix, containing an account of the treatment of the natives by the early voyagers, the settlement of New England by the forefathers, the Pequot war, narratives of persons carried into captivity, anecdotes of the Indians, and the most important late Indian wars to the time of the Creek war. By Samuel G. Drake. Third edition, with plates.
12mo. pp. 360. With frontispiece. *Boston.* 1825.

A second emission of Mr. Drake's edition was published in Boston, in 1827, and a third in 1828. In 1829, there was a reprint at Exeter, New Hampshire. In 1846, one at Cooperstown, New York; in 1854, one at Hartford, Conn., from the press of Silas Andrus & Son. These are duodecimos and believed to be from the same plates as the edition of 1825.

CITY BANK, PROVIDENCE, R. I. Proceedings of the Stockholders of, in reference to the last election of Directors, on the 4th July, 1836.
8vo. pp. 15. [No imprint.] 1836.

CLAGGETT, WILLIAM. A Looking-Glass for Elder Clarke and Elder Wightman, and the church under their care. Wherein is fairly represented the very image of their Transactions. It being a brief but true relation of the cause and prosecution of the differences between the Baptist Church, under the pastoral care of the aforesaid Elders, and John Rhodes, Capt. John Rogers, William Claggett and several others that were members of the aforesaid Church, with some remarks thereon.
12mo. pp. 230. *Printed for J. Rhodes, J. Rogers, W. Claggett, &c., and to be sold by J. Rhodes, Shopkeeper in Newport, on Rhode Island, in New England.* 1731.

CLAP, REV. NATHANIEL, A. M. "A broken heart acceptable with God through Christ." A sermon preached at Newport, March 27, 1715, on a murder committed by Jeremiah Meacham. (The Prisoner being present at the meeting, and addressed by the preacher,) with the dying words of the criminal at the execution at Newport on Rhode Island; April 12, 1715.
16mo. pp. 143. *Boston.* 1715.

Mr. Clap was a minister of the first Congregational Church, in Newport, nearly 50 years. He was born in Dorchester, Massachusetts, in 1668, graduated at Harvard College in 1690, and began to preach in Newport in 1695. The celebrated George Whitefield, in speaking of Mr. Clap, upon whom he called, in Newport, in 1740, says, he was the most remarkable man he ever beheld. "He looked like a good old puritan and gave one an idea of what stamp those old men were, who first settled New England." He died Oct. 30, 1745, in the 78th year of his age.

CLARKE, ABRAHAM LYNSEN, A. M., Rector of St. John's

Church, Providence. The secrets of masonry illustrated and explained; in a discourse preached at South Kingstown, before the Grand Lodge of the State of Rhode Island; convened for the installation of Washington Lodge, September 3d, A. L. 5799.

8vo. pp. *Providence. Bennett Wheeler.* 1799.

CLARK JOHN. Ill Newes from New-England: or a narrative of New England's Persecution. Wherein is declared that while old England is becoming new, New England is becoming old. Also four proposals to the Honoured Parliament and Council of State, touching the way to propagate the Gospel of Christ (with small charge and great safety) both in old England and New. Also four conclusions touching the faith and order of the Gospel of Christ as of his last will and testament, confirmed and justified. By John Clark, Physician, of Rhode Island in America.

4to. pp. 76. *London. Printed by Henry Hills, living in Fleet Yard, next door to the Rose and Crown, in the yeare* 1652.

——— The same. (*Mass. Hist. Coll.* 7th series, vol. 1.)

In this book the author introduces the substance of a curious tract said by Prof. Elton, in his notes to Callender's Discourse, p. 110, to have been issued the preceding year, called "A Brief Discourse touching New England, as to the matter in hand, and to that part of it, sci. RHODE ISLAND, where my residence is, together with the occasion of my going out, with others from the Mathatusets Bay, and the many providential occurrences that directed us thereto, and pitched us thereon." This is followed by "A faithful and true relation of the persecution of Obadiah Holmes, John Crandall and John Clark, merely for conscience sake towards God, by the principal members of the church or commonwealth of the Mathatnsets in New England, which rules over that part of the world; wherein is shown their discourteous entertainment of strangers, and how that spirit by which they acted, would order the whole world if either brought under them, or should come in unto them. Drawn forth by the aforesaid John Clark."

Dr. John Clark was the founder, in 1644, of the first Baptist church in Newport, and became its pastor. This was the second Baptist church in America. He was sent to England in 1611 with Roger Williams, as an agent of the colony, in which capacity he acted for twelve years. In 1663 he procured the charter by which Rhode Island was governed for nearly a century, and returned to his pastoral charge in Newport. He was elected three years successively, Deputy Governor, and, although he constantly exerted himself to promote the civil prosperity of the colony, he continued to labor as the pastor of the church referred to, until his death, which took place on the 20th of April 1676, in the sixty-seventh year of his age. Dr. Clark was ever distinguished for his piety and beneficence. He was one of Rhode Island's ablest legislators, and had the honor of contributing much towards establishing the first government in the world that gave to all, equal civil and religious liberty.

CLARKE, THOMAS M. Bishop of Rhode Island. Primary charge to the clergy of the Diocese of Rhode Island: Printed by order of the Convention.
8vo. pp. 19. *Providence. G. H. Whitney.* 1855.

―――― Oration before the municipal authorities and others of the city of Providence, July 4, 1860.
8vo. pp. 32. *Providence. Knowles, Anthony & Co.* 1860.

―――― Address in commemoration of Washington's Birth day, before the First Light Infantry of Providence, Feb. 22, 1861.
12mo. pp. 24. *Providence. Cooke & Danielson.* 1861.

CLEVELAND, HON. C. F. Letter to Gov. King, refusing to deliver up Thomas W. Dorr. (*See Constitution.*)

COAL. An enquiry into the chymical character and properties of that species of coal lately discovered at Rhode Island; together with observations on the useful application of it to the arts and manufactures of the Eastern States.
12mo. pp. 21. *Boston. Snelling & Simons.* 1808.

―――― An address to the inhabitants of Rhode Island on the subject of their coal mines.
8vo. pp. 16. *New York. J. Seymour.* 1825.

COBBETT, THOMAS. The Civil Magistrate's Power in matters of Religion, modestly debated, impartially stated according to the Bounds and Grounds of Scripture, and answer returned to those objections against the same, which seem to have any weight in them. Together with a Brief answer to a certain Slanderous Pamphlet, called " Ill News from New England: or, A Narrative of New England's Persecution." By John Clark of Road-Island, Physician. By

Thomas Cobbett, Teacher of the Church of Lime in New England.

4to. pp. xii. 103, 2d part iv. and 52. *London. Printed by W. Wilson for Philemon Stephens, at the Gilded Sign in St. Paul's Churchyard.* 1653.

Dedicated to the Right Hon. Oliver Cromwell, Captain General of all the Forces of the Commonwealth of England, Scotland and Ireland. Grace, Mercy and Peace be multiplied.

This Treatise concerning the Christian Magistrate's Power, and the exerting thereof in and about matters of religion, written with much zeal and judgment by Mr. Cobbett of New England, I doe allow to be printed, as being very profitable for these times. February 7th, 1652. *Obadiah Sedgwick.*

CODDINGTON, WILLIAM. A demonstration of True Love unto you the Rulers of the Colony of the Massachusetts in New England; shewing to you that are now in authority, the unjust Paths that your Predecessors walked in, and of the Lord's Dealings with them in his severe judgments, for persecuting his Saints and Children. Which may be a warning unto you, that you walk not in the same steps, lest you come under the same condemnation. Written by one who was once in authority with them; but always testified against their persecuting Spirit, who am called William Coddington of Rhode Island.

Small 4to. pp. 20. *Printed in the year* 1674.

——— Five letters from, to John Winthrop and John Winthrop, Jun., 1640 to 1648, written from Newport, R. I.— Also, the case of William Coddington vs. William Dyre.

Winthrop Papers, in Mass. Hist. Coll. 4 series, Vol. VI.

——— Letters from, see *Besse, History of the Quakers.*

Coddington was a native of Lincolnshire, England, and came to Massachusetts in 1630, as one of the magistrates. He removed to Rhode Island in 1637. The following year we find his name first among those who agreed to incorporate themselves into a "bodie politic," on Rhode Island. He was chosen judge or chief ruler of the colony at Newport, which elected him Governor, until that colony was incorporated with that of Providence Plantations in 1647. Under this patent he was again elected Governor in 1674 and 1675. Gov. Coddington early embraced the sentiments of the Society of Friends, which he continued to hold till his death. He appears to have enjoyed a high reputation, and was ever active in promoting the welfare of the colony which he had assisted in founding. He was a worm advocate of liberty of conscience, as was shown by his acts, and which may be seen in his writings.

COIT, THOMAS W., D. D., Rector of Trinity Church, New Rochelle. Puritanism, or a churchman's defence against its aspersions by an appeal to its own history, &c.
12mo. pp. 528. *New York. D. Appleton & Co.* 1845.

This book contains many facts relating to the settlement of Rhode Island, with full reference to authorities.

COLLINS, HOWARD C., of South Kingston; Memoir of [died 2d month, 14th, 1767, aged 15 years, 4 months.]
12mo. pp. 8. *No date.*

COLORED SCHOOLS. Will the General Assembly put down Caste Schools?
8vo. pp. 8. *Providence.* 1857.

COMSTOCK, CHARLES, L. L. D. A history of South Kingston with a particular description of the Hornet's Nest Company, and the Cats let out of the Bag.
12mo. pp. *Newport. Printed by the author.* 1806.

CONNECTICUT BOUNDARY. Paukatuck, now the boundary between Connecticut and Rhode Island. April 17, 1663.
Mass. Hist. Coll., 1st series, Vol. 5.

COOKE, JAMES W., A statement of facts relating to the ordination at Grace Church, with the correspondence on the subject between the Rt. Rev. J. P. K. Henshaw, D. D., and the Rev. J. W. Cooke, Rector of St. Michael's Church, Bristol, R. I.
8vo. pp. 72. *Providence. C. Burnett, Jr.* 1847.
See Mulchahey, for reply to this pamphlet.

COOPER, JAMES FENIMORE. Memoir of Commodore O. H. Perry, [in vol. 2, of "Lives of Distinguished American Naval Officers."
12mo. *Auburn. New York.* 1846.

COWELL, BENJAMIN. Spirit of '76 in Rhode Island; or sketches of the efforts of the Government and People in the war of the Revolution; together with names of those who

belonged to Rhode Island Regiments in the army. With
Biographical notices, Reminiscences, &c. &c.
8vo. pp. 351.   *Boston. A. J. Wright.* 1850.

——— Oration pronounced before the Greene Association
on the 8th of August 1814, it being the anniversary.
8vo. pp. 19.   *Providence. Miller, Goddard & Man.*

CRANE, JOHN, D. D. A sermon delivered July 31, 1816,
at the installation of the Rev. William Preston to the pastoral care of the Pacific Church and Society in Providence.
8vo. pp. 15.   *Providence. Miller & Hutchins.* 1816.

THE CONSTITUTION OF 1842–43. Books relating to.

ADAMS, JOHN QUINCY. The Social Compact exemplified in
the Constitution of the Commonwealth of Massachusetts,
with remarks on the theories of Divine right of Hobbes and
others, concerning the origin and nature of government.
A Lecture delivered before the Franklin Lyceum, Providence, R. I., November 25, 1842.
8vo. pp. 32.   *Providence. Knowles & Vose.* 1844.

AN ADDRESS to the people of Rhode Island, from the convention assembled at Providence on the 22d day of February,
and again on the 12th day of March, 1834, to promote the
establishment of a State Constitution.
8vo. pp. 60.   *Providence. Cranston & Hammond.* 1834.

On page 27 of Considerations, &c., by E. R. Potter, it is stated (and has not
been contradicted that we know of) that the historical portion of this
address was contributed by Joseph K. Angell, Esq., the statistics by William H. Smith, Secretary of State under the People's Constitution, and
the remainder, including all the argumentative part, by Thomas W. Dorr.

ADDRESS adopted by the Democratic Convention holden at
Providence, December 20, 1841.
8vo. pp. 8.   *Providence.* 1842.
Signed by Fenner Brown, President; Anson Potter, Nathaniel Tompkins,
Nathan Bardin, John D. Austin, Randall Carder, Vice Presidents; and
Wm. Simons, Jr., Wm. J. Miller and Pardon M. Hale, Secretaries.

ADDRESS to the people of the United States.
12mo. pp. 15.   *Providence. October* 21, 1844.

CONSTITUTION OF 1842–43. Books relating to.

This address relates to the Constitution of Government adopted by Rhode Island in 1842, and is signed by N. R. Knight, William Sprague, Moses B. Ives, John Brown Francis, James F. Simmons, H. Y. Cranston, E. R. Potter, John Whipple, Wm. G. Goddard, Henry Bowen, Albert C. Greene, Joseph M. Blake, John Carter Brown, Alexander Duncan, Charles Jackson, and others.

[ADDRESS] To the Members of the General Assembly of the State of Rhode Island.
8vo. pp. 24. [*No imprint or date.*]

ARGUMENTS of Messrs. Whipple and Webster in the case of Martin Luther, Plaintiff in error, versus Luther M. Borden and others, in the Supreme Court of the United States, January term, 1848.
8vo. pp. 56. *Charles Burnett, Jun.* 1848.

CHARTER. The famous old Charter of Rhode Island granted by King Charles 2d in 1663. Also the Rhode Island Bill of Rights and the declaration of religious freedom.
8vo. pp. 8. *Providence. I. H. Cady.* 1842.

CHARTERS and Acts of Rhode Island, to be used in the case of Martin Luther vs. Luther M. Borden, et al.
8vo. pp. *Providence. Joseph S. Pitman.* 1845.

CHARTERS AND LEGISLATIVE DOCUMENTS illustrative of Rhode Island History: showing that the people of Rhode Island, from the foundation of the State until their Constitution of 1842, possessed and exercised the rights of self-government; and in what manner and under what form of government they declared their independence in 1775, became a member of the Confederation of the United States in 1778, and adopted the Constitution of the United States in 1790.
8vo. pp. 68. *Providence. Knowles & Vose.* 1844.

The following are the Documents contained in this volume:
1. Charter of 1643 under the authority of Parliament, pages 3 and 4
2. Letter of Oliver Cromwell to Rhode Island, 1655, page 5
3. Commission to John Clark, agent of Rhode Island, 1660, 6
4. Charter of 1663, granted by Charles II., 8
5. Acceptance of the charter by the people of Rhode Island, 19–21
6. Opinion of Chalmers, extract from Rawle, on Constitution U. S. 21
7. Declaration relating to Liberty of Conscience, by General Assembly, 22

BIBLIOGRAPHY OF

CONSTITUTION OF 1842–43. Books relating to.

8. Declaration of General Assembly in 1665 as to qualifications to vote, page 23
9. Order of the Assembly, 1667, respecting persons voting not freemen, 23
10. Act of 1663-4, regulating elections, 24
11. Act of 1666, regulating admission of freemen, 26
12. Act of 1723, value of freehold to be admitted free, 27
13. Act of 1729, same, 26
14. Act of 1742, same, 28
15. Act of 1746, same, 29
16. Act of 1767, same referred to, 30
17. Declaration of Rhode Island Independence, May, 1776, 31
18. Instructions to Delegates in Congress, May, 1776, 34
19. Resolutions appointing, and instructions to, delegates 1st Congress, 36
20. Appointment of delegates, and instructions, December, 1774, 37
21. Act of June, 1775, repealing an "Act regulating Appeals" to the King, 38
22. Instructions to delegates, August, 1775, respecting American fleet, 39
23. Acts and resolutions of the Assembly, approving Declaration of Independence, 39 and 40
24. Authority of delegates, Feb., 1778, to sign Articles of Confederation, 40
25. Articles of Confederation as to rights of the States, 41
26. Resolution of convention, U. S., in reference to the adoption of Constitution, 42
27. Act of General Assembly, R. I., calling a convention to consider Constitution U. S., Jan., 1790, 42
28. Ratification of the Constitution U. S., by R. I. convention, 44
Comments on the ratification and the rights of Rhode Island under the Constitution; extract from the "Federalist," 50, 51, 52
29. Law of Rhode Island as to the qualifications of freemen, 1798, and reference to law of 1822, 53
Reasons for the long continuance of the freehold qualification in Rhode Island. Facts showing that the government of Rhode Island did all that was necessary, at various times, for the forming a Constitution, 54 and 55
30. Act of January, 1821, calling a convention, 55
31. Act of June, 1834, calling a convention, 57
32. Resolutions of January, 1841, calling a convention, 58
33. Resolutions of May, 1841, in relation to the convention, 59
34. Resolutions of January, 1842, relating to convention, 60
35. Resolutions of January, 1842, respecting the "People's Constitution," 61
36. Act of June, 1842, calling a convention, 61
37. Resolution of convention, Sept., 1842, 63
38. Act of October, 1842, declaratory of the act of June, 1842, 64

CONSTITUTION OF 1842-43. Books relating to.

39. Organization of the government under the Constitution of 1842, page 64
40. Certificate of the Secretary of State to the truth of the copies
    and abstracts, 68

BURKE'S REPORT. Interference of the Executive in the affairs of Rhode Island.

Report of the select committee, to whom was referred the memorial of the Democratic members of the Legislature of Rhode Island, requesting, among other things, the House of Representatives to institute an enquiry into the fact of the adoption of a constitution by the people of Rhode Island in December, 1841, and its suppression by the then existing authorities of that State, through the interference and assistance of the President of the United States: also, the petition of Samuel Melroy and other citizens of Carroll county, in the State of Indiana, relating to the same subject; also, the message of the President of the United States, relating to the alleged interference in the affairs of the people of Rhode Island, by which they were prevented from establishing a government under the constitution adopted by them in December, 1841, with the documents accompanying.   [By Edmund Burke, Chairman.] (*Pub. Doc.*, 28*th Congress*, 1*st Session. House Representatives, Report No.* 536.)

8vo. pp. 1070.   *Washington. June.* 1844.

The following papers constitute the appendix to this Document:
No. 1. Testimony of James Harris,   page 102
    2. Report of the committee on the action of the General
       Assembly on the subject of the Constitution, March, 1842,   126
    3. Constitution of the State of Rhode Island, as adopted by
       the Convention at Providence, November, 1841.   135
    4. Address to the people of Rhode Island, from the Conven-
       tion assembled at Providence, Feb. and March, 1834,   151
    5. Proposed Constitution of Rhode Island, adopted by the
       People's Convention, Nov. 18, 1841,   185
    6. People's Convention,   203
    7. Proclamation of Joseph Joslin, President of the Conven-
       tion,   206
    8. Opinion of Hon. John Pitman, Judge U. S. District Court,   206
    9. Proposed Constitution of the State of Rhode Island, as
       adopted by the Convention assembled at Newport, June
       21, 1824,   209

11

CONSTITUTION OF 1842-43. Books relating to.

No.		page
10.	Constitution of Rhode Island, adopted November, 1842,	219
11.	Ratification of the Constitution of the United States by Rhode Island, 1790,	236
12.	Democratic State Convention, December, 1842,	239
13.	Testimony of Welcome B. Sayles,	247
14.	Proceedings of the Mass Convention, Newport, May 5, 1841,	256
15.	Resolutions of the Mass Convention, Providence, July 5, 1841,	359
16.	Address of the State Suffrage Committee, setting forth the principles of the suffrage movement.	261
17.	Address of the State Suffrage Committee, calling on the people to elect delegates to a convention to form a constitution,	269
19 to 72.	Various depositions,	374
73.	Vote on the question of the adoption of the People's Constitution, December, 1841,	253
77.	Papers filed, with case of Martin Luther vs. Luther M. Borden, et al,	357
78.	Proceedings of a convention of delegates in Rhode Island, met for the purpose of ratifying the Constitution of the United States, 1790,	376
79.	Report of Benjamin Hazard on the extension of suffrage in 1829,	377
80.	Resolutions of the General Assembly of Rhode Island, January, 1831, upon a memorial for the poor of Smithfield,	401
81.	Petition of Elisha Dillingham and 580 others for the abrogation of the charter, January, 1841,	402
82.	Declaration of the principles of the Rhode Island Suffrage Association, made Feb. 7, and April 13, 1841,	403
83.	Resolutions adopted at a mass meeting in Newport, May 5, 1841,	404
84.	Resolutions adopted at a mass meeting in Providence, July 5, 1841,	407
85.	Resolutions of the General Assembly of Rhode Island, May 1, 1841,	409
86.	A call to the people of Rhode Island to assemble in convention, May 5, 1841,	410
87,	Address of the State Committee, of the suffrage convention at Newport, May 5, 1841, for the purpose of calling a convention to form a Constitution for the State,	412
88.	Constitution as finally adopted by the People's Convention which assembled at Providence, November 18, 1841,	420
89.	Resolution of the People's Convention, declaring the adoption of the People's Constitution,	436

RHODE ISLAND. 87

CONSTITUTION OF 1842–43. Books relating to.

No.		page
90.	An act, calling a convention to frame a written constitution for the State,	439
91.	Extract from the records of the House, May 7, 1841.	442
92.	do. do. do. do. January, 1842,	443
93.	Proposed act to change the day of annual election, etc.,	444
94.	An act to provide for calling a convention for the purpose of forming a new constitution or form of government,	444
95.	An act to amend "an act to provide for calling a convention to form a new constitution," etc.,	446
96.	Proceedings of the Charter Assembly, respecting Mr. Atwell's bill, proposing the People's Constitution for adoption or rejection,	447
97.	Organization of the government under the People's Constitution, January 13, 1842,	447
98.	Journal of the Senate under the People's Constitution, 1842,	448
99.	Journal of the House of Representatives, under the constitution of the State, May 3, 1842,	451
100.	Acts and Resolutions of the Legislature under the People's Constitution,	461
101.	Table of the population of Rhode Island,	470
102.	State of votes for general officers in the elections, from 1822 to 1841,	471
103.	Copy of an act declaring martial law,	472
104.	Proclamation of the People's Constitution,	472
105.	Agreement of parties to the action,	473
106.	List of persons voting at the elections of the 27th, 28th and 29th of December, 1841, for the purpose of adopting the People's Constitution,	474
107.	Charter of 1643, under the authority of Parliament,	623
108.	Letter from Oliver Cromwell, March 29, 1655,	625
109.	Charter of Rhode Island, granted by Charles II, 1663,	625
140.	Declaration by the General Assembly, relating to suffrage, 1664,	635
141.	Declaration by the General Assembly, in relation to the qualification of voters,	635
142.	Order of the General Assembly, respecting persons voting who are not freemen, 1667,	636
143.	Act of the General Assembly, prescribing proxy voting in 1663,	636
144.	Act of 1666, regulating the admission of freemen,	638
145.	Act fixing the freehold qualification of voters, passed 1723,	639
146.	Act relating to the same subject, passed in 1729,	639
147.	Act relating to the same subject, passed in 1742,	639
148.	Act relating to the same subject, passed in 1746,	640
149.	Legislation in relation to Suffrage; and acts of 1798 and 1822,	641

CONSTITUTION OF 1842–43. Books relating to.

No. 150. Act of 1821, calling a convention to frame a written constitution, page 642
151. Act of 1834, calling a convention to frame a constitution, 643
152. Resolution of January, 1841, for the same purpose, 644
153. Resolution of June, 1841, relating to the same subject, 645
154. Resolution of January, 1842, relating to the same subject, 646
155. An act in amendment of the act regulating the admission of freemen, 646
156. Resolution of the General Assembly relating to the people's constitution, 647
158. Resolution of the convention, asking for a declaratory act, 647
159. Act of October, 1842, declaratory of the act of June, 1842, 648
160. Organization under the constitution of 1842, 648
160. a Report of the committee appointed to count the votes given at the adoption of the existing constitution of Rhode Iisland, 651
161. Message from the President of the United States, relative to the employment of United States troops in Rhode Island, and transmitting documents relative to the recent difficulties there, April 9, 1844, 652
162 to 211. Various documents accompanying President Tyler's message, 655
212. Chief Justice Durfee's charge to the Grand Jury, at the March term of the Supreme Court at Bristol, Rhode Island, 1842, 706
213. Organization of the government under the People's Constitution, and message of Gov. Dorr, May 3, 1842, 707
214. Governor Dorr's address to the people of Rhode Island, August, 1843, 731
215. Proclamation of Governor King, suspending martial law in Rhode Island, Aug. 1, 1842, 767
216. Correspondence between the Hon. H. Clay and Hon. J. B. Francis, 763
217. Indictment vs. Wm. H. Smith, and certificate of commitment, 771
218. Indictment vs. Burrington Anthony, 776
218 a Indictment vs. Hezekiah Willard, 778
219. Indictment vs. Wm. P. Dean, and certificate of imprisonment, 782
220. Indictment vs. Benjamin Arnold, 786
221. Indictment vs. Chas. H. Campbell and Andrew Thompson, 790
222 to 226. Indictments vs. Joseph Gavitt, Sylvester Harris, David Parmenter, Geo. S. Nichols, and Martin Luther, 792
227–28. Indictment vs. B. M. Bosworth, Wilmarth Heath, with reprints of their trials, 804
228–33. Miscellaneous articles and papers, 813

CONSTITUTION OF 1842–43. Books relating to.

No. 234–5	Laws relating to the military, passed by the General Assembly, January, 1842,	page 819
236–37.	Laws relating to the military, passed by General Assembly, January, 1843,	833
238.	An act to regulate the election of civil officers, etc.,	842
239.	Speech of Thomas W. Dorr, on the right of the people of Rhode Island to form a constitution, Nov. 18, 1841,	851
240.	Report of the trial of Thomas W. Dorr, on the charge of treason,	865
241.	Proceedings of the United States Senate in relation to the difficulties in Rhode Island,	1018
242.	Statement of Mrs. A. H. Lord, and indictment against her,	1068

THE CLOSE of the late Rebellion in Rhode Island. An extract from a letter, by a Massachusetts man, resident in Providence. (1st and 2d editions.)
8vo. pp. 16.   *Providence. B. Cranston & Co.* 1842

CONSTITUTION of the State of Rhode Island and Providence Plantations, as adopted by the convention, assembled at Newport, June 21, 1824.
8vo. pp. 18.   *Providence. Jones & Maxcy.* 1824.

CONSTITUTION. Draft of a constitution of the State of Rhode Island and Providence Plantations, as revised by a committee appointed by the convention, assembled at Providence, November, 1841. Printed by order of the Convention.
8vo. pp. 24.   *Providence. Knowles & Vose.* 1841.
Known as the People's Convention.

CONSTITUTION. Articles of a constitution adopted by the People's Convention, held October 4, 1841, and postponed to November 16, for final consideration. Published by order of the convention.
8vo. pp. 16.   *Providence. Office of the New Age.* 1841.

CONSTITUTION of the State of Rhode Island and Providence Plantations, as finally adopted by the convention of the people assembled at Providence on the 18th of Nov., 1841.
8vo. pp. 22.   *Providence. New Age Office.* 1841.
Joseph Joslin, President of the Convention ; W. H. Smith and John S. Harris, Secretaries. This is known as the People's Constitution.

CONSTITUTION OF 1842–43. Books relating to.

CONSTITUTION. How the People's Constitution was made for Rhode Island, without the aid of the Law or of the Legislature.
8vo. pp. 4. double columns. [*Providence.* 1841.]

CONSTITUTION. Proposed constitution of the State of Rhode Island and Providence Plantations.
8vo. pp. 32. *Providence. Knowles & Vose.* 1842.

CONSTITUTION of the State of Rhode Island and Providence Plantations, as adopted by the convention assembled at Providence, November, 1841.
8vo. pp. 26. *Providence. Knowles & Vose.* 1842.
Henry Y. Cranston, President; Thomas A. Jenckes, Secretary. This is known as the Landholders' Constitution.

CONSTITUTION of the State of Rhode Island and Providence Plantations, as adopted by the convention assembled at Newport, September, 1842.
8vo. pp. 24. *Providence. Knowles & Vose.* 1842.
James Fenner, President; H. Y. Cranston, Vice-President; Thomas A. Jenckes and W. W. Updike, Secretaries.

CONSTITUTION. Message of Governor Fenner, to the General Assembly, relative to the interference of Congress in the national affairs of Rhode Island, with the Protest and Declaration of the select committee thereon, made to the General Assembly of Rhode Island, at its March Session, A. D. 1844. See March schedule, 1844.
The Protest and Declaration was also printed in a separate sheet.

THE CONSPIRACY to defeat the Liberation of Governor Dorr; or the Hunkers and Algerines identified, and their policy unveiled; to which is added a report of the case *ex parte* Dorr; comprising motion to Supreme Court of the United States; petitions of sundry citizens of Rhode Island; affidavits showing the treatment of Governor Dorr by the inspectors of the prison; argument of counsel, and the decision of the Court.
8vo. pp. 47. *New York. John Windt.* 1845.

CONSTITUTION OF 1842–43. Books relating to.

CONVENTION. Journal of the convention assembled to frame a Constitution for the State of Rhode Island, at Newport, September 12, 1842. Printed by order of the House of Representatives, at its January session, 1859.
8vo. pp. 69.   *Providence. Knowles, Anthony & Co.* 1859.

COOKE, PARSONS. An essay on the Gospel's relation to the Civil Law. 2d edition.
8vo. pp. 22.   *Boston. S. N. Dickinson.* 1843.

COWELL, BENJAMIN. A letter to the Hon. Samuel W. King, late Governor of the State of Rhode Island, May, 1842, 2d edition, with an appendix.
8vo. pp. 32.   *Providence. H. H. Brown.* 1842.

CRANE, REV. S. A., Address on the occasion of the return of the Kentish Guards and volunteers, July 1, 1842, after the suppression of the late rebellion in this State.
8vo. pp. 12.   *Providence. B. F. Moore.* 1842.

DAVIS, JOHN. Governor of Massachusetts. Message to the Legislature of Massachusetts, relative to arms loaned to Rhode Island, Sept. 1842.
8vo. pp. 13.   *Mass. Senate. Doc. No. 76, September.* 1842.

DECLARATION. Leonard Wakefield vs. Knowles, Vose and Anthony.
8vo. pp. 12.   *November* 13. 1843.

The defendants were charged with libel, for printing in the Providence Journal "the following scandalous and false words:" "The President has appointed Leonard Wakefield, Dorr's chaplain at Chepatchet, postmaster at Cumberland Hill. This Wakefield, as our readers know, was one of the most noisy and most active of the *Soverinnity.*," etc.

A DEMOCRATIC CATECHISM. Containing the self-evident and fundamental principles of Democracy. "The people are sovereign."
12mo. pp. 20.   *Providence. B. T. Albro.* 1846.

DORR, THOMAS W. Political Frauds exposed, or a narrative of the proceedings of "The Junto in Providence," concerning the Senatorial Question, from 1833 to 1838.— By Aristides.
8vo. pp. 24.   [*Providence.* 1838.]

CONSTITUTION OF 1842–43. Books relating to.

DORR. Report of the trial of Thomas Wilson Dorr, for Treason; including the testimony at length; arguments of counsel—the charge of the Chief Justice—the motions and arguments for a new trial, and an arrest of judgment; together with the sentence of the Court, and the speech of Mr. Dorr before sentence. From notes taken before the trial.
8vo. pp. 115.   *Providence. B. F. Moore.* 1844.

——— Report of the trial of Thomas Wilson Dorr, for treason against the State of Rhode Island; containing the arguments of counsel, and the charge of Chief Justice Durfee.
8vo. pp. 181.   *Boston. Tappan & Dennett.* 1844.

The following are the contents of this pamphlet:
Preface,—Arraignment of the Prisoner; Impannelling of the jury; Challenge to the array in the third writ of venire; Names of the jurors sworn; Opening of Alfred Bosworth, Esq., for the prosecution; Evidence for the Prosecution; Argument of Mr. Bosworth upon the evidence; Opening of George Turner, Esq., for the defence; Evidence for the defence; Argument of Mr. Turner on the Question of Treason against a State; Reply of Mr. Bosworth; Argument of Thomas W. Dorr, in close, on the same question; Closing argument of Mr. Turner upon the evidence; Closing argument of Thomas W. Dorr; Closing argument of Joseph M. Blake, Esq., Attorney General; Charge to the jury by Chief Justice Durfee.

——— The case of Thomas W. Dorr explained. [By Geo. Turner, counsel of Gov. Dorr.]
8vo. pp. 11.   *No date.*

——— Merits of Thomas W. Dorr and George Bancroft, as they are politically connected. By a citizen of Massachusetts, [Geo. Ticknor Curtis.]
8vo. pp. 36.   *Boston. John H. Eastburn.* 1844.

——— The same. Second edition, with an appendix.
8vo. pp. 41.   *Boston. John H. Eastburn.* 1844.

THE DORRIAD; Or the Hero of the Two Flights. [A Poem.]
12mo. pp. 12.   *Boston. Justin Jones.* 1842.

DORRIANA. Prospectus of a new and highly interesting work in two volumes, to be published in "The only Democratic

CONSTITUTION OF 1842-43. Books relating to.

City," as soon as a sufficient number of subscribers can be obtained to warrant the undertaking. The work will be entitled DORR-IANNA, or a logical, historical, tragical, magical, sympathetical, and democratical account of the late glorious Revolution in Rhode Island; containing a true and complete history of all the sayings, doings, adventures and brilliant achievements of His Excellency, Thomas Wilson Dorr, Governor and Commander-in-Chief of Rhode Island and Providence Plantations. By a Sympathizer.
4to. pp. 4.   *Providence. June* 17, 1842.

DAW'S DOINGS, or the History of the late war in the Plantations. By Sampson Short-and-fat, author of Quozziana. With wood cuts.
12mo. pp. 68.   *Boston. Wm. White & H. P. Lewis*. 1842.

DUFF. Petition of Henry J. Duff and others for an alteration of the State Constitution, May, A. D. 1846.
8vo. pp. 4.   [1846.]

DURFEE. Charge of Chief Justice Durfee, delivered to the Grand Jury at Bristol, 1842. Published by request of the Grand Jury.
8vo. pp. 16.   *Providence.* 1842.

EVANS, EASTWICK. Essay on State Rights. The object of which is to define and illustrate the spirit of our institutions and of liberty, and to renovate our political elements.
8vo. pp. 40.   *Washington.* 1844.

THE EVENTFUL DAY, in the Rhode Island Rebellion. A poem. By a Looker on.
12mo. pp. 12.   *Providence. H. H. Brown*. 1842.

FACTS involved in the Rhode Island Controversy, with some views upon the rights of both parties.
8vo. pp. 43.   *Boston. B. B. Mussey*. 1842.

FACTS for the people; containing a comparison and exposition of votes on occasions relating to the Free Suffrage movement in Rhode Island.
12mo. pp. 12.   *Providence. Knowles & Vose*. 1842.

CONSTITUTION OF 1842-43. Books relating to.

GODDARD, WILLIAM G. An address to the people of Rhode Island, delivered in Newport, May 3, 1843, in presence of the General Assembly, on the occasion of a change in the Civil Government of Rhode Island, by the adoption of the constitution which superseded the charter of 1663.
8vo. pp. 80.   *Providence. Knowles & Vose.* 1843.
* This is a pamphlet of great historical value, on account of the numerous notes appended to it.

GOODELL, WILLIAM. The rights and the wrongs of Rhode Island ; comprising views of liberty and law, of religion and rights, as exhibited in the recent and exciting difficulties in that State.
8vo. pp. 120.   *Press of Oneida Institute, N. Y.* 1842.
(From the Christian Investigator, No. 8, Whitesboro, N. Y., Sept. 1842.)

GRAY, FRANCIS C. Oration before the Phi Beta Kappa Society of Brown University, Providence, R. I., on Commencement day, Sept. 7, 1842.
8vo. pp. 40.   *Providence. B. Cranston & Co.* 1842.

HALLETT, BENJAMIN F. The right of the people to establish forms of government. Mr. Hallett's argument in the Rhode Island Causes before the Supreme Court of the United States, January, 1848. No. 14, Martin Luther *vs.* Luther M. Borden and others. No. 77, Rachel Luther *vs.* the same.
8vo. pp. 71.   *Boston. Beals & Greene.* 1848.

KENNEDY, Mr., of Indiana, speech of, on the resolution authorizing the committee on the Rhode Island controversy to send for persons and papers. Delivered in the House of Representatives, March 13, 1844.
8vo. pp. 7.   *Washington. Globe Office.* 1844.

KENYON, ARCHIBALD. The object and principles of Civil Government, and the duty of Christians thereto. Being a discourse preached before the West Baptist Church and Society, August 14, 1842.
8vo. pp. 11.   *Providence. B. T. Albro.* 1842.

CONSTITUTION OF 1842-43. Books relating to.

KING, GOV. SAMUEL WARD. Message to the General Assembly, April Session, 1842, relative to the proceedings of the insurrectionists, transmitting a letter from President Tyler, dated April 11, 1842.
In the Schedule. 1842.

LETTER to the Hon. James F. Simmons. By a Rhode Island Conservative.
8vo. pp. 8. *Providence.* 1845.

LETTERS of the Hon. C. F. Cleveland and the Hon. Henry Hubbard, Governors of Connecticut and New Hampshire, to Samuel Ward King, the Charter Governor of Rhode Island, refusing to deliver up Thomas Wilson Dorr, the Constitutional Governor of said State, to the usurping authorities thereof. Also letters of the Hon. Marcus Morton, [James Buchanan and Martin Van Buren,] to the Suffrage Clam-bake at Medbury Grove, Seekonk, Mass., August 30, 1842.
8vo. pp. 17. (double col's.) *Fall River. Thomas Almy.* 1842.

LUTHER vs. BORDEN. Supreme Court of the United States, No. 124. Martin Luther, Plaintiff in error, vs. Luther M. Borden et al., in error to the Circuit Court of the United States for the district of Rhode Island.
8vo. pp. 149. *Washington. J. & G. S. Gideon.* [1844.]

In the Plaintiff's schedule are the following papers:

Proceedings of Convention, May 29, 1790,	page 38
Report of Committee on Suffrage, June session, 1829,	39
Resolutions of General Assembly, January session, 1841	66
Petition of E. Dillingham and others,	67
Declaration of principles of the Suffrage Association, 1841,	68
Resolutions of the Mass Convention in Newport,	69
Resolutions of the Mass Convention at Providence, July 4, 1841,	72
Resolutions of the General Assembly, May session, 1841,	74
Act of General Assembly, calling convention rejected, May 7, 1841,	75
Minority report on said act, by S. Y. Atwell,	77
Proceedings of House of Representatives, relative to said act,	77
A call to the people to assemble in convention, July 21, 1841,	78
Address of State Committee, May 5, 1841,	81
People's Constitution adopted, December, 1841,	89

CONSTITUTION OF 1842-43. Books relating to.

<u>Copy from Records, House of Representatives, January session,</u>
1842,   page 106
Journal of the Senate under the People's Constitution,   112
Journal of the House of Representatives, under ditto,   116
Acts passed under the People's Constitution,   131
Table of Population,   140
Certificate of the number of votes polled for ten years past, etc.   141
Certificate containing act establishing martial law,   141
Act of General Assembly, calling convention, June session, 1842,   141
Copy of Records of House of Representatives, March session, 1842,   144
Proclamation from the President of the People's Convention,   144

MEMORIAL of the Democratic members of the Rhode Island Legislature, protesting against the course pursued by the President, during the late difficulties, and requesting the House of Representatives to make certain specified enquiries in relation thereto, Feb. 19, 1844.
8vo. pp. 4. 28th Con. 1st Sess. House Rep. Doc. No. 136. 1844.

McCLERNAND, Mr. of Illinois, speech of, on the resolution reported by the Select Committee on the Rhode Island controversy. Delivered in the House of Representatives, March 19, 1844.
8vo. pp. 8.   Washington. 1844.

McKENZIE. A Discourse against Life-taking. Delivered by request, before the Rhode Island Quarterly Meeting, in Tiverton, August 24, 1842. By James A. McKenzie, Pastor of Roger Williams Baptist Church, Providence.
8vo. pp. 23.   Providence. J. Whittemore & Batcheller. 1842.

MIGHT AND RIGHT. By a Rhode Islander, with portrait of Thomas W. Dorr.
12mo. pp. 324.   Providence. A. H. Stillwell. 1844.

PEET, REV. EDWARD W. A sermon on the occasion of Public Thanksgiving, for the happy termination of the late civil dissentions in Rhode Island. Delivered in Grace Church, Providence, July 21, 1842.
8vo. pp. 16.   Providence. Isaac H. Cady. 1842.

PITMAN, JOHN. A reply to the letter of the Hon. Marcus

CONSTITUTION OF 1842–43. Books relating to.

Morton, late Governor of Massachusetts, on the Rhode Island question. By one of the Rhode Island people.
8vo. pp. 32. *Providence. Knowles & Vose.* 1842.

POTTER, HON. ELISHA R. Considerations on the questions of the adoption of a Constitution and extension of Suffrage in Rhode Island.
8vo. pp, 64. *Boston. Thomas H. Webb & Co.* 1842.

—— Speech of, on the memorial of the Democratic members of the Legislature of Rhode Island, Delivered in the House of Representatives, March 7th, 9th, and 12th, 1844.
8vo. pp. 13. *Washington. Globe Office.* 1844.

POTTER, J. B. M. Oration delivered at Kingston, R. I., July 4, 1843.
8vo. pp. 24. *Boston. Thomas H. Webb & Co.* 1843.

PROCEEDINGS in the Rhode Island Legislature, on sundry resolutions of the State of Maine.
8vo. pp. 27. *Providence. Knowles & Vose.* 1845.

PROCEEDINGS of the citzens of East Greenwich and vicinity on the return of the Kentish Guards and volunteers, Friday, July 1, 1842; after the suppression of the late rebellion in this State; with an address by the Rev. S. A. Crane.
8vo. pp. 12. *Providence. B. F. Moore.* 1842.

PROTEST of the Legislature of Rhode Island against the right of the Congress of the United States, to decide or enquire into the question whether the constitution of the State, legally, peaceably, and freely adopted by the people thereof, in November, 1842, s, or is not, the lawful constitution of the State.
8vo. pp. 6. *28th Con. 1st Sess. House Rep. Doc. No.* 232. 1844.

PROTEST AND DECLARATION of the State of Rhode Island and Providence Plantations against any interference by the Congress, or by the House of Representatives of tne Congress of the United States, with the internal government and constitution of said State.
4to. pp. 3. [*Providence. March.* 1844.]

CONSTITUTION OF 1842–43. Books relating to.

PROTEST of the minority of the members of the Legislature of Rhode Island against the protest and declaration of the majority of the same Legislature, April 16, 1844.
8vo. pp. 4. *28th Con. 1st Sess. House Rep. Doc. No. 233.* 1844.

RANDALL, DEXTER. Democracy vindicated, and Dorrism unveiled.
8vo. pp. 100. *Providence. H. H. Brown.* 1846.

RATHBURN, MR., of New York, speech of, on the resolution authorizing the committee on the Rhode Island controversy to send for persons and papers. Delivered in the House of Representatives, March 9, 1844.
8vo. pp. 8. *Washington. Globe Office.* 1844.

THE RECENT CONTEST in Rhode Island; an article from the North American Review, for April, 1844.
8vo. pp. 69. *Boston. Otis, Broaders & Co.* 1844.

A REPLY to the letter of the Hon. Marcus Morton, late Governor of Massachusetts, on the Rhode Island Question. By one of the Rhode Island people.
8vo. pp. 32. *Providence. Knowles & Vose.* 1842.

REPORT of a committee of the Massachusetts Legislature, concerning the loan of arms by the Adjutant General, [to Rhode Island,] Feb. 8, 1843.
8vo. pp. 37. *Mass. House of Reps. Doc. No. 24.* 1843.

REPORT of a joint special committee, relative to Wm. T. Olney, [on complaint of being forcibly taken from his home in Massachusetts to Bristol, R. I., where he was confined in jail.] Feb. 1843.
8vo. pp. 10. *Mass. House of Reps. Doc. No. 93.* 1843.

REPORT of the committee on the action of the General Assembly of Rhode Island, on the subject of the Constitution. [By the Hon. R. K. Randolph.] With an act in relation to offences against the sovereign power of the State.
8vo. pp. 15. *Schedule. March Session.* 1842.

CONSTITUTION OF 1842–43. Books relating to.

RHODE ISLAND MEMORIAL. Report of Mr. Causin, from the minority of the select committee, on the memorial of the Democratic members of the Rhode Island Legislature, and other documents connected with the subject, dissenting from the views of the majority of said committee.
8vo. pp. 172.   Doc. House of Reps. 28th Con. 1st session, Report No. 581.   June, 1844.

Schedule of documents appended to this report:
No. 1. Charter of Charles the Second, 1663, page 41
  2. Proceedings of the people accepting it, 50
  3. Act of 1663, regulating voting, 52
  4. Act of 1665, requiring voters to be of competent estates 53
  5. Act of 1666–7, regulating the admission of freemen, 53
  6 to 10. Acts 1723-1729-12-16 and 6), fixing qualification, 54
  11. Act renouncing allegiance to the King of Great Britain, passed at the May session of the General Assembly, of Rhode Island, 1776, 56
  12. Proceedings of the Assembly ratifying the Declaration of Independence, July, 1776, 57
  13. Act of Assembly, Feb. 1778, ratifying articles of confederation, 58
  14. Act of 1789, calling a convention to consider the Constitution of the United States, 59
  15. Proceedings of the above-named convention, 60
  16. Act of 1798, regulating voting; fixes qualification at $134, 65
  17. Bill extending suffrage, passed by the Senate in 1811, 65
  18. Act of Assembly, 1821, for calling a convention to form a constitution, with the votes thereon, 66
  19. Act of Assembly, 1822, for calling a convention to form a constitution, with the votes thereon, 67
  20. Act of 1824, calling a convention. The convention formed a constitution which was rejected by the people, 68
  21. Act of 1834, calling a convention. This convention dissolved without completing a constitution, 69
  22. Act of Assembly, January, 1841, calling a convention, 70
  23. Act of May, 1841, apportioning delegates to convention, 71
  24. Constitution adopted by the meeting denominated the "People's Convention," December, 1841, 71
  25. Communication from the "People's Convention," to the Legislature, January, 1842, 88
  26. Act of January, 1842, extending the right of voting upon the constitution framed by the legal convention, to all who might be admitted to vote under it, 92
  27. Resolutions passed by the Legislature of Rhode Island, January

CONSTITUTION OF 1842-43. Books relating to.

	1842, condemning the proceedings of the "People's Convention," as revolutionary,	92
28.	Resolutions of the Rhode Island Suffrage Association, Jan. 1842, declaring their intention to support the "People's Constitution" by force,	93
29.	Constitution framed by the legal convention which assembled in November, 1841, and finally adjourned, Feb. 1842, commonly called the "Landholders' Constitution." Required residence only to vote. Rejected by the people in March, 1842. Report of the vote appended,	94
30.	Report of committee of the Legislature, March, 1842, with resolutions, and an act passed at that session, sometimes called the "Algerine Act,"	107
31.	Law of Rhode Island, defining and punishing treason, 1838,	117
32.	Law for punishing treason in Virginia,	117
33.	Proclamation of Governor King, April, 4, 1842,	118
34.	Statement made by Messrs. Whipple, Francis and Potter, to the President of the United States, April, 1842,	119
35.	The President's letter in reply,	122
36.	Letter from the Hon. John Whipple to Gov. King,	124
37.	President Tyler's second letter to Gov. King, May, 1842,	125
38.	Act of June, 1842, calling a new convention,	126
39.	Act of October, 1842, explaining an ambiguity in act of June,	128
40.	Constitution framed by the convention called under the act, No. 38, which met at Newport, Sept. 1842, and completed its labors at East Greenwich, Nov. 1842. Adopted by the people in November, 1842, and now in force,	129
41.	Resolutions of the Legislature for discontinuing the prosecutions on account of the late insurrection, and for releasing military fines, etc.,	143
42.	Table of population and of votes of the people on several occasions, within the last five years,	145
43.	Chief Justice Durfee's charge to the Grand Jury, at the Supreme Court at Bristol, March, 1842,	146
44.	Report of the case, Luther vs. Borden,	157
45.	Protest of the Legislature of Rhode Island, against the interference of Congress in the internal affairs of that State.	167

See, also, *Mr. E. R. Potter's speech*, *Mr. Rathbun's speech*, *Mr. C. B. Smith's speech*, *Mr. McClernand's speech*; *Protest and Declaration*; *Constitution*; *Message of Gov. Fenner*; *and President Tyler's message*.

SHERMAN. Report of the Committee on the petition of Henry J. Duff and others. By Sylvester G. Sherman, Esq., chairman of the Committee. Made to the House of Representatives of the Legislature of Rhode Island, at the January session, 1847.

8vo. pp. 16.   *Providence. M. B. Young.* 1847.

CONSTITUTION OF 1842-43. Books relating to.

SIEGE OF CHEPACHET. [A poem.]
8vo. pp. 8.   No date.
"This book is dedicated to the three-tail Bashaw of Tripoli, and all the Barbary powers. By Roger Dogherty, alias Peter Madicanscutter."

SMITH, Hon. C. B., of Indiana. Speech of, on the memorial of the "Democratic members" of the Legislature of Rhode Island. Delivered in the House of Representatives of the U. S., March 14, 1844.
8vo. pp. 16.   *Washington, Standard Office.* 1844.

STATEMENT submitted by Messrs. John Whipple, John. B. Francis and E. R. Potter, to the President of the United States, relative to the affairs of Rhode Island. President Tyler's reply to Governor King; and letter from Mr. Whipple to Gov. King.
8vo. pp. 8.   1842.

STETSON, Mr., of New York. Speech of, touching the opinions of Mr. Van Buren on the right of suffrage, in reply to Mr. Caleb B. Smith. Delivered in the House of Representatives, March 20, 1844.
8vo. pp. 8.   *Washington. Globe Office.* 1844.

STORY. Charge of Mr. Justice Story on the Law of Treason, delivered to the Grand Jury of the Circuit Court of the United States, holden at Newport, for the Rhode Island District, June 15, 1842. Published at the request of the Grand Jury and the Rhode Island Bar.
8vo. pp. 8.   *Providence. H. H. Brown.* 1842.

SUFFRAGE. An address to the citizens of Rhode Island, who are denied the right of Suffrage. (Periodical of the Social Reform Society, No. 3.)
12mo. pp. 8.   *New York.* 1840.

―――― Preamble and Constitution of the Rhode Island Suffrage Association, adopted Friday evening, March 27, 1840.
12mo. pp. 9.   *Providence. B. T. Albro.* 1840.
The formation of this Association was the beginning of the great movement for the extension of Suffrage and formation of a Constitution in Rhode Island. It was drawn up by Jacob Frieze.

Constitution of 1842–43. Books relating to.

——— The Banner of Freedom; a collection of patriotic songs, original and selected, designed for the Rhode Island Suffrage Association. Edited by Miss Ann Page.
12mo. pp. 24. *Providence. S. M. Millard & Co.* 1841.

——— Popular Liberty and Equal Rights. An oration delivered before the mass convention, of the Rhode Island Suffrage Association, held on the Dexter training ground, in Providence, July 5th, 1841. By Wm. S. Balch.
12mo. pp. 23. *Providence. B. F. Moore.* 1841.

——— Considerations on the question of the adoption of a Constitution, and extension of suffrage in Rhode Island. By Elisha R. Potter.
8vo. pp. 64. *Boston. T. H. Webb & Co.* 1842.

——— Address on the right of Free Suffrage. *See Luther.*

——— [Address] to the Members of the General Assembly of Rhode Island.
8vo. pp. 24. [*No date.*]
Relates to the Suffrage question, and attributed to the Hon. John Pitman.

——— Facts for the people: containing a comparison and exposition of votes on occasions relating to the free suffrage movements in Rhode Island.
8vo. pp. 12. *Providence. Knowles & Vose.* 1842.
Attributed to Jacob Frieze.

——— A concise history of the efforts to obtain an extension of suffrage in Rhode Island, from the year 1811 to 1842. By Jacob Frieze.
12mo. pp. 171 *Providence. B. F. Moore.* 1842.

——— Report of the Committee on the subject of an extension of Suffrage. Signed, B. Hazard.
8vo. pp. 26. *R. I. Schedule. June Session.* 1829.

——— The Garland of Gratitude; respectfully dedicated to the Constitutional Suffrage Ladies of Rhode Island.
8vo. pp. 12. *Providence.* 1842.

CONSTITUTION OF 1842-43. Books relating to.

TREADWELL, Francis C., counsellor at law. Treason defined. 12mo. pp. *New York. People's Rights Office.* 1844.

TUCKER, Mark, D. D. A discourse preached on Thanksgiving Day, in the Beneficent Congregational Meeting House, Providence, July 21, 1842. Published by Request. 8vo. pp. 16. *Providence. B. F. Moore.* 1842.

UNITED STATES TROOPS IN RHODE ISLAND. Message from the President of the United States, [John Tyler] in answer to a resolution of the House of Representatives, relative to the employment of the United States Troops in Rhode Island, and transmitting documents in relation to the recent difficulties in that State, April 10, 1844. 8vo. pp. 179.

28th, Cong. 1st Sess. H. of Rep. Doc. No. 225. 1844.

The following documents accompany the message:

No. 1. Affidavit of Samuel Currey relative to the arming the suffrage men.
2. Resolution of the Suffrage party in Cumberland, to be ready at a moment's warning, to carry into effect the "People's Constitution.
3. Letter from Governor King to the President of the United States.
4. Letter from President Tyler in reply.
5. Letter from Henry Bowen, Secretary of State of Rhode Island, transmitting affidavits of Messrs. Stoddard, Hoppin, Currey, Frieze, Robinson and Wilkinson.
6. Letter from John Whipple to the President, asking an audience for the committee appointed by Gov. King to wait on him.
7. Statement of the Rhode Island committee, of the political condition of the State of Rhode Island, April 10, 1842.
8. Letter from Gov. King to the President, May 4, 1842, with resolutions of the General Assembly of R. I., as to the insurrectionary movements in that State, and calling for his interference.
9. The President's reply to Governor King, May 7, 1842.
10. "Letter from Thomas W. Dorr, insurgent Governor of R. I. to the President, transmitting resolutions of the insurgent Assembly of Rhode Island, that the President of the United States and Congress be informed that the Government and Assembly were elected, and the latter in session."
11. "Letter from the President of the United States to the Governor of Rhode Island, (private and confidential,) May 9, 1842; giving his views of the policy to be pursued by the Government of Rhode Island towards the insurgents.

CONSTITUTION OF 1842–43. Books relating to.

12. The Governor of Rhode Island to the President in reply, May 12, 1842.
13. Letter from E. R. Potter, to the President of the United States, May, 15, 1842.
14. The President in reply to Mr. Potter, May 20, 1842.
15. Letter from Thomas A. Jenckes, private Secretary to Gov. King, transmitting Gov. Dorr's proclamation to the people of Rhode Island.
16. Letter from Gov. King to the President, stating that Dorr, since his flight, is organizing troops, and in consequence calls for military aid.
17. The President's reply to Gov. King, May 28, 1842.
18. Copies of letters of the Secretary of War to Col. Bankhead and Gen. Eustes, and of the President's instructions; also of the President's directions to the Secretary of War to proceed to Rhode Island.
19. Letter from Daniel Webster to the President, with a report in relation to the state of affairs in Rhode Island, June 3, 1842.
20. From Col. Bankhead to the Secretary of War—reports the expected invasion of Rhode Island by Dorr in great force, &c., &c.
21. From E. J. Mallett to Postmaster General, confirming rumor that 48 kegs of gunpowder had been stolen by the insurgents from a powder house.
22. From Thomas M. Burgess to the President, relative to the proceedings of the insurgents.
23. The President's reply to Mr. Burgess.
24. The affidavits of Messrs. Peckham, Harris, Shelley and Keep, in relation to the insurgents.
25. From Adjutant Townsend, stating that Col. Bankhead had returned to New York.
26. From Col. Bankhead to the Secretary of War—reports that he has had an interview with Gov. King. He had returned to Providence.
27. From Col. Bankhead, to Adj. Gen. Jones.
28. From ditto to ditto in relation to Dorr's military force.
29. From Messrs. Simmons, Sprague and Tillinghast, to the President of the United States, June 27, 1842, on the state of affairs in Rhode Island.
30. From the President to the Secretary of War, instructing him to publish a proclamation and other duties, in case of a requisition being made for the power and force of the United States.
31. Extracts from letters of the Hon. E. R. Potter, and from the President in reply,
32. From Wm. H. Smith and John S. Harris, Secretaries of the People's Convention, transmitting to the Governor of Rhode Island the People's Constitution.

CONSTITUTION OF 1842–43. Books relating to.

33. Depositions of Charles Martin, J. F. Pond and Wm. S. Slater, rela.
tive to the movements of the insurgents.
34. Military orders, through General Scott, from April 11 to June 11,
1842.

VIEWS of the Society of Friends in relation to Civil Government.
12mo. pp. 16.   *Providence. Joseph Knowles.* 1850.

VINTON. Loyalty and Piety ; or the Christian's civil obligations defined. A discourse preached in Trinity Church, Newport, R. I. By Francis Vinton, Rector, on Thursday, July 21, 1842. The day of public thanksgiving.
8vo. pp. 23.   *Providence. Burnett & King.* 1842.

WAYLAND, FRANCIS. The affairs of Rhode Island. A discourse delivered in the meeting-house of the First Baptist Church, Providence, May 22, 1842. (1st & 2d editions.)
8vo. pp. 32.   *Providence. B. Cranston & Co.* 1842.

———— "The affairs of Rhode Island." Being a review of Dr. Wayland's "Discourse," a vindication of the sovereignty of the people, and a refutation of the doctrines and doctors of Despotism. By a member of the Boston Bar.
8vo. pp. 30.   *Boston. B. B. Mussey.* 1842.

This review is attributed to John A. Bolles, Esq.

———— A Discourse delivered in the First Baptist Church, Providence, R. I., on the day of Public Thanksgiving, July 21, 1842.
8vo. pp. 31.   *Providence. H. H. Brown.* 1842.

MR. WEBSTER's argument in the Supreme Court of the United States, in the case of Martin Luther vs. Luther M. Borden and others, January 27th, 1848.
8vo. pp. 20.   *Washington.* 1848.

WHIPPLE, JOHN. Address of, to the people of Rhode Island on the approaching election.
8vo. pp. 16.   *Providence. Knowles & Vose.* 1843.

WHIPPLE AND WEBSTER. The Rhode Island Question.

CONSTITUTION OF 1842–43. Books relating to.

Arguments of Messrs. Whipple and Webster, in the case of Martin Luther, Plaintiff in error, vs. Luther M. Borden and others, in the Supreme Court of the United States, January, 1848.
8vo. pp. 56.   *Providence. Charles Burnett, Jr.* 1848.

NOTE TO THE CONSTITUTIONS.—The Convention which framed the People's Constitution, met in Providence, on the first Monday in October, 1841, and finally completed its labors on the 18th day of November following. The Constitution was submitted to the people of the State, for their adoption or rejection, on the 27th day of December, to be voted for on that and the five succeeding days. The vote, as returned, was 13,944 in favor of the Constitution, and 56 against it. The act calling the Convention which framed the Landholders' Constitution, was passed by the General Assembly, at its January session, in 1841. The Convention met on the first Monday of November following,—framed a Constitution, and submitted it to the people of the State, for their adoption or rejection, on the 21st, 22d, and 23d days of March, 1842. The vote, as returned, was 8,013 in favor of the Constitution, and 8,689 against it. Showing a majority of 676 votes against it. It was called the "Landholders' Constitution" from the fact that none but the owner of real estate and the oldest son of such landholder, were allowed to vote in the election of delegates to the Convention that framed it. At the June session of the General Assembly, 1842, an act was passed, calling another Convention to frame a Constitution. The Convention met at Newport, on the second Monday in September, 1842, and framed a Constitution, which was submitted to the people of the State, for their adoption or rejection, on the 21st, 22d, and 23d days of November following. The vote, as returned, was 7,024 in favor of the Constitution, and 51 against it. Showing a majority of 6,973 votes in its favor. This Constitution is the present supreme law of the State. The "People's Constitution" party took no part in the question.

COTTON JOHN. The Bloudy Tenent, washed and made white in the Bloud of the Lambe; being discussed and discharged of Bloud Guiltinesse by just defence. Wherein the great questions of the present time are handled, viz:— How farre Liberty of Conscience ought to be given to those that truly feare God? And how farre restrained to turbulent and pestilent persons, that not only raze the Foundation of Godlinesse, but disturb the Civill Peace where they live? Also, how farre the Magistrate may proceed in the Duties of the first Table? And that all Magistrates ought to study the Word and Will of God, that they may frame their Government according to it. Discussed as

they are alledged from divers Scriptures, out of the Old and New Testament. Wherein also the practice of Princes is debated, together with the Judgement of ancient and late writers of most precious esteeme. Whereunto is added a Reply to Mr. Williams' answer to Mr. Cotton's Letter. By JOHN COTTON, Batchelor in Divinity, and Teacher in the Church of Christ, at Boston, in New England.
Small quarto, pp. 195 and 144. *London. Printed by Mathew Symmons, for Hannah Allen, at the Crowne in Pope's Head Alley.* 1647.

For a reply to this work, see Roger Williams. See also the work which follows this, the author of which is unknown.

——— Wholesome Severity reconciled with Christian Liberty, or the True Resolution of a present Controversie concerning Liberty of Conscience. Here you have the question stated, the middle way betwixt Popish Tyrannic and Schismatizing Liberty; approved and also confirmed from Scripture, and the Testimonies of Divines, yea, of whole Churches. The Chief Arguments and Exceptions used in *The Bloudy Tenent*, The Compassionate Samaritane M. S. to A. S. &c., examined. Eight distinctions added for qualifying and clearing the whole matter. And in conclusion, a Paraenetick to the five Apologists for choosing accommodation rather than toleration. Imprimatur. Ia. Crawford. December 16, 1644.
4to. pp. 40. *London. Christopher Meredith.* 1645.

COZZENS, WILLIAM, Governor of Rhode Island, Wm. H. Cranston, Mayor of Newport, A. H. Dumont, chairman of the Public Schools, and Henry Rousmaniere, Commissioner of Public Schools. Addresses at the dedication of the " Trustees of the Long Wharf School House," on the 20th of May, 1863.
8vo. pp. 106. *Newport. Pratt & Messer.* 1863.

CRANE, John, D. D. A sermon delivered July 31, 1816, at the installation of the Rev. Willard Preston to the pastoral care of the Pacific Church and Society in Providence.
8vo. pp. 15. *Providence. Miller & Hutchens.* 1816.

CRANSTON, Capt. Robert B., of the Newport Artillery. Proceedings of a General Court Martial, holden in Newport, August 1, 1817. As officially reported by the Judge Advocate.
8vo. pp. 24.   *Providence. Jones & Wheeler.* 1817.

CURREY, Samuel, Argument for the heirs at Law in the Halsey Will Case.
8vo. pp. 19.   *Providence. Knowles, Anthony & Co.* 1859.

CURTIS, GEORGE WILLIAM. A Rhyme of Rhode Island and the Times; pronounced before the Sons of Rhode Island in New York, at their first anniversary held in the Hall of the New York Historical Society, May 29, 1863.
8vo. pp. 16.   *New York. C. A. Alvord.* 1863.

This poem is appended to Dr. Vinton's oration on the Annals of Rhode Island

BAILEY, MRS. CHARLOTTE F. Report upon the disabled Rhode Island soldiers; their names, condition, and in what hospitals they are. Made to Governor Sprague, and by him presented to the General Assembly of Rhode Island, January session, 1863.
8vo. pp. 24.   *Providence. Alfred Anthony.* 1863.

Mrs. Bailey was commissioned by Gov. Sprague to visit the United States Hospitals, in and near Philadelphia and Washington.

DANFORTH, WALTER R. An oration delivered before the Providence Association of Mechanicks and Manufacturers, April 8, 1822, being the anniversary of the election of officers.
8vo. pp. 22.   *Providence. Miller & Hutchins.* 1822.

——— An oration pronounced in the Universalist Chapel, on Thursday, July 4, 1833.
8vo. pp. 22.   *Providence. John Hutchins.* 1833.

DEANE, CHARLES. Some notices of Samuel Gorton, one of the first settlers of Warwick, R. I., during his residence at Plymouth, Portsmouth, and Providence; chiefly derived from early manuscripts, with a brief introductory memoir.
4to. pp. 41.   *Boston. Coolidge & Wiley.* 1850.

DEHON, REV. THEODORE, A. M. Rector of Trinity Church, Newport. A discourse delivered in Newport, R. I., before the congregation of Trinity Church, the Masonic Society

and the Newport Guards, the Sunday following the intelligence of the death of General George Washington.
8vo. pp. 19.   *Newport. Henry Barber.* 1800.

———— A discourse delivered in Providence, Sept. 6, 1804, before the Female Charitable Society, for the relief of indigent widows and children.
8vo. pp. 20.   *Providence. Heaton & Williams.* 1804.

———— A discourse delivered in Trinity Church, in Newport, on Thursday, 27 Nov. 1805; an appointed day of public Thanksgiving and Praise.
8vo. pp. 14.   *Newport. Ann Barber.* 1806.

Dr. Dehon was born in Boston in 1776, and graduated at Harvard College in 1795. After being Rector of Trinity Church, in Newport, he removed to Charleston, South Carolina, where he was elected Bishop in 1812. He died Aug. 6, 1817, aged 41. Bishop Dehon was considered a man of superior talents, and much esteemed for his social virtues. In 1821, two volumes of his sermons were published.

D'WOLF, JOHN. An address delivered before the citizens of Bristol, R. I., July 4, 1821.
8vo. pp. 24.   *Published by request.* 1821.

D'WOLF, JAMES. For discourse on the death of, see *Griswold.*

DEWEY, REV. ORVILLE. The Pulpit as a field of exertion, talent and piety. A sermon delivered at the installation of the Rev. Edward B. Hall, as pastor of the First Congregational Society in Providence.
8vo. pp. 36.   *New Bedford. Benjamin Lindsey.* 1832.

DEXTER ASYLUM. Rules and Regulations for the government of, established at a town meeting of the Freemen of the town of Providence, July 26, 1828.
8vo. pp. 14.   *Providence. Smith & Parmenter.* [1828.]

———— First annual report of the Board of attending and consulting physicians and surgeons of.
8vo. pp. 12.   *Providence. Smith & Parmenter.* 1829.

DEXTER GENEALOGY. Being a record of the families descended from the Rev. Gregory Dexter, with notes and biographical sketches of each parent. By S. C. Newman, A. M.
12mo. pp. 108.   *Providence. A. Crawford Greene.* 1859.

DIX, JOHN ROSS. A hand-book of Newport and Rhode Island, with wood cuts.
12mo. pp. xii and 170.   *Newport. C. E. Hammett.* 1852.
DORRANCE vs. FENNER. Report of the case, John Dorrance against Arthur Fenner, tried at the December term of the court of Common Pleas, in the county of Providence, A. D. 1801. To which is added the proceedings in the case Arthur Fenner vs. John Dorrance. Carefully compiled from the notes taken at the trial.
8vo. pp. 116.   *Providence. Bennett Wheeler.* 1802.

DORR. Report of the Trial of Thomas Wilson Dorr, for Treason against the State of Rhode Island, containing the arguments of counsel, and the charge of Chief Justice Durfee. By Joseph S. Pitman.
8vo. pp. 131.   *Boston. Tappan & Dennett.* 1844.

—— Political Frauds exposed; or a narrative of the proceedings of "The Junto in Providence," concerning the Senatorial Question, from 1833 to 1838.   By Aristides.
8vo. pp. 24.   [*Providence.* 1838.]

—— Address to the people of Rhode Island, August, 1843. (See Burke's report No. 214.)

—— Message to the General Assembly upon the organization of the government under the People's Constitution, May 3, 1842. (See Burke's Report, No. 213.)

—— Speech of, on the right of the people of Rhode Island to form a constitution; delivered in the People's Convention on the 18th day of November, 1841. (See Burke's Report, p. 851.)

—— Report of the trial of Thomas Wilson Dorr, for Treason, including testimony at length—arguments of counsel—the charge of the Chief Justice—the motions and arguments on the questions of a new trial and in arrest of judgment; together with the sentence of the court, and the speech of Mr. Dorr before sentence. From notes taken at the trial.
8vo. pp. 115. double col's.   *Providence. B. F. Moore.* 1844.
Prepared for the press by George Turner and Walter S. Burges, Attorneys for the defence.

—— The Life and Times of Thomas Wilson Dorr, with outlines of the political history of Rhode Island. By Dan King, with portrait.
12mo. pp. 368. *Boston. Printed for the author.* 1859.

DOWNER, SILAS. A discourse delivered in Providence, in the colony of Rhode Island, on the 25th day of July, 1768, at the dedication of the tree of Liberty, from the summer-house in the tree. By a Son of Liberty.
8vo. pp. 16. *Providence. Printed and sold by John Waterman at his printing office at the paper mill.* 1768.

The following account of this event is taken from the Providence Gazette, July 30, 1768:

"On Monday last, (25th,) at five in the afternoon, being the time appointed for dedicating the great Elm Tree, at Captain Joseph Olney's, in this town, to be the tree of Liberty, there was a very great concourse of very respectable people of this and the neighboring towns, many coming from a considerable distance out of the Province of Massachusetts Bay, to assist on the occasion. An animated discourse was delivered from the summer-house in the tree, by a Son of Liberty, wherein was briefly pointed out the Terrors of Colonization of the first Planters of these colonies; a Declaration of our Rights, and a particular enumeration of our Grievances, together with a designation of the means of Redress. After which followed the Directions thus: the people in the summer-house, laying their hands on the tree, the gentleman who gave the discourse pronounced these words aloud: "We do, in the name and behalf of the true sons of "Liberty, in America, Great Britain, Ireland, Corsica, or wherever they "may be dispersed throughout the world, dedicate and solemnize thereto, "this tree, to be a *Tree of Liberty*. May all our councils and deliberations "under its venerable Branches, be guided by wisdom, and directed for "the support and maintenance of that liberty which our renowned Fore-"fathers sought out, and found under trees, and in the wilderness. May it "long flourish, and may the sons of Liberty often repair hither, to confirm "and strengthen each other. When they look towards their sacred Elm, "may they be penetrated with a sense of their duty to themselves and "their posterity; and may they, like the House of David, grow stronger "and stronger, while their enemies, like the House of Saul, shall grow "weaker and weaker, Amen."—The whole conducted with great order and quiet.

The following account contains additional particulars of this event:

"In July, 1768, the Sons of Liberty were called upon to attend the dedication of the Tree of Liberty. Almost every town then had either its liberty tree or its liberty pole. The liberty tree of Providence was a little north of the north side of Olney street, in front of a public house kept there by Captain Joseph Olney. Samuel Thurber, in a note kindly communicated to me when in his 81st year, says: 'He,' Captain Olney, 'had a large, old fashioned, two story, elm shedded house, in the form of an L, with a large yard in front. In this yard stood the largest elm tree that I ever saw. A flight of steps was erected, leading, perhaps twenty feet up to where three or four limbs set out. There a convenient seat was fixed for, say, ten or twelve people to sit in and enjoy themselves in the shade. The dedication of this tree took place on the 25th day of July. A large concourse of people assembled. An animated discourse was delivered from the seat or summer-house on the tree, by Silas Downer." *Staples Annals of Providence, p. 221.*

DOYLE, THOMAS. [of Rhode Island.] Five years in a Lottery Office, or an exposition of the Lottery System in the United States.
12mo. pp. 62. Boston. *S. N. Dickinson.* 1841.

DRAKE, SAMUEL G. Biography and history of the Indians in North America, comprising a general account of them, and details in the lives of all the most distinguished chiefs and others who have been noted among the various Indian nations upon the continent, etc. etc.
8vo. pp. 720. 11th edition. *Boston. B. B. Mussey & Co.* 1851.

This work was first published, in 1832, in a small duodecimo volume, under the title of "Indian Biography." The following year a second edition was issued under the above title. Each successive edition has been enlarged. Very large numbers of each edition have been sold. No other such work contains as much on our aborigines as this. The Indians of Rhode Island and their wars, are noticed at length.

——— Old Indian Chronicle.
22mo. pp. 208. *Boston.* 1836.

This book consists of five early tracts, four of which relate to King Philip's War, accompanied by notes by Mr. Drake, and a chronology of Indian events.

DROWNE, SOLOMON., M. D. An oration delivered in the First Baptist Meeting-House, in Providence, at the celebration, February 23, A. D., 1824, in commemoration of the Birth Day of Washington, and in aid of the cause of the Greeks.
8vo. pp. 24. *Providence. Brown & Danforth.* 1824.

——— Annual address delivered before the Rhode Island Society for the encouragement of Domestic Industry, October 15, 1823.
8vo. pp. 18. *Providence. Carlile & Brown.* 1826.

—— A Funeral oration in memory of the Hon. James M. Vernon, Esq., late a Judge in the Western Territory; delivered at Marietta, Ohio, January 13, 1789. 8vo.

—— Biographical notice of, by the Rev. T. Stafford Drowne in sketches of Rhode Island Physicians, p. 25–34.

See *Historical Magazine* for March, 1857—*History of the Town of Foster*, by C. C. Braman, in the Providence Journal, 1858–59. Sketch of the life of,—By Prof. Wm. G. Goddard, in Providence Journal, 1838—and in the American Quarterly Register, vol. 11, p. 357 ; and Sketch of his life, with several of his letters, in "*New York City, during the American Revolution.*" Printed for the Mercantile Library Association, 4to. 1861.

Dr. Drowne was born in Providence, in 1753, and graduated at Brown University in 1773. After visiting Europe he returned to Providence, and entered upon the practice of medicine. For several years he was a surgeon in the army of the revolution. Ill health obliged him to remove to the West, where he labored in his profession, in Ohio and Western Pennsylvania for nine years. In 1801, he returned to his native State, and settled in the town of Foster, where he passed the remainder of his life, in professional and agricultural pursuits. In 1811, Dr. Drowne was appointed Professor of Materia Medica and Botany in Brown University. Botany was his favorite study, and, besides lecturing to the students, he had private classes of citizens. He died in 1834, at the age of 81 years.

DUDLEY, GOVERNOR JOSEPH. Queen Anne's Instructions to, in 1702. (*Mass. Hist. Collections*, 3d series, *Vol.* IX.)

These instructions give Governor Dudley "all the powers and authorities of any Captain General, over the colonies of Rhode Island, Providence Plantations and the Narragansett Country."

DUFF, HENRY J. and others. Petition of, for an alteration of the State Constitution, presented to the General Assembly, May, 1846. Report of the committee on the petition of Henry J. Duff, and others, by Sylvester G. Sherman, Esq., chairman of the committee, made to the House of Representatives of Rhode Island, January, 1847. 8vo. pp. 4 and 16. [*Providence.*] *M. B. Young.* [1847.]

DUMONT. Articles of Faith and Church Covenant of the United Congregational Church, of Newport, R. I., with a brief notice of the origin and history of the Church. Prepared at the request of the Church by the Pastor, Rev. Henry Dumont, A. M.
12mo. pp. 46. *Newport. James Atkinson.* 1834.

This church dates its origin in the year 1640.

DUMMER, JEREMIAH. A Defence of the New England charters. *Pulchrum est Patriæ benefacere, etiam benedicere haud absurdum est. Sallust.*
8vo. pp. 60. London. 1721.

——— The same work.
8vo. pp. 88. London. 1765.

Dummer was the agent of Massachusetts in England, and a distinguished scholar. "This very able defence was written some time before; but it was now published in the apprehension that a bill would be brought into the House of Commons at their next session to disfranchise the charter governments." *Holmes' Annals.*

DURFEE, HON. JOB. Late Chief Justice of Rhode Island, the complete works of, with a memoir of the author, edited by his son.
8vo pp. xxvi and 523. *Providence. Gladding & Proud.* 1849.

Among other articles, this volume includes the following:

What Cheer; or Roger Williams in Banishment. A Poem.
History of the subjection and extermination of the Narragansetts. A Lecture.
The Idea of the supernatural among the Indians. A Lecture.
A Discourse delivered before the Rhode Island Historical Society, Wednesday, January 13, 1847.
The Character of Chief Justice Eddy.

——— What Cheer; or Roger Williams in Banishment. A Poem.
12mo. pp. *Providence.* 1832.

——— A discourse delivered before the Rhode Island Historical Society, on the evening of Wednesday, January 13, 1847. Published at the request of the Society.
8vo. pp. 42. *Providence. C. Burnett, Jr.* 1847.

——— Charge to the Grand Jury at the March term of the Supreme Judicial Court, at Bristol, R. I., A. D. 1842.
8vo. pp. 16. 1842.

——— An oration before the municipal authorities and citizens of Providence, July 4, 1853.
8vo. pp. 29. *Providence. Knowles. Anthony & Co.* 1853.

———— Discourse on the character of, see *R. G. Hazard*.

Judge Durfee was born in Tiverton, R. I., in 1790, and graduated at Brown University, in 1813. He enjoyed a high reputation as a lawyer, and was besides favorably known as a poet. In 1821, and again in 1823, he was elected to Congress. In 1834 he was promoted to the bench of the Supreme Court; and in 1836 was Chief Justice of that Court, which office he held till his death in 1847.

ASTBURN, Rt. Rev. MANTIN, D. D. The Blessedness of the upright in their end: A Sermon preached in St. Michael's Church, Bristol, Rhode Island, on Wednesday, Feb. 28, 1855. At the Funeral of Rev. John Bristed, formerly Rector of said Church.
8vo. pp. 22. *Bristol, R. I.* 1835.

EAST GREENWICH. History of, see *Eldredge.*

EASTON, JOHN. Narrative of the causes which led to Philip's Indian war, of 1675 and 1676, with other documents concerning this event, in the office of the Secretary of the State of New York. Prepared from the originals, by Franklin B. Hough.
4to. pp. xxiii. and 207. *Albany, N. Y. J. Munsell.* 1856.

The papers in this volume are mostly letters containing accounts or rumors of Indian hostilities ; the Proceedings of the government of New York in consequence of these disturbances ; Reports obtained from the captives escaped from the enemy ; and other documents incidentally relating to the war. 105 *copies printed.*

——— The same on large paper, imp. 4to.
5 copies only printed.

John Easton was the son of Governor Nicholas Easton. He held the office of Attorney General of Rhode Island, from 1651 to 1675. Was Deputy Governor and Assistant at various times; and from 1690 to 1695 was elected Governor. He died at Newport, December 12, 1705, at the age of 88 years, and was buried in the Coddington burial place.

EDDY, SAMUEL. Reasons offered by, for his opinions, to the First Baptist Church in Providence, from which he was compelled to withdraw, for Heterodoxy.
8vo. pp. 19.　　　[*Providence.*] *Jones & Wheeler.* 1818.

──── A review of the reasons offered by S. Eddy, Esq., for his opinions, to the First Baptist Church in Providence, from which he was compelled to withdraw for heterodoxy. From the Christian Disciple, published in Boston.
8vo. pp. 12.　　*Providence. Miller & Hutchins.* 1819.

Judge Eddy was born in Johnston, R. I., March 31, 1769, and graduated at Brown University in 1787. In 1798, he was elected Secretary of State, which office he held for twenty-one years, when he was elected a member of Congress. He held this office during three successive terms, from 1819 to 1825. Subsequently he was appointed Chief Justice of the Supreme Judicial Court of Rhode Island, which position he occupied for eight years, when ill health compelled him to resign it. Judge Eddy was a man of extensive literary acquirements. He died February 3, 1839, aged 69 years.

EDMUNDSON. A Journal of the Life, Sufferings and Labour in the work of the ministry, of that worthy elder and faithful servant of Jesus Christ, William Edmundson, who departed this life the 31st of the 6th month, 1712.
8vo. pp.　　　　　　　　　　　　　　　　　*London.* 1713.

──── The same work, second edition.
8vo. pp. LXXV. and 371. Contents and Index.　*London.* 1774.

Mr. Edmundson was a distinguished preacher of the Society of Friends, and made no less than three voyages to America previous to the year 1700. He was born in 1627, and served in Cromwell's army. Subsequently he joined the Quakers, and became a most zealous apostle among them. In 1671, " he had movings of the spirit" to come to America, and soon after that, sailed in company with George Fox. He visited the West Indies, Virginia, Maryland, New Jersey, New York, and New England, and gives an interesting account of his travels in these climes as a missionary. He was in Rhode Island with George Fox. When at Newport, he says: " One Roger Williams, an old priest, and an enemy to truth, had put forth fourteen propositions, as he called them, which he would maintain against the Quakers that came from Old England, and challenged a dispute of seven of them at Newport, and the other seven at Providence." This is the famous controversy mentioned by Williams, to engage in which, he rowed a canoe, when 73 years of age, from Providence to Newport.

ELDREDGE, JAMES H., M. D. and Daniel H. Greene. History of East Greenwich. A series of articles published in the

East Greenwich *Weekly Pendulum*, commencing June 8, and ending November 17, 1860.

These contain sketches of the most prominent professional men, and the most important incidents from the settlement of the town in 1677 to the present century.

ELDRIDGE, ELLEANOR. Memoirs of.
12mo. pp. 128.   *Providence. B. T. Albro.* 1838.
The subject of this memoir was a colored woman, born in Warwick in 1785.

———— Eleanor's Second Book.
12mo. pp. 127.   *Providence. B. T. Albro.* 1847.

ELLERY, WILLIAM, LIFE OF, by Edward T. Channing, Sparks' American Biography. Vol. 6.

ELLERY, ABRAHAM REDWOOD. An oration delivered July 4, 1793, in the Baptist meeting house in Newport.
8vo. pp. 24.   *Warren. N. Phillips.* 1796.

ELLIS, JAMES, A. M. A narrative of the rise, progress and issue of the late Law suits relative to the property held and devoted to pious uses, in the first precinct in Rehoboth ; containing the substance of the Records which show for whose use and benefit the property was originally intended; together with some observations on certain constitutional principles, which respect the support of Public Worship, and the equal protection and establishment of all regular denominations of christians. By James Ellis, A. M.
12mo. pp. 76.   *Warren, (R. I.) Nathaniel Phillips.* 1795.
Mr. Northrop, a Baptist Elder of Narragansett, and the Rev. Isaac Backus, were involved in the controversy to which the above pamphlet refers.

ELTON, Rev. ROMEO, D. D. Callender's Historical Discourse, with notes. See *Callender*.

———— Life of Roger Williams the earliest legislator and true champion for a full and absolute liberty of conscience.
18mo. pp. viii. and 173.   *Providence. Geo. H. Whitney.* 1853.

———— Same.
18mo. pp. viii. and 173.   *London. Albert Cockshaw.* 1852.

———— Literary remains of the Rev. Jonathan Maxcy, D. D., President of Brown University, with a memoir.
8vo. pp.   *New York.* 1844.

Dr. Elton is a native of Connecticut, and graduated at Brown University in 1812. He was Professor of Ancient Languages in that institution, from 1825 to 1843, and has since resided in England.

EMMONS, WILLIAM. An oration on the death of Mr. Levi Hoppin, a member of the Sophomore Class at Brown University, pronounced March 27, A. D. 1805. In the University Chapel.
8vo. pp. 12. *Providence. J. Carter.* [1805.]

EXAMINATION, by Chemical Analysis and otherwise, of substances emptied into the Public Waters of the State, from Gas and other manufactories, sewerage and other sources, to ascertain if any injury results therefrom to any of the Fisheries in said public waters, in the vicinity of the city of Providence, 1860.
8vo. pp. 31. *Providence. A. Crawford Greene.* 1861.

A report made to the General Assembly of the State of Rhode Island, by a special committee, consisting of Messrs. Geo. Lewis Cooke, C. C. Van Zandt and George B. Peck. The Chemical Analyses are by Professors G. I. Chace and N. P. Hall, of Brown University.

———— See also *Waters of the State.* Report of Committee on.

EVANGELICAL CONSOCIATION and Home Missionary Society of Congregational Churches in Rhode Island. Proceedings of. June 1836.
8vo. pp. 20. *Providence. B. Cranston & Co.* 1836.

———— The Same. June 1837.
8vo. pp. 24. *Providence. B. Cranston & Co.* 1837.

———— The same. June 1838.
8vo. pp. 24. *Providence. B. Cranston & Co.* 1838.

EVANGELICAL CONSOCIATION of the Congregational Churches of Rhode Island. Minutes of the Annual Meeting of, held at Little Compton, June 8–10, 1852. With a report of the Home Missionary Society.
8vo. pp. 24. *Providence. B. T. Albro.* 1852.

———— Same. Held at Barrington, June 14, 1853.
8vo. pp. 24. *Providence. M. B. Young.* 1853.

―――― Same. Held at Pawtucket, June 12, 1855, with reports of the Benevolent Societies and of Religion.
8vo. pp. 22. *Providence. M. B. Young.* 1855.

―――― Same. Held at Little Compton, June 14, 1859.
8vo. pp. 23. *Providence. M. B. Young.* 1859.

FACTORIES. Report of the Commissioner appointed to ascertain the number, ages, hours of labor, and opportunities for education of children, employed in the Manufacturings Etablishments of Rhode Island ; made to the General Assembly [of Rhode Island] at its January session, 1853. Printed by order of the Senate.
8vo. pp. 8.   *Providence. Sayles, Miller & Simons.* 1853.

FALL RIVER, Historical Sketch of, see *Fowler.*

FARLEY, Rev. FREDERICK A. A discourse delivered at the dedication of Westminster Church in Providence R. I., March 5, 1829.
8vo. pp. 31.   *Boston. Leonard C. Bowles.* 1829.

FARMERS' EXCHANGE BANK, GLOCESTER. Report of the Committee appointed by the General Assembly of the State of Rhode Island and Providence Plantations, at the February Session, A. D. 1809, to enquire into the situation of the Farmers' Exchange Bank, in Glocester, with the documents *accompanying the same.* Published by order of the General Assembly, 1809.
8vo. pp. 56.   *Providence. American Office.* 1809.

FESSENDEN, G. M. History of Warren, Rhode Island, from the earliest times, with particluar notice of Massasoit and his family.
18mo. pp. 125.   *Providence. H. H. Brown.* 1845.

FOBES, PERES, A. M. A sermon, delivered in the Baptist Meeting House in Providence, July 31, 1791, occasioned by the death of the Rev. James Manning, D. D., President of Rhode Island College.
8vo. pp. 40. *Providence. J. Carter.* 1791.

FENNER, ARTHUR vs. John Dorrance. Report of the Case of, See *Dorrance.*

FENNER, JAMES, a Letter to. By a Republican.
8vo. pp. 8. *No date.*

———— Letter to. 1811 and 1831.
12mo. pp. 16. *No date.*

FERGUSON. Memoir of the Life and Character of Rev. Samuel Hopkins, D. D., formerly pastor of the First Congregational Church in Newport, Rhode Island; with an appendix; by John Ferguson, pastor of the East Church in Attleborough, Mass.
18mo. pp. viii. and 196. *Boston. Leonard W. Kimball.* 1830.

FIELD. Report of the trial of Albert S. Field, indicted for the murder of Jonathan Gray, before the Supreme Court of Rhode Island, at Providence, March term, 1826.
8vo. pp. 48. *Providence. Miller & Grattan.* 1826.

FISK, ISAAC. An Eulogy on Mr. Samuel Smith Adams, member of the Senior class of Brown University, who died February 6. 1812, aged 22 years. Pronounced at the University Hall, April 18, 1812.
8vo. pp. 16. *Providence. Jones & Wheeler.* 1812.

FISH, JOSEPH, A. M. Pastor of a church in Stonington. A sermon preached at Westerly in the Colony of Rhode Island, August 27, 1755, in the South Meeting House, to a number of religious people, on a day of fasting and prayer (observed by them) for success to our Armies, with a more particular reference to the expedition against Crown Point, in which some of them had near relations.
8vo. pp. 32. *Newport. J. Franklin.* [1755.]

———— A sermon preached at the Ordination of the Rev. Wm. Vinal to the pastoral charge of the first Congregational

church of Christ in Newport, Rhode Island, October 29,
1746, with the charge of the Rev. Mr. S. Checkley, and the
right hand of fellowship by the Rev. Mr. J. Cotton. By
Joseph Fish, A. M., Pastor of the Second church of Christ
in Stonington.
8vo. pp. 55.   *Newport, R. I. Widow Ann Franklin.* 1747.

FOWLER, SAMUEL M. Letters to seceding Masons. See
Anti-Masonry

FOWLER, ORIN, A. M. An Historical Sketch of Fall River
from 1620 to the present time ; with notices of Freetown
and Tiverton ; in three discourses. Delivered January
24, 1841.
8vo. pp. 24. *Fall River. Benjamin Earl.* 1841.

FORMS. A collection of Forms, adapted to the use of Justices
of the Peace, Public Notaries, Sheriffs and Constables,
Overseers of the Poor, Town Councils, Executors and
Administrators, Courts of Probate and Military Officers,
etc. Conformable to the Laws and Usages of the State of
Rhode Island.
12mo. pp. 352. *Providence. John Miller.* [1824.]

——— The same. Conformable to the Revised Statutes and
Usages of the State of Rhode Island.
12mo. pp. iv. and 303. *Providence. Geo. H. Whitney.* 1859.

FOURTH OF JULY ORATIONS, delivered in Providence.

Rev. Enos Hitchcock, D. D.	Providence. J. Carter. 1793.
George Tillinghast, A. M.	Providence. Carter & Wilkinson. 1794.
Jonathan Maxcy, A. M.	Providence. Carter & Wilkinson. 1795.
Paul Allen, Jr., A. B.	Providence. Carter & Wilkinson. 1796.
George R. Burrill, Esq.	Providence. Carter & Wilkinson. 1797.
Samuel W. Bridgham.	Providence. Carter & Wilkinson. 1798.
Jonathan Maxcy.	Providence. John Carter. 1799.
Jonathan Russell.	Providence. B. Wheeler. 1800.
Tristam Burges.	Providence. John Carter. 1801.
Rev. Nathaniel Bowen.	Providence. John Carter. 1802.
Asa Messer, A. M.	Providence. John Carter. 1803.
Henry Wheaton, (before Tammany Society.)	
	Providence. Jones & Wheeler. 1810.
Tristam Burges.	Providence. Jones & Wheeler. 1810.
Emerson Paine.	Providence. H. Mann & Co. 1813.
Benjamin F. Allen.	Providence. 1817.

Albert G. Greene. Providence. John Miller. 1823.
William Hunter. Providence. Smith & Parmenter. 1826.
Albert G. Greene. Providence. Smith & Parmenter. 1827.
David Pickering. Providence. Smith & Parmenter. 1828.
Tristam Burges. Providence. W. Marshall & Co. 1831.
Walter R. Danforth. Providence. John Hutchens. 1833.
John Whipple, (Municipal.) Providence. Knowles, Vose & Co. 1838.
L. M. Sargent, (Temperance.) Providence. 1838.
Thomas P. Rodman. Providence. B. T. Albro. 1840.
Thomas Durfee. Providence. Knowles, Anthony & Co. 1853.
Jerome B. Kimball. Providence. Knowles, Anthony & Co. 1856.
Thomas M. Clark, D. D. Providence. Knowles, Anthony & Co. 1860.
Samuel L. Caldwell, D. D. Providence. Knowles, Anthony & Co. 1861.
Rev. Augustus Woodbury. Providence. Knowles, Anthony & Co. 1862.
Rev. John G. Adams. Providence Knowles, Anthony & Co. 1863.

——— Delivered in Newport.
William Hunter, Newport. Henry Barber. 1795.
Abraham Redwood Ellery. Warren. N. Phillips. 1796.
William Marchant. Newport. Henry Barber. 1797.
Paul M. Mumford. Newport. O. Farnsworth. 1801.
William Hunter. Newport. Mercury Office. 1801.
Noah Bisbee, Jr. Newport. A. Barber. 1805.
Samuel Austin, D. D. Newport. William Simons. 1822.
Joseph H. Patten. Providence. Carlile & Brown. 1826.
Asher Robbins. Providence. Miller & Hammond. 1827.
Henry James. Boston. Ticknor & Fields. 1861.

——— Delivered in Bristol.
John D'Wolf. 1821.

——— Delivered in Kingston.
James B. M. Potter. Boston. T. H. Webb & Co. 1844.

——— Delivered in Warren.
Levi Haile. Warren. S. Randall. 1821.
Philip S. Gardner. Warren. S. Randall. 1822.

——— Delivered in Westerly.
Samuel Hassard. Stonington. W. & J. B. Stone. 1828.

——— Delivered in Clayville.
Tristam Burges. Providence. 1829.

——— Delivered in Warwick.
George F. Man. Providence, Knowles, Vose & Co. 1838.
Thomas K. King. Providence. George H. Whitney. 1854.

Fox, George and John Burnyeat New England Fire-Brand Quenched. Being an answer unto a Slanderous Book, Entituled, George Fox digged out of his Burrows, &c. Printed at Boston in the year 1676, by Roger Williams of Providence in New England. Which he Dedicateth to the King, with Desires, that if the Most High please, Old and New England may flourish, when the Pope and Mahomet, Rome and Constantinople are in their Ashes, of a Dispute upon xiv. of his Proposals, held and debated betwixt him, the said Roger Williams, on the one part ; and John Stubs, William Edmundson and John Burnyeat on the other. At Providence and Newport, in Rode Island, in the year 1672. In which his Cavils are Refuted, and his Reflections reproved. In two parts. As Also, an Answer to R. W's appendix, &c. With a Postcript confuting his Blasphemous Assertions, viz: Of the Blood of Christ, that was Shed, its being Corruptible and Corrupted ; and that Salvation was by a Man that was Corruptible, &c. Whereunto is added a Catalogue of his Railery, Lies, Scorn and Blasphemies; and his Temporising Spirit made manifest. Also, the Letters of W. Coddington, of Rode Island, and R. Scot, of Providence, in New England, concerning R. W. And Lastly, some Testimonies of Antient and Modern authors concerning the Light, Scriptures, Rule and the Soul of Man. By George Fox and John Burnyeat.

4to. pp. 256. and 14 preliminary leaves.

[*London.*] *Printed in the Year MDCLXXIX.*

———— Something in Answer to a letter which I have seen of John Leverat, Governour of Boston, to William Coddington, Governour of Rode Island. Dated 1677. Wherein he mentions my name, and also wherein John Leverat justifies Roger Williams' Book of Lyes.

4to. pp. 11. [At. p. 7 and 9, signed G. F.] *London.* 1677.

This is George Fox's answer to Roger Williams' book, entitled George Fox "*Digged out of his Burrows.*"

Fox, George. Cain against Abel, representing New England's Church Hierarchy, in opposition to her Christian Protestant Dissenters.

Small 4to. pp. 48. *London.* 1675.

The preface to this tract is addressed "To the New England Professors, that hanged the servants of the Lord for Religion. And all others that are found in their steps, Persecuting, Imprisoning, Hating and Killing their Brethren about Religion, as Cain did Abel his brother." Mary Dyer, a Quaker of Rhode Island, who was hanged in Boston, is doubtless one of the persons alluded to. At the end of the volume, the author gives the "Order from the Court at Boston" against the Quakers.

——— A Journal or Historical account of the Life, Travels, Sufferings, Christian Experiences and Labor of Love in the Ministry of that ancient, eminent and faithful servant of Jesus Christ, George Fox, who departed this life with great peace with the Lord, the 13th of the 11th month, 1690. Folio. *London*. 1694.

——— The same work.
2vols. 8vo. pp. 506 and 487. *London. W. Phillips*. 1827.

"One of the most extraordinary and instructive narratives in the World; which no reader of competent judgment can peruse without revering the virtue of the writer.—*Sir James Mackintosh*.

George Fox was the founder of the Society of Friends or Quakers. He was born in Leicestershire, England, in the year 1624, and died in 1690. In the course of his public ministrations he visited America twice, where he spent two years. He was much with the people of his sect in Rhode Island, and held a public discussion with Roger Williams, at Newport; for particulars of which, see *Edmundson*. Notwithstanding the severe language of Fox in the titles of his books quoted, William Penn, in speaking of him says, he was "civil beyond all forms of breeding, in his behaviour very temperate, eating little, and sleeping less. He had an extraordinary gift in opening the Scripture; but, above all, excelled in prayer. The reverence and solemnity of his address and behaviour, and the promptness and ferventness of his words, often struck strangers with admiration."

Publications of the Society of Friends officially sanctioned. This List has been kindly furnished me by Dr. Samuel Boyd Tobey, a distinguished member of the Society of Friends.

BROWN, MOSES. From the meeting for sufferings for New England, to the Several Quarterly and Monthly meetings belonging to the Yearly Meeting, eleventh of the 11th month, 1782. *Providence. John Carter.* 1782.

Address to Friends on the subject of establishing a Yearly Meeting
School.   1782.
Epistle of advice to Friends,   1783.
New Digest of Book of Discipline,   1785.
Job. Scott's Review of Relly's Treatise on Union,   1786.
Moses Brown's remarks on Samuel Shepley's Three Letters on Baptism 1792.
The Baptism of Christ, a Gospel Ordinance, by Job Scott,   1794.
Journal of the Life, Travels and Gospel labors of Job Scott,   1797.

Replication to Samuel Shepley, by Moses Brown, 1798.
Journal of Patience Brayton, 1801.
Church Discipline, by Job Scott, 1805.
Essay on the qualification and work of an elder in the Church of Christ,
  by Mary Mitchell, 1807.
Letters by Job Scott, 1807.
Correction of Mosheim's Ecclesiastical History regarding Friends, 1812.
Journal of Mary Mitchell, 1812.
Answer of Samuel F. Hussey to Asa Rand, 1821.
Epistle of New England Yearly Meeting to its subordinate meetings, 1827.
Advice from the Yearly Meeting to its subordinate meetings, 1828.
Testimony of Friends on the Continent of America, 1831.
Declaration of Faith by New England Yearly Meeting, 1836.
Address on the subject of trafficking in ardent spirits on voyages to the
  Pacific Ocean, 1836.
Address to Friends and others, on the subject of Slavery, 1837
Epistle to the members of the Society of Friends in New England, 1838.
Essay on Church Government, 1840.
Essay on Civil Government, 1840.
Memorials of deceased Friends, with an Introduction, 1841.
An Appeal to the professors of Christianity in the Southern States, and
  elsewhere on the subject of Slavery, 1842.
An Essay on some of the prominent Doctrines and Testimonies of deceas-
  ed Friends, 1843.
Memorials of deceased Friends, 1843.
Address to the Preparative Monthly and Quarterly Meetings of Friends
  within the limits of New England Yearly Meeting, 1844.
Epistle from New England Yearly Meeting to its subordinate meetings,
  and individual members, 1845.
A declaration of the New England Yearly Meeting of Friends, &c., 1845.
Narrative of facts that have tended to produce a secession in New England
  Yearly Meeting, 1845.
A statement of the several meetings composing the New England Yearly
  Meeting, 1848.
Books of Discipline revised and reprinted, 1849.
Memorials of deceased Friends, published in the years 1849-1850-1851-
  1852-1854-1856 and 1860.
Essay in vindication of the disciplinary proceedings of the New England
  Yearly Meeting, 1852.
Address relating to Colored Refugees, 1862.
Minutes of advice to Subordinate Meetings, 1863.
Minutes of New England Yearly meetings, published yearly, from 1846
  to 1863,

REVIEW of a Vindication of the Disciplinary Proceedings of the New England Yearly Meeting of Friends. 8vo. pp. 42.   *Philadelphia. Collins*, 1852.

For other books relating to the Society of Friends, see *Quakers*; *George For.*

FRANKLIN LYCEUM, Providence R. I., Charter and By-laws of.
12mo. pp. 16. *Providence. B. F. Moore.* 1843.

———— The Same, with list of members.
8vo. pp. 23. *Providence.* 1850.

———— Dedication of Lyceum Hall, Oration by Francis E. Hoppin; and Poem by Henry C. Whitaker; delivered on the opening of the new rooms, November 19, 1858, with a sketch of the other dedicatory exercises.
8vo. pp. *Providence. Printed by order of the Lyceum.* 1859.

FREE MASONRY. A discourse delivered at Providence, before the Grand Lodge of ancient and honorable fraternity of Free and Accepted Masons of the State of Rhode Island, June 24. 1794. By Abraham Lynson Clarke, A. M.
8vo. pp. 18. *Providence. Carter & Wilkinson.* 1794.

———— An oration delivered before Mount Vernon Lodge, on the aniversary election, Febuary 22, A. L. 5811. By John Holroyd, Esq., G. S.
8vo. pp. 16. *Providence. American Office.* 1811.

———— An address before the Grand Lodge of Rhode Island, June 24, 1830. By David Benedict.
8vo. pp. 21. *Pawtucket. Meacham & Fowler.* 1830.

FRIEZE, JACOB. A concise history of the efforts to obtain an extension of suffrage in Rhode Island; from the year 1811 to 1842.
12mo. pp. 179. *Providence. B. F. Moore.* 1842.

GAMMELL, WILLIAM. Address delivered before the Rhode Island Historical Society, at the opening of their Cabinet, on Wednesday, November 20, 1844.
8vo. pp. 30.
Providence. B. Cranston & Co. 1844.

——— Life of Roger Williams, Founder of the State of Rhode Island, with Portrait of Williams.
12mo. pp. ix and 221.
Boston. Gould, Kendall & Lincoln. 1854.

GAMMELL, PROF. WILLIAM. Sketch of the Educational and other Benefactions of the late Hon. Nicholas Brown, with portrait; 8vo. pp. 26. Reprinted from Barnard's American Journal of Education, for June, 1857.
8vo. pp. 26. *Providence.* 1857.

——— Life of Samuel Ward, Sparks' American Biography, Vol. 19.

GANO, STEPHEN., A. M. A Sermon occasioned by the death of the Rev. Joseph Snow, Pastor of a Congregational Church in Providence, R. I., who departed this life April 10, 1803, aged 88 years and 4 days. This sermon was preached in the meeting-house of the deceased, on Lord's day after April 17, 1803.
8vo. pp. 24. *Providence. J. Carter.* 1803.

GANO, REV. STEPHEN. Discourse at the interment of. See *Daniel Sharp.*

GARDNER AND POTTER vs. Hannah Gardner and others. An abridgment of the case of. [Relative to a will.]
8vo. pp. 18. *Providence. Walter R. Danforth.* 1826.

GENERAL TREASURY. Further report of the Finance Committee of the State, under the resolution of June session, 1851, on the affairs of the General Treasury. Jan. 1852.
8vo. pp. 12. *Providence. Sayles & Miller.* 1852.

GIBBS, CHARLES. Mutiny and Murder. Confession of Chas. Gibbs, a native of Rhode Island, who, with Thomas J. Wansley, was doomed to be hung in New York, on the 22d of April last, for the murder of the Captain and Mate of the Brig Vineyard, on her passage from New Orleans to Philadelphia, in November, 1830.
12mo. pp. 36. *Providence. Israel Smith.* 1831.

GIBBS, GEORGE. A discourse occasioned by the death of, and delivered in Trinity Church, Newport, Rhode Island, October 23, 1803. By Theodore Dehon, A. M. Rector.
8vo. pp. 19. *Newport. Ann Barber.* 1803.

THE GLEANER. Sustained by the Senior Department of the Girls' High School, Providence, Rhode Island. A periodical, 4 vols. 8vo. *Providence.* 1855-7.

GLEASON, BENJAMIN. An Oration on the Anniversary of American Independence. Pronounced before the Senior Class of Rhode Island College, in College Chapel, on the evening of July 5, 1802.
8vo. pp. 16. *Boston. Munroe & Francis.* 1802.

GODDARD, WILLIAM G. Professor of Belles Lettres in Brown University. An address to the Phi Beta Kappa Society of Rhode Island, delivered September 7, 1836.
8vo. pp. 30. *Boston. John H. Eastburn.* 1837.

——— Memoir of the Rev. James Manning, D. D., First

President of Brown University; with biographical notices of some of his pupils. With Portrait of Manning.
8vo. pp. 24. *Boston. Perkins & Marvin.* 1839.
Originally published in the May number of the American Quarterly Review for 1839.

—— Brief notices of the Life and Character of the late Nicholas Brown. From the Providence Journal of October 4, 1841.
12mo. pp. 15. *Providence.* 1841.

—— Address to the people of Rhode Island, delivered at Newport, on Wednesday, May 3, 1843, in presence of the General Assembly, on the occasion of the change in the Civil Government of Rhode Island, by the adoption of the Constitution, which superseded the charter of 1663.
8vo. pp. 80. *Providence. Knowles & Vose.* 1843.

—— Sketch of the Life of Dr. Solomon Drowne, in Providence Journal for 1838, and American Quarterly Register, vol. 11. p. 357.

—— A discourse in commemoration of the life and services of William G. Goddard, delivered at the request of the Faculty, in the chapel of Brown University, March 12, 1846. By Francis Wayland, D. D., President of Brown University.
8vo. pp. 31. *Providence. B. Cranston & Co.* 1846.
Professor Goddard was born in Providence, in 1793, and graduated at Brown University in 1812. For ten years he was editor and proprietor of the Rhode Island American, and from 1825 to 1842 Professor of Moral Philosophy and Metaphysics in Brown University. Professor Goddard was an easy and graceful writer, was well read in English literature, and had few equals in this branch of scholarship. Bowdoin College conferred on him the degree of Doctor of Laws. He died at Providence on the 16th February, 1846, aged 52 years.

GOODELL, WILLIAM. The rights and wrongs of Rhode Island. See *Constitution.*

GORDON. A full report of the trial of John Gordon and William Gordon, charged with the murder of Amasa Sprague; before the Supreme Court of Rhode Island, March term, 1844; with all the incidental questions raised in the trial carefully preserved—the testimony of the wit-

nesses nearly verbatim—and the arguments of the counsel, and a correct plate of all the localities described in the testimony, prepared expressly for this report. Reported by Edward C. Larned and William Knowles.
8vo. pp. 45.   *Providence. Transcript Office.* 1844.

GORDON. A full report of the arguments of Thomas F. Carpenter, Samuel Y. Atwell, and Joseph M. Blake, Attorney General, in the case of, The State vs. John and William Gordon, for the murder of Amasa Sprague, Supreme Judicial Court, March, 1844. Reported by Edward C. Larned.
8vo. pp. 38.   *Providence. Transcript Office.*

——— Petition of, to His Excellency, James Fenner, Governor of the State of Rhode Island.
8vo. pp. 8.   *Dated February* 10, 1845.

——— Last days of Gordon; being the trial of John and William Gordon, for the murder of Amasa Sprague before the Supreme Court of Rhode Island, with the principal witnesses in the case, and the arguments of the counsel, together with the full particulars of the execution of John Gordon, on the 14th of February, 1845. By an eye witness—also, William's full disclosure of what he avers to be facts in regard to the murder.
12mo. pp. 64.   *Boston. Skinner & Blanchard.* 1845.

GOOKIN, DANIEL. Historical Collections of the Indians in New England, of their several natures, numbers, customs, manners, religion and government, before the English planted there. Also a true and faithful account of the present state and condition of the Praying Indians, (or those who have visibly received the gospel in New England,) declaring the number of that people, the situation and place of their Towns and Churches; and their manner of worshipping God, and divers other matters appertaining thereto, &c., &c. Now first printed from the Original Manuscript.
Mass. Hist. Collection, 1st series, *Vol.* 1.   1792.

The Narragansetts and Pokanoketts of Rhode Island, are among the Indian tribes noticed in this memoir, which extends to eighty pages, and is followed by an account of the author.

GORTON, SAMUEL. · Simplicities Defence against Seven-headed Policy, or Innocency Vindicated, being unjustly accused and sorely censured, by that Seven-headed Church Government united in New England : or that Servant so Imperious in his Master's abseence, revived, and now thus re-acting in New England. Or the Combate of the United Colonies, not onely against some of the Natives and Subjects, but against the authority also of the Kingdome of England, with their execution of Laws, in the name and authority of the Servant, (or of themselves) and not in the name and authority of the Lord, or fountain of the Government. Wherein is declared an Act of a Great People and Country of the Indians in those parts, both Princes and People (unanimously) in their voluntary submission and subjection unto the protection and Government of Old England, (from the fame they hear thereof) together with the true manner and forme of it, as it appears under their own hands and seals ; being stirred up and provoked thereto, by the combate and courses abovesaid. Throughout which Treatise is secretly intermingled, that great Opposition, which is in the goings forth of those two grand Spirits, that are, and ever have been, extant in the World, (through the sons of men) from the beginning and foundation thereof.

4to. pp. —. Dedication 2. Epistle to reader 12 and III.

London. Printed by John Macock, and are to be sold by Luke Favvne, at his shop in Paul's Church-yard, at the sign of the Parrot. 1646.

——— Simplicities Defence against Seven-headed Policy, or a True Complaint of a Peaceable People, Being Part of the English in New England, Made unto the State of Old England, Against Cruell Persecutors, United in Church Government in those parts. Wherein is made manifest the manifold outrages, cruelties, oppressions and taxations, by cruell and close imprisonments, fire and sword, deprivation of goods, lands, and livelyhood ; and such like barbarous inhumanities, exercised upon the people of Providence

Plantations in the Nanhyganset Bay, by those of the Massachusetts, with the rest of the United Colonies, stretching themselves beyond the bounds of all their own jurisdictions, perpetrated and acted in such an unreasonable and barbarous manner, as many thereby have lost their lives. As it hath been faithfully declared to the Honorable Committee of Lords and Commons for Forrain Plantations; whereupon they gave present order for redress. The sight and consideration whereof hath moved a great Country of the Indians and Natives in those parts, Princes and people, to submit unto the crown of England, and earnestly to sue to the State thereof, for safeguard and shelter from like cruelties.

4to. pp.—. *London. Printed by John Macock, andare to be sold by George Wittington, at the Blue Anchor, neer the Royal Exchange, in Cornhill.* 1647.

——— "Simplicities Defence," with notes explanatory of the text; and appendixes containing original documents referred to in the work. By William R. Staples.

8vo. pp. 278. *Providence. Marshall, Brown & Co.* 1835.

The historical, biographical and explanatory notes of Judge Staples are of great interest, as well as the original documents appended to the work. It forms the second volume of the Collections of the Rhode Island Historical Society.

——— Saltmarsh returned from the Dead. *In amico Philalethe*, or, the Resurrection of James the Apostle, out of the grave of Cavnall Glosses, for the correction of the Universall Apostacy, which cruelly buryed him, who yet liveth. Appearing in the comely ornaments of his Fifth chapter, in an exercise, *June* 4, 1654. Having laid by his grave clothes, in a despised village remote from ENGLAND, but wishing well, and heartily desiring the true prosperity thereof.

4to. pp. xiv and 198.

London. Printed for Giles Calvert, and are to be sold at the black Spread Eagle, at the west end of Pauls. 1655.

——— An Antidote against the common Plague of the World, or an answer to a small Treatise, (as in water, face answereth to face,) entituled *Saltmarsh returned from the Dead;* and by transplacing the letters of his name, is *Smartlash*, ascend unto the throne of equity, for the arraignment of false interpretours of the word of God. Summoned out of all ages to appear under penalty of death, challenging the consent, or forbidding to gainsay the common approved priesthood of this Age.

4to. pp. 18, 62 and 296.

London. Printed by J. M., for A. C. 1657.

This work begins with a Dedicatory Preface of 18 pages to Oliver Cromwell, signed Samuel Gorton, and dated at Warwick, in the Naniganset Bay, October 20, 1656. This is followed by an "Epistle to the Reader," of 62 pages, signed S. G., Preface, one page. The main body of the work, extending to 296 pages, follows, and an addenda of 3 pages of faults in printing "Saltmarsh returned from the Dead." At page 269 are copies of letters which passed between Gorton and certain Quakers, who arrived at Boston, from England, but were forbidden to land "lest the purity of that religion professed in the churches of New England should be defiled with Errour."

GORTON. An Incorruptible Key composed of the ex. Psalme, wherewith you may open the rest of the Holy Scriptures; Turning itselfe onely according to the composure and art of that lock, of the closure and secrecy of that great mystery of God manifest in the flesh, but justified only by the spirit which it evidently openeth and revealeth out of

Fall and resurrection; Sin and righteousnesse; Ascension and descension: Height and depth; First and last; Beginning and ending; Flesh and spirit; Wisdom and foolishnesse; Strength and weaknesse; Mortality and immortality; Jew and Gentile; Light and darknesse; Unity and multiplication; Fruitfulness and barrenness; Curse and blessing; Man and woman; Heaven and earth; Life and death; Allsufficiency and deficiency; Kingdome and Priesthood; God and man.

And out of every unity made up of twaine, it openeth that great twoleafed gate, which is the sole entrie into the City of God, or new Ierusalem, into which none but the king of glory can enter; and as that pater openeth the doore of the sheepfold, by which whosoever entereth is the shepheard of the sheep. See Isa. 45. 1. Psal. 24, 7, 8, 9, 10. Iohn. 10, 1, 2, 3. Or, (according to the signification of the word translated Psalme) it is a pruning knife, to lop off from the Church of Christ all superfluous twigs of earthly and carnall commandements, Leviticall services or Ministery, and fading and vanishing Priests, or Ministers, who are taken away and cease, and are not established and confirmed by death, as holding no correspondency with the princely dignity, office and ministery of our Melchisedek, who is the onely Minister and Ministery of the sanctuary, of that true tabernacle which the Lord pitcht and not man. For, it supplants the old man, and implants the new; abrogates the old Testament or Covenant, and confirms the new, unto a thousand generations, or in generations forever.

By SAMUEL GORTON, GENT., and at the time of the penning hereof, in the place of Indicature (upon Aquethneck, alias Road Island) of Providence Plantations, in the Nauhyganset Bay, New England.
4to. Dedication pp. 22. Table 10, 120 and 119.
        Printed in the Yeere. 1647.

—— Some Notices of Samuel Gorton, one of the first settlers of Warwick, Rhode Island, during his residence at Plymouth, Portsmouth and Providence; chiefly derived from early manuscripts; with a brief introductory memoir. By Charles Deane.
4to. pp. 44.   *Boston. Coolidge & Wiley.* 1850

Samuel Gorton came to this country from England, and landed in Boston in the year 1636, soon after which he removed to Plymouth. On the 20th June, 1639, he was admitted an inhabitant at Aquednock, or Rhode Island In the Introduction to his edition of Simplicitie's Defence, Judge Staples. thus speaks of him: "He was the founder of a religious sect. In an age and among people where conformity to an established religion was enforced by the civil power, Gorton dared to think for himself, and to avow his thoughts. And such were the powers of his mind, or the truth of his position, that he soon gathered a company who adopted and avowed his peculiar principles, notwithstanding the reproaches and penalties to which such avowals subjected them. Though his followers cannot be called illiterate, still such were the circumstances with which they were surrounded, that they left but scanty written memorials, either of their leader or themselves. Gorton probably wrote more than them all; but his writings are chiefly of a polemic or religious character, and contain but few allusions to himself.

His work entitled "Simplicitie's Defence," etc., although chiefly theological, contains, as he says in the Dedication, "a more particular and full relation of what hath passed betwixt some other Colonies and New England and ourselves." This was first printed in London in 1646, and again in 1647. Though the long titles to these are quite different, the body of the work is the same. This narrative was answered by Winslow, in a work entitled "*Hypocrsie Unmasked*," London, 1646, and again under the title of "*The Danger of Tolerating Levellers:*" both works being the same, with different titles only. Besides the works of Gorton, the titles of which are given, he prepared for the press a Commentary on the Lord's Prayer, the manuscript of which, in his own hand writing, is now in the possession of the Rhode Island Historical Society.

Gorton always had the confidence of his fellow-townsmen; and during his long life filled various offices of the town of Warwick, where he lived, or of the Colony. He died in 1677. Besides his Biography by Mr. Mackie there is a candid and brief memoir of him, by Judge Staples, prefixed to his edition of Simplicitie's Defence; but the reader who would fully understand his character and principles, must study the histories of Winthrop, Morton and Johnston, who were contemporary with him. The notes and illustrative documents appended by Judge Staples to Simplicitie's Defence, are copious and very valuable.

GRACE CHURCH, in Providence. A sketch of the rise and progress of. Compiled by a clergyman, for the Providence Journal. (J. A. E.) 1857.
8vo. pp. 4. *From the Providence Journal*. 1857.

GRANGER, REV. J. N. A sermon occasioned by the death of the Rev. Zabdiel Bradford, delivered before the Pine Street Baptist Church, in Providence, June 10, 1849.
8vo. pp. 23. *Providence. Weeden & Peck.* 1849.

——— Discourse on the character and services of. See *Wayland*.

GRAY, FRANCIS C. Oration before the Phi Beta Kappa Society of Brown University, Providence, R. I., on Commencement Day, September 17, 1842.
8vo. pp. 40. *Providence. B. Cranston & Co.* 1842.

GREENE, GENERAL NATHANAEL. Memoir of the Life and Campaigns of the Hon. Nathanael Greene, Major General in the army of the United States, and Commander of the Southern Department, in the War of the Revolution. By Charles Caldwell, M. D. (Portrait and facsimile of letters of Washington and Greene.)
8vo. pp. xxii. and 452. *Philadelphia. Robert Desilver.* 1819.

——— Sketches of the Life and Correspondence of. Compiled chiefly from original materials. By William Johnson, of Charleston, S. C. Portrait.
2vols. 4to. pp. xii. and 515; xi. and 476.
Charleston, S. C. 1822.

——— Life of, by Geo. W. Greene, in Sparks' American Biography, Vol. 20. *Boston.* 1846.

———— The life of. Edited by William Gilmore Simms, Esq. 12mo. pp. 393.   *New York. G. F. Coolidge & Bro.* 1849.

GREENE, NATHANAEL. The Life, Letters and Despatches of Major General Nathanael Greene, from original manuscripts in the possession of his family. With a Life by his Grandson, George Washington Greene. With Portraits, Maps and Battle Plans.
7vols. 8vo.   *Boston. Little, Brown & Co.*
A prospectus has been issued for the publication of this work.

GREENE, ALBERT G. An oration delivered in commemoration of the 47th anniversary of the Declaration of American Independence, July 4, 1823, before the citizens of Providence.
8vo. pp. 16.   *Providence. John Miller.* 1823.

———— Recollections of the Jersey Prison Ship; taken and prepared for publication, from the original manuscript of the late Capt. Thomas Dring, of Providence, R. I., one of the prisoners.
12mo. pp. xvi. and 167.   *Providence. H. H. Brown.* 1829.

———— An address to the citizens of Providence, (R. I.) on the anniversary Celebration of the birth day of Washington, February 22, 1825, delivered in the Universalist Chapel, at the request of the "First Light Infantry."
8vo. pp. 22.   *Providence. J. B. Yerrinton.* 1825.

———— Anniversary Celebration of the Philermenian Society of Brown University. September 6, 1825. Ode for the occasion.   *Providence.* 1825.
The music for the ode was composed expressly for the occasion by Oliver Shaw, a celebrated teacher and composer of Providence.

———— Address to the patrons of the Manufacturers' & Farmers' Journal and Independent Enquirer, for the New Year, 1826.
8vo. pp. 8.   *Providence. Journal & Enquirer.* 1826.

———— Oration pronounced before the Young Men of the Town of Providence, July 4, 1827.
8vo. pp. 28.   *Providence. Smith & Parmenter.* 1827.

———— Anniversary Poem pronounced before the Philermenian Society, at their Thirty-fourth Celebration, September 20, 1828.
8vo. pp. 8. Providence. Smith & Parmenter. 1829.

GREENE, GEORGE WASHINGTON. A discourse delivered before the Rhode Island Historical Society, on the evening of Tuesday, February 8, 1849. Published at the request of the Society.
8vo. pp. 22. Providence. Gladding & Proud. 1849.

GREENE, WILLIAM. Some of the Difficulties in the administration of a Free Government; a discourse pronounced before the Rhode Island Alpha of Phi Beta Kappa Society, July 8, 1851.
8vo. pp. 40. Providence. John F. Moore. 1851.

GREENE vs. BRIGGS. Report in the case of William H. Greene vs. Nathan M. Briggs, et al. The plaintiff's opening argument, and the opinion of the U. S. Circuit Court for the Rhode Island District. By Joseph S. Pitman, Counsellor at Law.
8vo. pp. 60. Boston. Little, Brown & Co. 1853.

GREENWOOD, ISAAC. A Lecture read at a quarterly meeting of the Providence Association of Mechanics and Manufacturers, July 9, 1798. See Stone's Hist. of the Association.

GRISWOLD, ALEXANDER V. Memoir of the Life of the Right Rev. Alexander Viets Griswold, D. D., Bishop of the Protestant Episcopal Church in the Eastern Diocese. By John S. Stone, D. D., Rector of Christ's Church, Brooklyn, New York, with an appendix; to which is added a sermon, charge and pastoral letter of the late Bishop. Portrait.
8vo. pp. xi. and 620. Philadelphia. Stavely & McCalla. 1844.

———— A sermon preached at Bristol, R. I., July 9, 1808, at the funeral of the Hon. William Bradford, Esq. By Alexander V. Griswold, Rector of St. Michael's Church, in Bristol.
8vo. pp. 15. Bristol. Golden Dearth. 1808.

―――― A discourse delivered in Bristol, Rhode Island, February 11, 1838, occasioned by the decease of the Hon. James D'Wolf and Mrs. Ann B. D'Wolf, his wife.
12mo. pp. 14.   *Bristol. W. H. S. Bayley.* 1838.

Bishop Griswold was born in Simsbury, Connecticut, April 22, 1766. He was admitted to Holy Orders in 1795. After officiating for nine years in his native State, he removed to Bristol, R. I., in 1804 and became Rector of St. Michael's Church. In 1811 he was consecrated the first Bishop of the Eastern Diocese of New England. In 1829 he removed to Salem, Mass., and became Rector of St. Peters Church, there. A few years later he relinquished parochial duties and took up his residence in Boston, where he died February 15, 1843, at the age of 77 years. His biographer, Dr. Stone, says : " Perhaps not once in an age, if ever, are we presented with an instance of earlier and indomitable love of learning than that which was exhibited in the first years of Bishop Griswold." His published sermons, together with his official addresses, charges and correspondence, denote a vigorous and highly cultivated mind.

GUILD, REUBEN A. An Account of the Writings of Roger Williams.
8vo. pp. 11.   *Providence. S. S. Rider.* 1862.

M. Guild also has in preparation a work with the following title :

―――― Memoirs of the Life, Times and Correspondence of the Rev. James Manning, D. D., First President of Brown University ; Comprising Annals of the College from its Commencement to the close of the Year 1791 ; to which is added a Brief History of the University down to the present time ; with Biographical Sketches of Manning's Friends and Pupils, and Illustrative Documents.
2 vols. small quarto.

A prospectus just issued by the author, states that the first volume will be put to press, whenever a sufficient number of subscribers can be obtained to warrant the expense.

HAKLUYT RICHARD. Divers voyages touching the discoverie of America, and the ilands adjacent unto the same, made first of all by our Englishmen, and afterward by the Frenchmen and Britons; and certaine notes of advertisements for observations, necessarie for such as shall heereafter make the like attempt. With two mappes annexed heereunto for the plainer understanding of the whole matter.
small 4to. unpaged. *Imprinted at London, for Thomas Woodcocke, dwelling in Paule's Church Yard, at the signe of the blackbeare.* 1582.

This rare volume contains seven articles or voyages, the 5th of which is "The relation of John Verarzanus, a Florentine, of the lande by him discovered in the name of his Majestie, written in Diepe, the cyth of July, 1524." It is mentioned in this Bibliography, inasmuch as it contains the earliest known account of Rhode Island. Verazzano first discovered Block Island, which he called 'Claudia' Island, after the wife or mother of Francis the 1st. He entered Newport harbor, where he remained fourteen days, meanwhile making an exploration of what is now known as Narragansett Bay.

—— The voiages, navigations, traffiques and Discoveries of the English nation, and in some few places, where they have not been, of strangers, performed within and before the time of these hundred yeares, to all partes of the Newfound world of America, or the West Indies, from 73 deg. of Northerly to 57 of Southerly latutude: etc., etc.
3 vols. folio. Black-letter. *Imprinted at London by George Bishop, Ralfe Newberie and Robert Barker. Anno Dom.* 1598–1599–1600.

In the third volume, at page 295, is the relation of Verazzano's voyage referred in the first work of Hakluyt.

A new edition of Hakluyt's voyages was published in London in 1809-12, in 5vols. 4to. with the addition of certain voyages printed in the first edition and omitted in the second. Two hundred and fifty copies only were printed, besides seventy-five copies on large paper. Both are now scarce and command high prices.

The narrative of Verrazzano may also be found in *Ramusio's Navigationi et Viaggi*, 3 vols. folio. Venetia, 1583-88. From this it was translated for, and appears in the Collections of the New York Historical Society. It is also included in the publications of the Hakluyt Society, of London.

HAGUE, WILLIAM. An Historical Discourse delivered at the Celebration of the second centennial anniversary of the First Baptist Church, in Providence, November 7, 1839. By William Hague, Pastor of the Church.

12mo. pp. 192.   *Providence. B. Cranston & Co.* 1839.

HAGUE, WILLIAM, D. D. True Friendship. A discourse commemorative of the Life and Character of the Rev. John Overton Choules, D. D. Delivered in the Second Baptist Church, Newport, R. I., on Sunday, Feb. 24, 1856.

8vo. pp. 76.   *New York. Sheldon, Blakeman & Co.* 1856.

HALL, REV. EDWARD B. Discourses comprising a history of the First Congregational Church, in Providence. Delivered June 19th, 1836, after the close of a century from the formation of the Church.

8vo. pp. 62.   *Providence. Knowles, Vose & Co.* 1836.

——— A Discourse occasioned by the death of William Ellery Channing, delivered in the First Congregational Church, Providence, October 12, 1842.

8vo. pp. 34.   *Providence. B. Cranston & Co.* 1842.

——— Discourse in behalf of the Children's Friend Society, Delivered in the First Baptist meeting house, Providence, October 7, 1845.

8vo. pp. 16.   *Providence. C. Burnett, Jr.* 1845.

——— The value of a Man. A Discourse occasioned by the death of the Hon. Henry Wheaton; Delivered Sunday evening, March 19, 1848, in the First Congregational Church, Providence. R. I.

8vo. pp. 23.   *Providence. C. Burnett, Jr.* 1848.

——— An address before the R. I. Peace Society at its 27th Annual Meeting, June 30, 1844.
8vo. pp. 24. *Providence. H. H. Brown.* 1844.

——— A Discourse delivered before the Rhode Island Historical Society, February 6, 1855, On the Life and Times of John Howland, late President of the Society.
8vo. pp. 36. *Providence. Geo. H. Whitney.* 1855.

——— A Lecture on the pleasures and vices of the City, delivered Sunday evening, March 30, 1856. Published by request.
8vo. pp. 31. *Providence. Knowles, Anthony & Co.* 1856.

——— Sermon on the installation of. See *Dewey.*

HALL, J. PRESCOTT. An address delivered at Middletown, R. I., on the 21st of September, 1854, before the Aquidneck Agricultural Society.
8vo. pp. *Newport. Cranston & Norman.* 1854.

HALLETT, B. F. Argument in the Rhode Island causes before the Supreme Court of the United States. Martin Luther vs. Luther M. Borden and others, and Rachel Luther vs. the Same.
8vo. pp. 71. *Boston. Beals & Greene.* 1848.

HALSEY WILL CASE. See *Currey.*

HAMILTON. The Whig Party; its objects—its principles—its candidates—its duties—and its prospects. An address to the people of Rhode Island, published in the Providence Journal, in a series of articles during the months of September and October, 1844.
8vo. pp. 31. *Providence. Knowles & Vose.* 1844.

HARD-SCRABBLE CALENDAR. Report of the Trials of Oliver Cummins, Nathaniel G. Metcalf, Gilbert Humes and Arthur Farrier, who were indicted with six others for a Riot, and for aiding in pulling down a Dwelling House, on the 18th October, at Hard-Scrabble.
8vo. pp. 32. *Providence. Printed for the Purchaser.* 1824.

HARRIS, SAMUEL F., of Cincinnati. Class of 1858. An

oration and poem, (the latter by John M. Hay, of Warsaw, Illinois,) delivered in the Chapel of Brown University, on Class day, June 10, 1858. Printed for private distribution.
8vo. pp. 43.   *Providence. Knowles, Anthony & Co.* 1858.

HART, REV. LEVI, A. M.   A Discourse on 1 Corinthians, xv. 17. Addressed to the Second Congregational Church in the City of Newport, Rhode Island, at the ordination of the Rev. William Patten to the evangelical ministry, and pastoral office over them, May 24, 1786. Charge by the Rev. Ezra Stiles.
8vo. pp. 30.   *Providence. John Carter.* 1786.

HART, LEVI, D. D.   A Discourse delivered at Newport, Rhode Island, at the funeral of the Rev. Samuel Hopkins, D. D., Pastor of the First Congregational Church, there, who died on the 20th of December, A. D. 1803, in the eighty-third year of his age, and sixtieth of his ministry.
12mo. pp. 24.   ? *Newport.* 1804.

HASSARD, SAMUEL, A. M.   An oration delivered at the Union Meeting House, in Westerly, R. I., July 4, 1828.
8vo. pp. 24.   *Stonington. W. & J. B. Stone.* 1828.

HAYES, WINGATE.   The Revision of the Laws; prepared for the Providence Journal, of June 30, 1857.
8vo. pp. 12.   *Providence. Knowles, Anthony & Co.* 1857.
A history of the several codes of the Laws of Rhode Island, and their revi sions from the first code adopted in 1647 to that of 1857. Mr. Hayes was one of the commissioners on the last revision.

HAZARD, BENJAMIN.   Report on the subject of an extension of Suffrage, to the General Assembly of Rhode Island, June, 1829.
8vo. pp. 26.   1829.

———— Report of the committee appointed by the House of Representatives, of the State of Rhode Island, &c., to enquire into the expediency of increasing the Banking capital within said State.
8vo. pp. 40.   *Providence. Smith & Parmenter.* 1826.

―――― Argument of, in the case of the Providence Bank vs. the State of Rhode Island.
8vo. pp. 22. *January.* 1830.

―――― Letters addressed to the Hon. John Quincy Adams, in refutation of charges made by that gentleman against a committee of the Legislature of Rhode Island, and against the Legislature itself.
8vo. pp. 46. *Providence. Marshall, Brown & Co.* 1834.

Benjamin Hazard was born in Middletown, Rhode Island, September 18, 1770; graduated at Brown University in 1792, and was admitted to the bar in 1796. He commenced practice in Newport, and ere long became one of the most distinguished men in his profession in the State. In 1809, he was elected a member of the General Assembly, which place he continued to fill for thirty-one successive years, a portion of which period he was Speaker of the House. In the sphere where he had so long moved, he felt himself perfectly at home, and his influence was most potent. As a debater, he held a high rank. On all committees of the Assembly he was most diligent, and his reports able. That upon Banking, mentioned above, is yet referred to, as the most able essay on the subject ever produced in the State. Mr. Hazard died in Newport, March 10, 1811, aged 69 years.

HAZARD, EBENEZER. Historical Collections; consisting of State Papers, and other authentic documents; intended as materials for an History of the United States of America.
2 vols. 4to. *Philadelphia. T. Dobson.* 1792-94.

This valuable collection of State Papers embraces those relating to Columbus, Cabot, Sir Humphrey Gilbert, Sir Walter Raleigh, various Patents, Charters of the several English Colonies in America; with a great variety of documents relating to these colonies and New France. These are taken from Hakluyt's Voyages, Rymer's Foedera, Rushworth's Historical Collections; the Public Records of the Colonies, and from rare works relating to America.

The following list embraces such as relate to Rhode Island in vol. 1:

Report of Arbitrators at Providence, containing proposals for a form of Government, 1640.
Patent for Providence Plantations, March 14, 1643.
Letter to the Governor and Assistants of Massachusetts Bay, in favor of Roger Williams.
Letters from Roger Williams, President of Providence Plantations, to the General Court of Massachusetts and Deputies, assembled at Boston, 1656.
League of Peace entered into by Massasoit, an Indian sachem, and the first settlers of Plymouth.
Letters from William Arnold (of Pawtuxet) to the Governor of Massachusetts, 1651-1652.

RHODE ISLAND. 147

Passport for Samuel Gorton, May 15,	1646.
Remonstrance and Petition of the Governor and Company of Massachusetts to the Earl of Warwick and other Commissioners for Foreign Plantations, in way of answer to the petition and declaration of Samuel Gorton.	
The Parliament's Commissioner's Letter to Massachusetts, about Samuel Gorton, May 25,	1647.

The following in Volume 2, are from the records of the United Colonies of New England :

A Message from the Commissioners to the Narragansett Indians, September, 1643,	page 11
Settlement of dispute between the Narragansetts and Uncas, 1644,	25
War with the Narragansetts determined upon,	29. 292
Treaty between the Commissioners of the United Colonies and the Sagamores of the Narragansett and the Nyantick Indians, 1645,	40
Declaration of War against the Narragansetts, 1645,	45
Queries to the Sachem Ninegrit, and others of the Narragansetts, with their replies relative to their position with the English and Dutch, 1658,	206
Treaty of Peace with the Narragansetts, October, 1675,	536
Sentence of Massachusetts to hang Mary Dyer, of Rhode Island, a Quaker,	566
Declaration of the General Court of Massachusetts, respecting the Quakers, with reference to Mary Dyer,	567
Order of Massachusetts to proceed against Samuel Gorton and his Company, with other references to,	10–153–199
Letter from the Commissioners to Governor Coddington of Rhode Island, September 15, 1651,	196
Letter from the Commissioners to the Government of Rhode Island, September 13, 1661,	448
Letter from the Commissioners to Rhode Island, requesting the removal of the Quakers, September 12, 1657,	370
Letter from Rhode Island to Massachusetts, in answer, relative to the removal of the Quakers, October 13, 1657,	552
Documents relating to the jurisdiction of the Narragansett Country, 1662,	462–99
Proposal of Rhode Island to be received into the combination with the United Colonies, 1648,	
Letter from the Commissioners to Rhode Island, relative to the seizure of a vessel, 1658,	285
Reply of Governor Easton to the same, September 16, 1658,	293
Charter of Rhode Island, July 8, 1663,	612

For a variety of other references to, see Indexes, at the end of each volume.
"In a few years after the English had established themselves at Plymouth, in New England, their settlements became so extensive, and were so distant from each other, as to render their situation very insecure. Surrounded by enemies, distracted by internal divisions, and too far from their mother country, to receive seasonable assistance from her, they were led to con-

sult their common safety ; and for that purpose, the few principal colonies, (Massachusetts, Plymouth, Connecticut, and New Haven), confederated in 1643. They gave to Commissioners, annually chosen, the management of such affairs as concerned the Union generally, while each retained its sovereignty in other respects. The Commissioners held both stated and occasional meetings, and kept regular journals of their proceedings, which have acquired the name of the Records of the United Colonies of New England. *Preface to Hazard's State Papers, Vol. 2.* These records have lately been reprinted in the "Plymouth Records," by the State of Massachusetts. They contain much relating to Rhode Island.

HAZARD, ROWLAND G. Address before the Pawcatuck Temperance Society, at Westerly, July 4, 1843.
12mo. pp. 30.

———— Address before the Washington County Association, for the improvement of Public Schools, January 3, 1845.
8vo. pp. 42. *Providence. B. F. Moore.* 1845.

———— Essay on the Philosophical character of Channing.
8vo. pp. 40. *Boston. James Munroe & Co.* 1845.

———— A Discourse delivered before the Rhode Island Historical Society, on the evening of Tuesday, January 18th, 1848; on the character and writings of Chief Justice Durfee. Published at the request of the Society.
8vo. pp. 45. *Providence. Charles Burnett, Jr.* 1848.

———— Remarks of, in the General Assembly, January, 1851, on the act introduced by him to equalize the charges for carrying freight on the Stonington Rail Road.
8vo. pp. 12. *Providence. Sayles & Miller.* 1851.

———— Narragansett Speech.
8vo. pp. 15. [double columns.] *October* 21, 1856.

HAZARD, THOMAS R. Report on the Poor and Insane in Rhode Island ; made to the General Assembly at its January session, 1851. Printed by order of the General Assembly, [with a view of the Butler Hospital, and an appendix on the Indian Tribe.]
8vo. pp. 119. *Providence. Joseph Knowles.* 1851.

———— Facts for the Laboring Man. By a Laboring Man.
8vo. pp. 102. *Newport. James Atkinson.* 1840.
This volume contains a great many facts relating to the early history of manufacturing in Rhode Island.

—— A Constitutional Manual for the National American Party, in which is examined the question of Negro Slavery in connection with the Constitution of the United States. By a Northern man, with American principles.
8vo. pp. 30. *Dated, Vaucluse, R. I.*, 1 mo. 28, 1856.

—— An appeal to the people of Rhode Island, in behalf of the Constitution and Laws.
8vo. pp. 163. *Providence.* 1857.
This relates to the celebrated case of *Ives vs. Hazard.*

—— Letter addressed to Robert H. Ives, in reply to his published statements in relation to the case in equity, Ives vs. Hazard.
8vo. pp. 48. *Newport. George T. Hammond.* 1859.

—— Memorial of, [to the General Assembly of Rhode Island] asking for the removal of the State Reporter, and the impeachment of Chief Justice Ames, etc.
8vo. pp. 16. *Providence. A. Crawford Greene.* [1861.]

HENSHAW, Rt. Rev. J. P. K. A Vindication of the Protestant Episcopal Church, in an address on the occasion of the laying of the corner stone of Grace Church, in Providence, on Tuesday, April 8, 1845. By the Rt. Rev. J. P. K. Henshaw, D. D., Rector of Grace Church, and Bishop of Rhode Island.
12mo. pp. 16. *Providence. B. F. Moore.* 1845.

—— A statement of facts relating to the late ordination at Grace Church, with the correspondence on the subject between the Rt. Rev. J. P. K. Henshaw, D. D., and the Rev. James W. Cooke, Rector of St. Michael's Church, Bristol, R. I.
8vo. pp. 72. *Providence. Charles Burnett, jr.* 1847.

—— Review of the Rev. J. W. Cooke's Pamphlet, entitled "A Statement of facts relating to the Ordination at Grace Church," in two letters addressed to the Bishop of the Diocese. By the Rev. James Mulchahey, minister of St. Mary's Church, Portsmouth, R. I.
8vo. pp. *Providence. C. Burnett, Jr.* 1847.

―――― A discourse delivered in Grace Church, Providence, on the occasion of the Third Jubilee, or one hundred and fiftieth anniversary of the Society for the Propagation of the Gospel in Foreign Parts, on the first Sunday after Trinity, June 22, 1851.
8vo. pp. 36. *Providence. J. F. Moore.* 1851.

This discourse contains a history of the founding of the Protestant Episcopal Church in Rhode Island, which was coeval with that of the Society itself. Bishop Henshaw was born in Middletown, Connecticut, June 13, 1792, and graduated at Middlebury College, Vermont, in 1808. He pursued his theological studies with Bishop Griswold. He was ordained at the age of twenty-one, and in 1816, was ordained minister of St. Ann's Church, Brooklyn, N. Y. The following year, he accepted the Rectorship of St. Peter's Church, Baltimore. Dr. Henshaw's labors closed in Maryland in 1843, when he was consecrated Bishop of Rhode Island. While on a visit to Maryland, he died suddenly of appoplexy, July 19, 1852, at the age of sixty years. His influence was felt wherever he was disposed to exert it, and he is said to have controlled, in a remarkable manner, the congregations to which he was accustomed to minister.

―――― Sermon on the consecration of, as Bishop of Rhode Island. See *Whittingham.*

―――― Funeral Sermon on the death of. See *McJilton.*

THE HIGH SCHOOL MAGAZINE, issued by the English and Scientific Department of the Boys' High School, Providence, Rhode Island. 1st number issued March, 1858.

HINTS to the Farmers of Rhode Island. By a Freeman.
8vo. pp. 18 *Providence. Office of Republican Herald.* 1829.

Relates to the controversy about the act providing for the use of Broad Rimmed Wheels.

―――― What a Ploughman said about the " Hints to Farmers," made last April by men of " Trade."
8vo. pp. 33. *Kingston. May.* 1829.

Attributed to Tristam Burges.

HISTORICAL SOCIETY. The Charter, Constitution and Circular of the Rhode Island Historical Society ; Incorporated June, A. D., 1822.
8vo. pp. 8. *Providence. Jones & Wheeler.* [1822.]

HISTORICAL SKETCH, Covenant and Articles of Faith, of the

Fifth Congregational Church, North Main Street, Providence, Rhode Island.
18mo. pp. 24.   *Providence. Allbro & Hall.* 1849.

HITCHCOCK, ENOS. D. D. An oration in commemoration of the Independence of the United States of America; delivered in Providence, July 4, 1793.
8vo. pp. 19.   *Providence. Printed by J. Carter.* 1793?

────── A discourse delivered at the dedication of the New Congregational Meeting-house in Providence; and also at the West Parish in Brookfield, November 10, 1795, on a like occasion.
8vo. pp. 17.   *Brookfield, Mass. Rice & Waldo.* 1795.

────── A Funeral Sermon, occasioned by the death of Sarah Bowen, consort of the Hon. Jabez Bowen, Esq., who died March 17, 1800, in the 58th year of her age. Delivered in the Benevolent Congregational Church.
8vo. pp. 24.   *Providence. John Carter, Jun.* 1800.

────── Discourse on Education; delivered at the Meeting-house on the West side of the river, in Providence, November 16, 1785.
4to. pp. 16.   *Providence. Bennett Wheeler.* 1777.

────── Funeral Discourse on. See *Tappan*.

Dr. Hitchcock was born in Massachusetts, and graduated at Harvard College in 1767. Three years after, he was ordained pastor of the second church in Beverly, Massachusetts; and on the breaking out of the Revolutionary War, he entered the army as Chaplain. On the 1st of October, 1783, he was installed as pastor of the First Congregational Church in Providence. He was a man of large benevolence, and was greatly interested in the subject of education, and was one of the earliest promoters of Free Schools. Besides the books mentioned above, Dr. Hitchcock wrote a book of Catechetical Instructions, and Forms of Devotion; Memoirs of the Bloomsgrove Family, 2 vols.; An essay on the Lord's Supper; and various funeral discourses. He died in 1803, aged 58 years.

HOLDEN, RANDALL. Letter to the Governor of Massachusetts, together with the worshipful assistants, and our loving neighbors there. From the Hutchinson Papers.
       Mass. Hist. Col. 3d Series. Vol. 1.

HOLLISTER, G. H. Mount Hope, or Philip, King of the Wampanoags; an Historical Romance.
12mo. pp. 280.   *New York. Harper & Brothers.* 1851.

HOLMAN, NATHAN. A funeral oration, delivered in the chapel of Rhode Island College, on Wednesday, June 29, 1796; occasioned by the death of Mr. Alva Spalding, a member of the Junior Class.
8vo. pp. 14.   *Providence. Joseph Fry.* 1796.

HOLME, BENJAMIN. A collection of the Epistles and Works of Benjamin Holme. To which is prefixed an account of his Life and Travels in the work of the ministry through several parts of Europe and America; written by himself.
8vo. pp. vii. and 194.   *London. Luke Hinde.* 1753.
The author, who was a Quaker, visited and labored in Rhode Island in the conrse of his missionary travels, of which he gives an account.

HOLMES, ABIEL. The Life of Ezra Stiles, D. D., L. L. D. A Fellow of the American Philosophical Society; of the Academy of American Arts and Sciences; a corresponding member of the Massachusetts Historical Society; Professor of Ecclesiastical History in Yale College. By Abiel Holmes, A. M., Pastor of the First Church in Cambridge.
8vo. pp. 403.   *Boston. Thomas & Andrews.* 1798.
Dr. Stiles was for many years a settled minister in Newport.

HOME FOR AGED WOMEN. Charter, Constitution and By-laws of, established in Providence, 1856. Incorporated January, 1857.
12mo. pp.   *Providence. H. H. Brown.* 1857.

—— Annual Reports of, from April, 1857, to May, 1862. 1 to 6.

HOPKINS, STEPHEN. A true Representation of the Plan formed at Albany, for uniting all the British Northern Colonies, in order to their common safety and defence; containing abstracts of the authorities given by the several governments to their commissioners; and of several letters from the Secretaries of State, and Lords Commissioners for Trade and Plantations, concerning such Union. To-

gether with a Representation of the state of the English and French Colonies in North America; and the said plan of Union, with the doings of the Commissioners thereon; and some remarks on the whole.
Folio. pp. 14. ———— *Dated Providence, March 29, 1755.*
The Commissioners from Rhode Island were Stephen Hopkins and Martin Howard. The Colonies represented were Massachusetts Bay, New Hampshire, Connecticut, Rhode Island, New York, New Jersey, Pennsylvania, Maryland, Virginia, North Carolina and South Carolina.

—————— An Historical account of the planting and growth of Providence, R. I. First printed in the Providence Gazette from January 12th to March 30, 1765. It was never completed as intended, owing to the disastrous occurrences of the times.

—————— The same, reprinted in Mass. Historical Collections, 2d series. Vol. ix.

—————— [Letter to the people of Rhode Island, giving "some public account of such parts of my conduct as have been most censured."]
Folio. pp. 5. *Dated Providence, March 31, 1757.*
For reply to the above from Samuel Ward, Esq., see *Ward*.

—————— The Grievances of the American Colonies candidly examined.
    Midst the low murmurs of submissive fear
    And mingled rage, my Hampden rais'd his voice,
    And to the Laws appeal'd.—*Thomson*.
8vo. pp. *Printed by authority at Providence.* 1765.

—————— The same.
8vo. pp. 47. *London. J. Almon.* 1766.
A large number of pamphlets was published in London, New York and Boston during this and the following years, relative to the rights of the Colonies in general, but more particularly of the Stamp Act, Gov. Hopkins' work was twice reprinted in London, and was immediately followed by a pamphlet, the title of which follows this. To the latter came a reply from James Otis, entitled: "A Vindication of the British Colonies," one of the most remarkable works of the day. See *Otis*, and the works which follow. For further particulars relating to this most exciting period, see Bancroft's History, Vol. v.; and Frank Moore's Diary of the Revolution.

A LETTER from a gentleman at Halifax, to his friends in Rhode

Island, containing remarks upon a pamphlet entitled "The Rights of the Colonies examined."
Small 4to. pp. 22. *Newport. S. Hall.* 1765.

Stephen Hopkins was one of the most remarkable men that Rhode Island ever produced. For nearly a half century he was in public life. He first appears as clerk of one of the Courts; next as a member of the General Assembly; then as Judge, and subsequently as Chief Justice of the Supreme Court. He was Governor of the State, at various times from 1755 to 1768; one of the signers of the Declaration of Independence, and Member of the American Congress from 1774 to 1779. He was born in 1707, and died in 1785.

———— For an address to the public concerning negroes, see *Stiles*.

HOPKINS, SAMUEL, D. D. The Life and Character of Miss Susanna Anthony, who died in Newport, Rhode Island, June 23, 1791, in the sixty-fifth year of her age. Consisting chiefly in Extracts from her Writings, with some Brief Observations on them.
8vo. pp. 193. *Worcester, Mass. Leonard Worcester.* 1796.

———— The same work.
8vo. pp. 168. *Hartford. Hudson & Goodwin.* 1799.

———— Memoirs of Miss Susanna Anthony, &c. By Samuel Hopkins. A new edition, with a recommendatory preface. By Dr. Ryland, Mr. Fuller and Mr. Sutcliff.
8vo. pp. ii. and 241. *Clipstone. J. W. Morris.* 1802.

———— Sketches of the Life of the late Rev. Samuel Hopkins, D. D. Pastor of the First Congregational Church in Newport, written by himself; interspersed with marginal notes, extracted from his private diary, to which is added a Dialogue, by the same hand, on the nature and extent of true Christian submission; also, a serious address to Professing Christians; closed by Dr. Hart's Sermon at his funeral: with an introduction to the whole, by the Editor. Published by Stephen West, D. D., Pastor of the Church in Stockbridge, Mass. Portrait.
18mo. pp. xxii. and 240. *Hartford. Hudson & Goodwin.* 1805.

Dr. Hopkins was the founder of the Hopkinsian School of Divinity. He was born in Waterbury, Connecticut, in 1721, graduated at Yale College in

1741; studied theology under the celebrated Jonathan Edwards; was ordained minister of Great Barrington, Conn., from which place he was dismissed by an ecclesiastical council in 1769. In 1770, he was settled in the ministry at Newport, R. I.

The war of the revolution interrupted his labors, when he preached elsewhere. In 1780, he returned to Newport, but found his congregation so dispersed and impoverished, that he had no prospect of a maintenance. Nevertheless, he continued to preach in Newport, deriving his subsistence from his friends. He died in 1802, at the age of 82. In addition to the books mentioned above, which appertain to Rhode Island, Dr. Hopkins was the author of many theological works. He also wrote "A Dialogue, showing it to be the duty and interest of the American States to emancipate all their African Slaves," which was published in 1776. A collected edition of his works, including his System of Doctrines, with a memoir of his Life and Character, was published by the Doctrinal Tract and Book Society,, in Philadelphia, in 1853, in 3 vols. 8vo.

"The celebrity of the author, who, with Edwards and Bellamy, completes the American triumvirate of eminent writers in the same strain of divinity, would have rendered this work much more popular and useful, had he kept clear of a bold and grating sentiment,—that 'God has foreordained all the moral evil which does take place,' and which he endeavors to defend with more ingenuity than success,"—*Dr. E. Williams' C. P.*

―――― Memoir of the Life and Character of. See *Ferguson*.

―――― Reminiscences of, illustrative of his Character and Doctrines. See *Patten*.

―――― Memoir of the Life and Character of. See *Park*.

―――― Funeral Sermon on the death of. See *Hart*.

For additional notices of Dr. Hopkins, see *Whittier's old Portraits and modern Sketches. The Biographical Dictionaries of Allen and Blake; W. Ellery Channing's Works; and the Christian Examiner.* vol. xxxiii. p. 109.

HOPPIN. Report of the Special Committee on the memorial of certain citizens of Providence, in relation to the election of William W. Hoppin.

8vo. pp. 14. *Providence. Sayles, Miller & Simons.* 1853.

HOPPIN, LEVI. Oration on the death of. See *Wm. Emmons*.

HOPPIN, FRANCIS E. Oration by, delivered upon the occasion of the opening of the new rooms of the Franklin Lyceum, November 19, 1858.

8vo. pp. *Providence. Knowles, Anthony & Co.* 1859.

HOUGH, FRANKLIN B. Narrative of the causes which led to King Philip's War. See *Easton*.

Hovey, Alvah, D. D. A memoir of the Life and Times of the Rev. Isaac Backus, A. M.
12mo. pp. 369.   Boston. *Gould & Lincoln.* 1859.
This volume contains much petaining to the religious history of Rhode Island, and especially the Baptist History.

Howland, John. A Lecture read at a Quarterly meeting of the Providence Association of Mechanics and Manufacturers, January 4, 1799.
4to. pp. 14.   *Providence. Bennett Wheeler.* 1799.

—— The same. Reprinted in Stone's Sketch of the Association, which see   1860.

—— An Address delivered before the Providence Association of Mechanics and Manufacturers, April 9, 1810. Being the Anniversary of the choice of officers in the Association.
8vo. pp. 25.   *Providence. Jones & Wheeler.* 1810.

—— An Oration delivered before the Providence Association of Mechanicks and Manufacturers, April 13, 1818.
8vo. pp. 24.   *Providence. Miller & Hutchins.* 1818.

—— Address delivered before the Providence Assoication of Mechanics and Manufacturers, on the occasion of opening Mechanicks' Hall, January 10, A. D., 1825. By John Howland, President of the Association.
8vo. pp. 12.   *Providence. H. H. Brown.* 1830.

—— The Same. Reprinted, with the by-laws and list of members.   1850.

—— A Biographical sketch of the Rev. James Manning, D. D., formerly President of Brown University.
8vo. pp. 16.   *Providence.* 1815.
An article in the January number of the Rhode Island Repository for 1815.

——Letter from John Howland, Esq., relative to the Rhode Island Regiment, commanded by Col. Christopher Lippitt, in the years 1776 and 1777.
12mo. pp. 11.   *Providence. H. H. Brown.* 1831.

—— Notices of the military services rendered by the mili-

tia as well as by the enlisted troops of the State of Rhode Island during the revolutionary war.
12mo. pp. 11. *Providence.* 1832.

—— Discourse on the Life and Times of. See *E. B. Hall.*

———. Life and Recollections of. See *E. M. Stone.*

John Howland was a direct descendant of John Howland born in 1592, one of the founders of the Plymouth colony. He was born in Newport, Rhode Island, October 31st, 1757, and removed to Providence in his thirteenth year. He entered the army of the revolution at an early age, and was for half a century an active political associate of the leading statesmen of Rhode Island. Besides filling many offices of trust, he was President of the Rhode Island Historical Society for 21 years; an active member of the School Committee for 20 years; and for many years President of the Mechanics Association. His whole life was devoted to the public good, and to the advancement of the interests of others. He died November 5, 1854, at the age of 97 years.

HUBBARD, REV. H. G. A historical discourse delivered on the Fiftieth Anniversary of the organization of the First Baptist Church in Bristol, Rhode Island.
8vo. pp. 18. *Providence. A. Crawford Greene.* 1861.

HUBBARD, WILLIAM. The present state of New England, being a narrative of the troubles with the Indians in New England; to which is added a discourse about the war with the Pequods in the year 1637.
Small 4to. pp. 88. *London.* 1677.

HUBBARD, Gov. H. Letter to Gov. King, refusing to deliver up Thomas W. Dorr. (See Constitution.)

HUDSON, DAVID. History of Jemima Wilkinson, a Preacheress of the Eighteenth Century; containing an authentic narrative of her life and character; and of the rise, progress, and conclusion of her ministry.
12mo. pp. 208 and appendix 20.
Geneva, N. Y. S. P. Have. 1821.

HUMPHREYS. An Historical account of the Incorporated Society for the propagation of the Gospel in Foreign parts. Containing their foundation proceedings, and the success of their missionaries in the British Colonies to the year

1728. By David Humphreys, D. D., Secretary to the Honorable Society.
8vo. pp. xxxi. and 356.   London. 1730.

—— The Same.
8vo. pp. 135.   London. [1852.]

—— Reprinted also, in the " Church Review" of 1851-2.
In this volume is a particular account of the state of religion in Rhode Island, and of the founding of an Episcopal Church here in 1704, by the Rev. Mr. Honeyman. "Though the Island was full of persons of many persuasions, especially Quakers," says the author, "the Governor himself being such, yet by his prudent behaviour, he gave offence to none, and gained many to the Church."

HUNTER, WILLIAM. An Oration delivered in the Baptist Meeting-house, in Newport, July 4, A. D., 1795, on the celebration of the nineteenth anniversary of American Independence.
8vo. pp. 30.   Newport. Henry Barber. 1795.

—— An Oration, delivered in Trinity Church, in Newport, July 4, 1801.
8vo. pp. 32.   Newport. Mercury Office. 1801.

—— Oration pronounced before the citizens of Providence, on the 4th of July, 1826, being the Fiftieth anniversary of American Independence.
8vo. pp. 46. and 4.   Providence. Smith & Parmenter. 1826.
This pamphlet relates chiefly to the part taken by Rhode Island in the "splendid drama" of American Independence.

—— The Same. Second edition. pp. 46.   1826.

—— Annual Address, delivered before the Rhode Island Society for the Encouragement of Domestic Industry, October 20, 1821.
8vo. pp. 43.   Providence. Carlile & Brown. 1826.

Mr. Hunter was a native of Newport, Rhode Island, and graduated at Brown University in 1791. He soon after went to England, where he studied medicine, which he afterwards relinquished, and studied law at the Inner Temple, London. On his return to Newport, he was admitted to the bar, and soon rose to eminence in his profession. For many years he was a member of the General Assembly of Rhode Island. In 1811, he was elected a Senator in Congress, which place he held till 1821. In 1834, he was appointed Chargé des Affaires to Brazil, and in 1842, Minister

Plenipotentiary to the same Court. On his return to his native town in 1811, he retired from public life. Mr. Hunter was a man of varied and extensive learning. He died, December 3, 1819, aged 75 years.

HUNTINGTON, REV. DANIEL, A. M. A Poem, on the pleasures and advantages of true religion. Delivered before the United Brothers' Society, in Brown University, on their anniversary, August 31, 1819. Published by request.
8vo. pp. 23. *Providence.* 1819.

IMPRISONMENT FOR DEBT. Report of the Select Committee on the Bill "To abolish imprisonment for debt." By Wm. B. Lawrence and Seth W. Macy.
8vo. pp. 20.   October, 1851.

INDIANS. The number of Indians in Rhode Island. From an account of the number of Inhabitants of that colony, taken between the 4th of May and the 14th of June, 1774, and ordered to be printed by the General Assembly. —*Mass. Hist. Collection, 1st series, vol. x.*

——— Account of an Indian visitation, A. D., 1698, copied for Dr. Stiles, by the Rev. Mr. Hawley, Missionary at Marshpee, from the printed account published in 1693. *Ibid.*
Contains, among others, notices of the Indians in Little Compton and Nantucket.

——— King Ninegret's Tribe of Indians, A. D., 1761. *Ibid.*

——— Relation of the Indian Plot, of Miantenomo, Sachem of the Narragansetts, to destroy the English, 1642. —*Mass. Hist. Coll. 3d series, vol. 3.*

——— Indian Lands. Intrusion of Rhode Island people upon. 1669.—*Mass. Hist. Coll.*   *Ibid.*

——— Manuscripts relating to the Narragansett Indians, in the archives of the State, 1735 to 1842. 2 vols. folio.

—— Report of the Committee on the Indian Tribe, made to the General Assembly, October Session, 1852. By Elisha R. Potter. Published by order of the Senate. 8vo. pp. 8. *Providence. Sayles & Miller.* 1852.

INDIANS. For books relating to, see *Church's Indian Wars; Drake's Book of the Indians; Easton's Philip's Indian War; Gookin; Mather; New England's Tears for her Present Miseries; Niles; Hubbard; Irving.*

INDIAN WAR. The present state of New England, with respect to the Indian War. Wherein is an account of the true reason thereof, (as far as can be judged by men.) Together with the most remarkable passages that have happened from the 20th June, till the 10th of November, 1675. Faithfully composed by a Merchant of Boston, and communicated to his Friend in London.
Folio. pp. 19. *London. Printed for Dorman Newman.* 1675.

INDIAN WAR. A continuation of the State of New England; being a farther account of the Engagement betwixt the joint Forces of the United English Collonies and the Indians, on the 19th of December, 1675; with the true number of the slain and wounded, and the transactions of the English Army since the said Fight; With all the other passages that have there hapned, from the 10th of November, 1675, to the 8th of February, 1675–6.
Folio. pp. 20. *London. Printed for Dorman Newman.* 1676.

INDIAN WAR. A New and further Narrative of the State of New England; being a continued account of the Bloudy INDIAN WAR, From March till August, 1676. Giving a perfect relation of the Several Devastations, Engagements, and Transactions there; as also, the great successes lately obtained against the Barbarous Indians; the reducing of KING PHILIP, and the killing of one of his Queens, &c. Together with a catalogue of the losses in the whole, sustained on either side, since the said war began, as near as can be collected.
Folio. pp. 14. *London. Printed for Dorman Newman.* 1676.

INDIAN WAR. A true account of the most considerable occurrences that have hapned in the WARRE between the English and Indians in New England, From the 5th of May, 1676, to the fourth of August last ; as also, of the successes it hath pleased God to give the English against them.
Folio. pp. 10.　　　London. Benjamin Billingsley. 1676.

INDUSTRIAL STATISTICS of the State of Rhode Island, (Report on) from materials collected by the Rhode Island Society for the Encouragement of Domestic Industry, in accordance with a resolution of the General Assembly, January, 1860.
8vo. pp. 22.　　　Providence. A. Crawford Greene. 1861.

IRVING, WASHINGTON. Philip of Pokanoket. An Indian Memoir. *Sketch Book.*

IVES, THOMAS POYNTON. Obituary notice of, who died April 30th, 1835, by William G. Goddard. From the Providence Journal of May 5th 1835.
8vo. pp. 6.　　　Providence. 1835.

IVES, MOSES BROWN. A discourse in commemoration of the Life and Character of. By Francis Wayland.
8vo. pp. 25.　　　Providence. Knowles, Anthony & Co. 1857.

――― The Same. Large paper, 4to.

――― The late Moses Brown Ives. Extracts from the Providence Journal, August 8, and August 12, 1857. Providence Tribune and Providence Post. Resolutions adopted by various public bodies at the time of Mr. Ives's death, etc.
8vo. pp. 12.　　　Providence. Privately printed. 1857.

IVES AND HAZARD CASE. Books relating to.

――― Supreme Court in Equity, March term, 1853. No. 230. Robert Ives vs. Charles T. Hazard, Henry A. Middleton, Mumford Hazard. Opening argument for complainant.
8vo. pp. 30.　　　Providence. Knowles, Anthony & Co. 1855.

――― Same case. Closing argument for complainant.
8vo. pp. 19.　　　Providence. Knowles, Anthony & Co. 1855.

―――― Same case. March term, 1855. Arguments for Defendants.
8vo. pp. 127.　　　Providence. Knowles, Anthony & Co. 1855.

―――― Report of the Case of Ives vs. Hazard and others, in the Supreme Court of Rhode Island, September term, 1855. Present: Hon. William R. Staples, Chief Justice; Hon. George A. Brayton, Hon. Alfred Bosworth, Justices. From the 4th volume of Rhode Island Reports.
8vo. pp. 15.　　　Boston. Little, Brown & Co. 1858.

―――― Speech upon a resolution to appoint a committee, and to send for persons and papers to examine into the subject of the memorial of Geo. H. Calvert et al., and of Charles T. Hazard, delivered in the House of Representatives, February 3, 1858. Published in the Providence Journal.

―――― An appeal to the people of Rhode Island in behalf of the Constitution and the Laws; By Thomas R. Hazard. "And judgment is turned away backward, and justice standeth afar off, for truth is fallen in the street, and equity cannot enter."
8vo. pp. 163.　　　[Providence.] 1857.

―――― Letter addressed to Robert H. Ives, in reply to his published statements in relation to the case in equity, Ives vs. Hazard. By Thomas R. Hazard.
8vo. pp. 48.　　　Newport. George T. Hammond. 1859.

―――― Report of the Special Committee on Equity powers of Supreme Court.
8vo. pp. 8.　　　Providence. Knowles, Anthony & Co. 1859.

―――― Robert H. Ives vs. Charles T. Hazard and others. Deposition of Moses B. Ives.
8vo. pp. 6.　　　Providence. 1859.

―――― Speech of Thomas A. Jenckes, of Providence, upon the resolution to annul the decree of the Supreme Court in the case Ives vs. Hazard, et al., delivered in the House of Representatives of Rhode Island, on the 23d and 24th of February, 1859. Reported by William Henry Burr.
8vo. pp. 58.　　　Providence. Knowles, Anthony & Co. 1859.

—— Speech of Hon. Nathan F. Dixon, of Westerly, upon the resolution to annul the decree of the Supreme Court, in the case of Robert H. Ives vs. Charles T. Hazard, et al.
8vo. pp. 36. *Providence. Knowles, Anthony & Co.*

—— Speech of William P. Sheffield, of Newport, upon the resolution to annul the decree of the Supreme Court, in the case, Ives vs. Hazard, delivered in the House of Representatives, January 17, 1859.
8vo. pp. 11. *Providence. Knowles, Anthony & Co.* 1859.

—— Speech of Hon. Joseph M. Blake, upon the report of the case, Ives vs. Hazard, made to Chief Justice Samuel Ames, State Reporter.
8vo. pp. 16

—— To the people of Rhode Island: Ives vs. Hazard. By Charles T. Hazard.
8vo. pp. 4. *From the Providence Journal of February 9, 1860.*

—— Remarks of the Hon. Samuel Ames, reporter of the Decisions of the Supreme Court, in explanation of his report of the case, Robert H. Ives vs. Charles T. Hazard, et al.
8vo. pp. 25. *Providence. Knowles, Anthony & Co.* 1859.

—— The Rhode Island Controversy. A short history of the case of Ives vs. Hazard. From the Boston Law Reporter for June.
8vo. pp. 12. *Boston. Geo. C. Rand & Avery.* 1859.

—— Majority Report of the Special Committee on the petition of Charles T. Hazard.
8vo. pp. 7. *Providence. Knowles, Anthony & Co.* 1860.

—— "The astonishing Development." Ives vs. Hazard. From the Republican Herald, Providence, June 4, 1859.

—— To the people of Rhode Island: Memorial of Mumford Hazard. 8vo. 1858.

—— The General Assembly not Guilty; or, The Court vs. The Assembly. Reprinted from the Providence Post.
8vo. pp. 7. *Providence. [March. 1863.]*

———— Memorial of Thomas R. Hazard, asking for the removal of the State Reporter, and the impeachment of Chief Justice Ames, etc.
8vo. pp. 16.　　Providence. *A. Crawford Greene.* [1861.]

———— A Lawyer's unbought opinion, in the Ives and Hazard case, addressed to the Honorable General Assembly of the State of Rhode Island.
8vo. pp. 7.　　　　　　　　　　　　*January.* 1861.

———— Libel Suit of Chief Justice Ames against Thomas R. Hazard. Hon Joseph M. Blake's argument for defendant upon plaintiff's demurrer.
8vo. pp.　　Providence. *A. Crawford Greene.* 1862.

———— Newspaper history of, embracing editorials, communications, speeches, letters and documents relating to the Ives and Hazard case, from the Providence Journal, Post and Press; preserved in a bound volume, in the possession of J. R. Bartlett.

21

JACKSON, CHARLES T., M. D. Report on the Geological and Agricultural Survey of the State of Rhode Island, made under a resolve of the Legislature, in the year 1839.
8vo. pp. viii. and 312.
Providence. B. Cranston & Co. 1840.

JACKSON, HON. RICHARD, JUNIOR. Representative in Congress. Address from, to his constituents, March 16, 1812. 8vo. pp. 22. [*Washington.*] *no date.*

JACKSON, REV. HENRY. An Historical Discourse, delivered in the Central Baptist Meeting-house, Newport, R. I., January 8, 1854. Published by order of the Church. 8vo. pp. 45. *Newport, R. I. Cranston & Norman.* 1854.

——— An account of the Churches in Rhode Island, presented to an adjourned session of the Twenty-eighth Annual meeting of the Rhode Island Baptist State Convention, Providence, November 8, 1853.
8vo. pp. 134. *Providence. George H. Whitney.* 1854.
Contains a view of the First Baptist Meeting-house, Providence. Dr. Jackson was pastor of the Central Baptist Church, in Newport, R. I.

——— Discourse occasioned by the death of the Rev. Zalmon Tobey, September 17, 1858. (Preached at Warren,) October 3, 1858.
8vo. pp. 32. *Providence. Coggeshall & Stewart.* 1859.

——— A Discourse in commemoration of the 215th Anniversary of the Mite Society; and the Twenty-fifth Anniversary of the First Baptist Church in America.
8vo. pp. 32. *Providence. John R. Stickney.* 1854.

Henry Jackson, the second son of Richard Jackson, was born in Providence, June 16, 1798, and graduated at Brown University, in 1817. From 1822 to 1836, he was settled over the First Baptist Church, in Charlestown, Massachusetts. In December, of the same year, he became pastor of the First Baptist Church, in Hartford, Connecticut. On the 1st of January, 1839, he became pastor of the First Baptist Church, in New Bedford, Massachusetts, where he officiated for seven years. In January, 1847, he was settled as pastor of the Central Baptist Church, in Newport, Rhode Island, where he continued till his death, which took place, while traveling in the Railroad cars from Providence to Stonington, on the 2d of March, 1863. During the ministry of Dr. Jackson, he was actively engaged in promoting the cause of religion and education.

JACOBS, REV. BELA., A. M. Memoir of, compiled chiefly from his letters and journals, by his daughter, with a sketch of his character. By Barnas Sears.
12mo. pp. vii. and 305.
Boston. Gould, Lincoln & Edmonds. 1857.

Mr. Jacobs was a native of Rhode Island, and for many years a settled minister at Pawtuxet.

JAMES, CHARLES T., vs. the Atlantic DeLaine Company, et al. The Bill in Equity. T. A. Jenckes for complainant. R. W. Greene, A. Payne, Jas. B. Parsons, for respondents.
8vo. pp. 211. *Providence. Knowles, Anthony & Co.* 1859.

JAMES, HENRY. The Social Significance of our Institutions. An oration delivered in Newport, July 4, 1861.
8vo. pp. 47. *Boston. Ticknor & Fields.* 1861.

JOHNSON, LORENZO D. The Spirit of Roger Williams, with a portrait of one of his descendants.
16mo. pp. 94. *Boston. Published for the author.* 1839.

JOHNSON, EDWARD. A History of New England, from the English planting in the yeere 1628, untill the yeere 1652. Declaring the form of their government, Civil, Military, and Ecclesiastique. Their wars with the Indians, their troubles with the GORTONISTS, and other Heretiques. The manner of gathering the churches, the commodities of

the country, and description of the principall towns and havens, with the great encouragements to increased trade betwixt them and old England. With the names of all the Governors, Magistrates, and eminent Ministers.
Quarto. pp. 236. *London. Printed for Nath. Brooke.* 1654.

This work is better known by its inner title of "Wonder-working Providence." The author came in the fleet with Governor Winthrop, in 1630. In 1643, he went with Captain Cooke and forty men to Rhode Island, to take Samuel Gorton who had become obnoxious to the Massachusetts Government. For twenty-eight years he was a member of the General Court of Massachusetts, and at one time Speaker.

JOURNAL of the proceedings of the Congress held at Albany, in 1754:

An original manuscript Journal of the Commissioners of this Congress is among the Public Archives of the State of Rhode Island, in the office of the Secretary of State. The object of the convention was to treat with the Six Nations of Indians, and concert a scheme of general union for the British American Colonies. The Colonies represented were: New Hampshire, Massachusetts, Rhode Island, Connecticut, New York, Pennsylvania and Maryland. The delegates from Rhode Island were, Stephen Hopkins and Martin Howard, Jun'r. The whole number in attendance was twenty-five, among which were Dr. Franklin, Roger Wolcott, Jr., Gov. Colden, Sir William Johnson, and other distinguished men. Of this assemby, Hutchinson, in his "History of Massachusetts," Vol. III. p. 20, says, that it "was the most deserving of respect of any which had ever been convened in America, whether we consider the Colonies which were represented, the rank and character of the delegates, or the purposes for which it was convened."

Mr. Sparks, in his edition of Franklin's writings, in speaking of this convention and the plan of union which grew out of it, says:

"The prospect of a French war, and the hostile attitude already assumed by the tribes of Indians on the frontiers, induced the British Government to seek for the means of providing for a timely and efficient resistance in the Colonies. With a view to this end, an order was sent over by the Lords of Trade, directing that Commissioners should be appointed in the several provinces to meet at Albany. The immediate object was to conciliate the Six Nations, by giving them presents, and renewing a treaty, by which they should be prevented from going over to the French, or being drawn away by the Indians under their influence."

—— The same. Printed in the Massachusetts Historical Collections, 3d series, vol. v. See also, Stephen Hopkins,— "*A True Representation,*" etc.

JOURNAL of the Rhode Island Institute of Instruction. Edited by Henry Barnard.
3 vols. 8vo. *Providence.* 1845–1848.

EACH, HORACE A. Burrillville as it was, and as it is.
12mo. pp. vi. and 170.
     Providence. Knowles, Anthony & Co.

KENYON, ARCHIBALD. The Object and Principles of Civil Government, and the duty of Christians thereto. Being a discourse preached before the West Baptist Church and Society, August 14, 1842.
8vo. pp. 11.   Providence. B. T. Albro. 1842.

KIMBALL, JEROME BONAPARTE. An Oration, delivered before the Municipal Authorities of the city of Providence, July 4, 1856. Poem, by W. M. Rodman.
8vo. pp. 52.   Providence. Knowles, Anthony & Co. 1856.

KING, THOMAS K. An Oration, delivered before the Kentish Artillery and citizens of Apponaug, on the Seventy-eight Anniversary of American Independence, July 4, 1854.
8vo. pp. 29.   Providence. Geo. H. Whitney. 1854.

KINGSTON ACADEMY. A statement of facts relating to the funds of.
8vo. pp. 15.   Providence. E. A. Marshall. 1836.

KINNICUTT, THOMAS. An Oration, delivered before the Society of United Brothers, of Brown University, September 1, 1840. Published by request of the Society.
8vo. pp. 32.   Providence. Knowles & Vose. 1840.

KNIGHT, GOV. Address to the Farmers of Rhode Island, October, 1832.
8vo. pp. 15.   Providence. Cranston & Hammond. 1832.

KNIGHT, RICHARD. History of the General and Six Principle Baptists in Europe and America; In two parts. Published under the patronage of the Rhode Island Yearly Meeting.
8vo. pp. iv. and 367. Providence. Smith & Parmenter. 1827.

KNOWLES, JAMES D. Memoir of Roger Williams, the Founder of the State of Rhode Island.
12mo. pp. 457.   Boston. Lincoln, Edmonds & Co. 1834.

LAWS, CODE OF, 1647. Proceedings of the First General Assembly of "The incorporation of Providence Plantations," and the Code of Laws adopted by that Assembly. With notes, Historical and Explanatory. By William R. Staples, one of the Judges of the Supreme Court of Rhode Island.
8vo. pp. x. and 64. *Providence. Charles Burnett, Jr.* 1847.
The original manuscript of these laws is in a volume of the early records, in the Secretary of State's office.

BODYE OF LAWES of the Colonie of Rhode Island and Providence Plantations, 1663 to 1705; manuscript, folio.
This the earliest digest of the Colonial Laws. It was compiled by order of the General Assembly, and probably formed the basis of the collection of Public Laws, printed in the year 1719.

———— The Charter granted by His Majesty King Charles the Second, to the Colony of Rhode Island and Providence Plantations in America.
Folio. pp. 8. *Boston. In New England, &c.* 1719.

ACTS AND LAWS of His Majestie's Colony of Rhode Island and Providence Plantations in America.
Folio. pp. 102. *Boston. In New England. Printed for John Allen and Nicholas Boone, at the sign of the Bible, in Cornhill.* 1719.

ACTS AND LAWS of His Majesty's Colony of Rhode Island and

Providence Plantations in America. [Preceded by the Charter.]
Folio. charter. pp. 12. table xii. and 243.
 Newport, Rhode Island. Printed by James Franklin, and sold at his shop near the Town School House. 1730.

ACTS AND LAWS, of His Majesty's Colony of Rhode Island and Providence Plantations, in New England, in America.
Folio. charter. pp. 15. table xv. and 308.
 Newport, Rhode Island. Printed by the Widow Franklin, and to be sold at the Town School House. 1744.

ACTS AND LAWS of his Majesty's Colony of Rhode Island and Providence Plantations, in New England, in America. From Anno 1745 to Anno 1752.
Folio. pp. 110. *Newport, Rhode Island. Printed by J. Franklin, at the Printing office under the Town School House.* 1752.

ACTS AND LAWS of the English Colony of Rhode Island and Providence Plantations, in New England, in America.
Folio. pp. charter xv. table 46 and 272.
 Newport. Printed and sold by Samuel Hall, Printer to the Honorable General Assembly. 1767.

THE PUBLIC LAWS of the State of Rhode Island and Providence Plantations, as revised by a committee, and finally enacted by the Honorable General Assembly, at their session in January, 1798. To which are prefixed, the Charter, Declaration of Independence, Articles of Confederation, Constitution of the United States, and President Washington's Address of September, 1796. Published by authority. *Ignorantia legis neminem excusat.* Ignorance of the Law is no excuse for its violation.
8vo. pp. 652.
 Printed at Providence, by Carter & Wilkinson. 1798.

———— A Supplement to the Digest of the Laws, 1798. Public Laws of the State of Rhode Island and Providence Plantations, passed since the session of the Honorable General Assembly in January, A. D., 1798.
8vo. pp. 144. *Providence. Jones & Wheeler.* 1810.

LAWS OF RHODE ISLAND. Books relating to.

——— Public Laws of the State of Rhode Island, etc., passed since the session of the General Assembly in October, A. D., 1810. [With an index.]
8vo. pp. 168.   *various years.*

This volume is paged continuously from the preceding, and has no title page. It begins at p. 141, and terminates at p. 313. It includes the Public Laws to February 24, 1821. The laws of the May, June and October Sessions, 1821, were never printed separately, and are only to be found in the schedules.

——— Public Laws of the State of Rhode Island and Providence Plantations, passed at, and since the session of the General Assembly, in January, A. D., 1822.
8vo. pp. from 525 to 1099, and from 2000 to 2097.

These are the biennial publications of the laws, as ordered to be printed by the digest of 1822, and contain an index to each biennial publication. The volume is paged correctly from the digest of 1822, i. e., from 525 to 1099, when the printer, by a singular blunder, skipped to p. 2000, from which number, he continued to p. 2097.

THE PUBLIC LAWS of the State of Rhode Island and Providence Plantations, as revised by a Committee, and finally enacted by the Honorable General Assembly, at their session in January, 1822. To which is prefixed the Charter, Declaration of Independence, Articles of Confederation, Constitution of the United States, and President Washington's Address of September, 1796. Published by authority. *Ignorantia legis neminem excusat.*
8vo. pp. 524 and index xlvi.
                         Providence. Miller & Hutchins. 1822.

THE PUBLIC LAWS of the State of Rhode Island and Providence Plantations, as revised by a committee, and finally enacted by the General Assembly, in January, 1844. To which are prefixed, the Charter of Charles 2d, Declaration of Independence, Resolution of the General Assembly to support Declaration of Independence ; Proceedings of the Convention on the adoption of the Constitution of the United States by Rhode Island ; President Washington's Ad-

LAWS OF RHODE ISLAND. Books relating to.

——— dress, and Constitution of the State of Rhode Island and Providence Plantations.
8vo. pp. viii. and 594.   *Providence. Knowles & Vose.* 1844.

——— Second edition.
8vo. pp. 594.   *Providence. George H. Whitney.* 1852.

THE REVISED STATUTES of the State of Rhode Island and Providence Plantations, to which are prefixed the Constitutions of the United States and of the State. Published by authority of the General Assembly.
8vo. pp. xv. and 804.
    Providence. Sayles, Miller & Simons. 1857.

——— Supplement to the Revised Statutes No. 1. Being the Public Laws of the State of Rhode Island and Providence Plantations, passed by the General Assembly from January, 1857, to January, 1859, inclusive.
8vo. pp. 76.   *Providence. Knowles & Anthony.* 1859.

——— Supplement to the Revised Statutes, No. 2. May, 1859, to January, 1861, inclusive.
8vo. pp. 77 to 137.   *Providence. A. Crawford Greene.* 1861.

——— Ibid.   No. 3.   May, 1861, to January, 1863, inclusive.
8vo. pp. 137 to 273.   *Providence. Alfred Anthony.* 1863.

LAW CASES, for full titles, see the following:

ANGELL WILL CASE. See *Angell.*

AVERY. REV. E. K. Charged with murder of Sarah M. Cornell. See *Avery.*

AMES, SAMUEL VS. THOMAS R. HAAZRD, for libel. See *Hazard.*

ANTOINE, WOHLFAHRT, and others, for the murder of Field and Jenkinson. See *Wohlfahrt.*

DORRANCE, JOHN VS. ARTHUR FENNER. See *Dorrance.*

FIELD, ALBERT. Charged with murder of Jonathan Gray. See *Field.*

GREENE VS. BRIGGS. Maine Liquor Law. See *Greene.*

LAW CASES. Books relating to.

GORDON. Charged with the murder of Amasa Sprague. See *Gordon*.

GARDNER AND POTTER vs. HANNAH GARDNER. Will Case. See *Gardner*.

HALSEY WILL CASE. See *Currey*, for argument on.

HAZARD AND IVES CASE. See *Hazard & Ives*.

JAMES, CHARLES T. vs. ATLANTIC DELAINE CO. See *James*.

LUTHER vs. BORDEN. See under head of *Constitution*.

MALLETT vs. DEXTER. See *Mallett*.

POTTER, J. J. vs. JAMES SNOW. "Liquor Case." See *Potter*,

RIOTERS in Providence, October 18, 1824. Trials of. See *Hardscrabble*.

STATE OF RHODE ISLAND vs. WM. S. SPEAR. See *Spear*.

TAYLOR vs. PLACE. See *Taylor*.

TREVETT AND WEEDEN, case of. See *Trevett*.

WALKER, SARAH vs. JOHN MARTIN. See *Walker*.

WALMSLEY, AMASA E. Life and Confession of. See *Walmsley*. See also, *Reports of the Supreme Court of Rhode Island, and State Archives*.

LAWRENCE, WILLIAM BEACH. Speech of, in the Senate of Rhode Island, February 10, 1852, on the Maine Liquor Law Bill.
8vo. pp. 16. Providence. 1852.

———— Memoir of Henry Wheaton. Introduction to Mr. Lawrence's edition of Wheaton's *History of International Law*.

LAWTON, JOSIAH. Oration on the importance of Scientific Knowledge, delivered before the Providence Association of Mechanics and Manufacturers, at their 37th anniversary, April 10, 1826.
8vo. pp. Providence. Miller & Grattan. 1826.

LECTURE ON MYSTERIOUS KNOCKINGS. Mesmerism, &c.,

with a brief history of the Old Stone Mill, and a prediction of its fall ; delivered before the A N ti Quarian Society of Pappigassett. At Newport, R. I., February 14, 4199. By Benjamin Franklin Macy, D. F., D. D. F., A. S. S. Professor of Hyperflatinated Philosophy in the University of Hardscrabble. " Huic versatile ingenium sic pariter ad omnia fuit, ut natum ad id unum diceres quod-cunque ageret."
8vo. pp. 8.   *Newport. B. J. Tilley.* 1851.

LECRAW, J. B. A sketch of the Life, Works and Sufferings of a reformed man ; showing the misery to which intemperance brought him, and the means he could resort to to procure the inebriating draught. Written by himself.
12mo. pp. 36   *Pawtucket. B. W. Pearce.* 1844.

LEE, GEN. HENRY. The campaign of 1781 in the Carolinas ; with remarks, historical and critical, on Johnson's Life of General Greene, and appendix of original documents relating to the History of the Revolution.
8vo. pp.   *Philadelphia.* 1824.

LEIDY, JOSEPH., M. D. Contributions towards a knowledge of the Marine Invertebrate Fauna of the Coasts of Rhode Island and New Jersey, (in the Journal of Natural Sciences, of Philadelphia. Vol. 3. art, 11.)

LETTER to the Hon. James F. Simmons. By a Rhode Island Conservative.
8vo. pp. 8.   *Providence. April* 1. 1845.

LETTERS to James Fenner, Esq., in 1811 and 1831. [Signed Another Republican.]
8vo. pp, 16.   *Providence.*

LEXINGTON, STEAMER. A full and particular account of all the circumstances attending the loss of the steamboat Lexington, in Long Island Sound, on the night of January 13, 1840 ; as elicited in the evidences of the witnesses examined before the jury of inquest, held in New York, immediately after the lamentable event. A portion of the

profits of this work will be appropriated to the benefit of the destitute families of those who were lost.
8vo. pp. 32.　　　*Providence. H. H. Brown & Stillwell.* 1840.

LEXINGTON. Proceedings of the Coroner, in the case of the Steamer Lexington; lost by fire on the 13th of January, 1840.
8vo. pp. 89.　　　　　　　　　　　　*New York.* 1840.

LOTTERIES IN RHODE ISLAND. For account of, see *Doyle, Bartlett.*

LUTHER, SETH. Address to the working men of New England, on the state of education and the condition of the producing classes in Europe and America, etc. See *Education.*
8vo. pp. 39.　　　*Boston. Published for the author.* 1832.

——— An address on the right of Free Suffrage, delivered at the request of Freeholders and others, of Providence, Rhode Island, in the Old Town House, April 19, and repeated April 26, [1833,] at the same place. With an appendix, containing the Rhode Island Bill of Rights, and the rejected petition presented in 1829 to the Legislature of Rhode Island, by nearly 2000 petitioners, including 700 Freeholders, who were all denominated vagabonds and renegades, by Benjamin Hazard, who reported on that petition to the General Assembly.
8vo. pp. 25. and xvi.　　*Providence. S. R. Weeden.* 1833.

——— An address to the working men of New England on the State of Education, and on the condition of the producing classes in Europe and America. With particular reference to the effect of manufacturing, (as now conducted,) on the health and happiness of the poor, and on the safety of the Republic.
8vo. pp. 39.　　　*Boston. Printed for the author.* 1832.

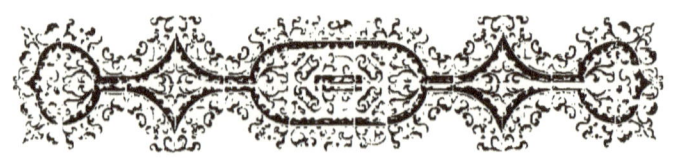ACHILTON, REV. J. N. The Sleep of the Beloved. A Funeral Sermon on the death of the Rt. Rev. John Prentiss Kewley Henshaw, D. D., Bishop of Rhode Island. Delivered in St. Stephen's Church, Baltimore, July 25, 1852.
8vo. pp. 20.   *Baltimore. Jos. Robinson.* 1852.

MACKENZIE, ALEXANDER SLIDELL. The Life of Commodore Oliver Hazard Perry.
2 vols. 12mo.   *New York. Harper & Brothers.* 1840.

MCKENZIE, REV. JAMES A. A discourse on Life-taking. See *Constitution of* 1842.

MACSPARRAN, REV. J., D. D. America Dissected, being a full and true account of all the American Colonies, showing the intemperance of the climates, excessive heat and cold, and violent changes of weather; terrible and mischievous thunder and lightning; bad and unwholesome air, destructive to human bodies; badness of money; danger from enemies; but above all, to the souls of the poor people that remove thither, from the multifarious wicked and pestilent houses that prevail in those parts: Published as a caution to unsteady people who may be tempted to leave their native country.
8vo. pp.   *Dublin. Printed and sold by S. Powell.* 1753.

This work was written in the Narragansett country, Rhode Island, where Dr. MacSparran resided as a missionary, for upwards of thirty years. Brief notices are given of all the British Colonies, but of Rhode Island his descriptions are more full. The original pamphlet is very rare. It was reprinted by Mr. Updike in the appendix to his "History of the Narragansett Church," with the addition of genealogical and biographical notes of of persons mentioned by the author.

MAINE LIQUOR LAW. Report in the case, William H. Greene vs. Nathan M. Briggs, et al. The Plaintiff's opening argument, and the opinion of the U. S. Circuit Court for the Rhode Island District. By Joseph S. Pitman, Counsellor at Law.

8vo. pp. 60. *Boston. Little, Brown & Co.* 1853.

MALLETT vs. DEXTER. The case in Equity, between Edward J. Mallett, et al., complainants, and Samuel Dexter, administrator, respondent.

8vo. pp. 134. *Providence. A. Crawford Greene.* 1852.

MAN, GEORGE F. An Oration, delivered before the citizens of the county of Kent, at Apponaug, Warwick, July 4, 1838.

8vo. pp. 23. *Providence. Knowles, Vose & Co.* 1838.

MANNING, REV. JAMES., D. D. First President of Brown University. Memoir of, with biographical notices of some of his pupils. By William G. Goddard, A. M., Prof. of Belles Lettres in Brown University.

8vo. pp. 24. *Boston. Perkins & Marvin.* 1839.

——— Obituary notice of the Rev. James Manning, D. D., First President of Brown University. Published in Rippon's Baptist Register.

pp. 241 to 247. *London.* 1791.

——— Sermon on the death of. See *Fobes.*

A more extended life of Dr. Manning, with his correspondence, by Reuben A. Guild, Librarian of Brown University, has been announced for publication. See *Guild.*

Dr. Manning was a native of New Jersey, and a graduate of Princeton College, in the class of 1762. In the summer of 1763, he came to Rhode Island, and used his influence in behalf of a college, which was incorporated by the General Assembly early in the following year. Soon after, he commenced a Latin School at Warren, where he also founded a Baptist Church, and in the year 1767, the Warren Association. In the year 1765, he was appointed President of Rhode Island College, now Brown University, which office he filled with distinguished success and usefulness until his death in 1791.. Upon the removal of the College from Warren to Providence, he became the Pastor of the First Baptist Church, which office he also held until a few months before his death. Dr. Manning was very active in the cause of public education, and was for many years Chairman of the School Committee of Providence. In 1786, he was unanimously appointed by the General Assembly to represent the State in the Old Federal Congress. His sudden death at the early age of 52, was universally lamented.

MAP. A topographical map of the State of Rhode Island and Providence Plantations. Surveyed Trigonometrically and in detail. By James Stevens, Topographer and Civil Engineer. *Newport.* 1831.

MAP. Chart of Narragansett Bay. Surveyed in 1832, by Capt. Alexander S. Wadsworth, Lieut. F. R. Gedney, Charles Wilkes, Jun'r, and George S. Blake, of the U. S. Navy. By order of the Hon. Levi Woodbury, Secretary of the Navy. *Washington.* 1833.

MAP OF RHODE ISLAND, by Stevens. With additions and corrections by S. B. Cushing and H. F. Walling.
Providence. 1846.

MAP of Massachusetts, Rhode Island and Connecticut. Compiled from the latest authorities.
New York. Phelps & Enign. 1843.

MAP OF THE STATE OF RHODE ISLAND and Providence Plantations. From surveys under the direction of Henry F. Walling, Civil Engineer. *Providence.* 1855.

——— The same. A new edition, showing the new Eastern Boundary of the State, including the towns of Pawtucket and East Providence.
New York. Published by John Douglas. 1863.

MAP OF THE CITY OF PROVIDENCE and Town of North Providence, from actual survey, by B. Lockwood and S. B. Cushing. 1835.

MAP OF THE CITY OF PROVIDENCE, from actual surveys. By Cushing & Walling, 1849. A map of the City of Providence, Rhode Island, from surveys under the direction of H. F. Walling. *Providence. E. Baker.* 1857.

MAP OF PROVIDENCE COUNTY, Rhode Island, with some of the adjacent towns, from orginal surveys, by H. F. Walling, C. E. *Providence.* 1851.

MAP OF BRISTOL COUNTY, Rhode Island, from original surveys, under the direction of Henry F. Walling, C. E.
Providence. 1851.

MAP OF NEWPORT COUNTY, Rhode Island, from original surveys, by H. F. Walling, assisted by O. Harkness, and J. Hannon. 1850.

MAP OF WASHINGTON COUNTY, Rhode Island; from original surveys, by H. F. Walling. *Providence.* 1857.

MAP OF NEWPORT, Rhode Island, from original surveys. Published by M. Dripps. *New York.* 1850.

MANUAL of the Free Evangelical Congregational Church, Providence, R. I.
18mo. pp. 28. *Providence. Gladding & Brother.* 1857.

MARCHANT, WILLIAM. An Oration, pronounced at Newport, July 4, 1797.
8vo. pp. 18. *Newport. Henry Barber.* 1797.

MASON, JOHN. A Brief History of the Pequot War; Especially of the memorable taking of their fort at Mistick, in Connecticut, in 1637. Written by Major John Mason, a principal actor therein, as their Chief Captain and Commander of Connecticut Forces. With an introduction, and some explanatory notes, by the Reverend Mr. Thomas Prince.
8vo. pp. x. and 22 *Boston, Printed and sold by S. Kneeland and T. Green, in Queen street.* 1736.

———— The same. *Mass. Hist. Coll.* 2d series. vol. VIII.

———— The same. 16mo. pp. *Boston.* 1736.

The following work, by an anonymous author, relates to the Pequot War:

———— A true relation of the late Battell fought in *New England*, between the English and the Pequot Salvages. In which were slaine and taken prisoners about 700 of the

Salvages, and those which escaped, had their heads cut off by the Mohocks; With the present state of things there. Small 4to. pp. 23. *London. Thomas Harper.* 1638.

Three editions of this work were printed in the years 1637 and 1638, as is evident from the variation in the title pages and text, all of which are in the library of John Carter Brown. For other accounts of the Pequot War, see *Church's History of King Philip's War; Drake's Book of the Indians; Easton's King Philip, and Indian Wars.*

MASON, GEORGE C. Newport Illustrated, in a series of Pen and Pencil sketches. By the Editor of the Newport Mercury. With wood-cuts.
12mo. pp. 110. *New York. D. Appleton & Co.* 1854.

——— Re-union of the Sons and Daughters of Newport, R. I., August 23, 1859. Printed by order of the committee of arrangements.
12mo. pp. 297. *Newport, R. I. F. A. Pratt & Co.* 1859.

MASONRY. The secrets of. See Mr. Clarke's Discourse on.
For books relative to the excitement against Free Masonry in 1831, and subsequently, see *Anti-masonry*.

MASSASOIT'S DAUGHTER; or, the French Captive. A Romance of Aboriginal New England. By A. J. H. Duganne.
12mo. pp. 115. *New York. Beadle & Company.* 1864.

MATHER INCREASE. The History of the war with the Indians in New England. From June 24, 1675, (when the first Englishman was murdered by the Indians), to August 12, 1676, when *Philip*, alias *Metacomet*, the principal author and beginner of the war was slain. Wherein the grounds, beginning and progress of the war, is summarily expressed. Together with a serious exhortation to the inhabitants of that land.
Small 4to. pp. 51 and 8.
London. Printed for Richard Chiswell. 1676.

MAURAN, EDWARD C. Annual Report of the Adjutant General of the State of Rhode Island, for the year 1861.
8vo. pp. 27. *Providence. Cooke & Danielson.* 1862.

——— The same, for the year 1862.
8vo. pp. 64. *Providence. Alfred Anthony.* 1863.

———— The same for the year 1863.
8vo. pp. 12 and 94   *Providence. Alfred Anthony.* 1864.
Previous to 1861, the Adjutant General's Reports were very brief and were never published in a separate pamphlet. They will be found among the minor reports appended to the schedules.

MENDON ASSOCIATION. The Christian Magazine. By Members of the Mendon Association. Printed for the Proprietors.
8vo.   *Providence. Barnum Field.* 1824.

MAXCY, JONATHAN., A. M. A Funeral Sermon occasioned by the Death of the Rev. James Manning, D. D., President of Rhode Island College. Delivered in the Baptist Meeting House in Providence, July 31, A. D., 1791.
8vo. pp. vi. and 30.   *Providence. Bennett Wheeler.* 1796.

MAXCY, REV. JONATHAN., A. M. President of Rhode Island College. An address to graduates at the Commencement of Rhode Island College, September 3, 1794.
8vo. pp. 8.   *Providence. Bennett Wheeler.* 1794.

———— An oration, delivered before the Providence Association of Mechanics and Manufacturers, April 13, 1795.
8vo. pp. 17.   *Providence. Bennett Wheeler.* 1795.
Appended are "Hymns performed at the anniversary election of the officers of the Association."

———— An oration, delivered in the Baptist Meeting House, in Providence, July 4, 1795, at the celebration of the 19th anniversary of American Independence. Published at the request of the town.
8vo. pp. 20.   *Providence. Carter & Wilkinson.* 1796.

———— A Sermon preached September 4, 1796, at the Dedication of the Meeting House, belonging to the Catholic Baptist Society in Cumberland.
8vo. pp. 22.   *Providence. Carter & Wilkinson.* 1796.

———— A Sermon, delivered in the Baptist Meeting House in Providence, on Lord's Day afternoon, October 14, 1798, occasioned by the death of Welcome Arnold, Esq., one of the Trustees of Rhode Island College, and member of the

General Assembly of this State, who departed this life September 29, 1798, in the 54th year of his age.
8vo. pp. 15. *Providence. Carter & Wilkinson.* 1798.

—— An oration, delivered in the First Congregational Meeting House, in Providence, on the Fourth of July, 1799.
Small 4to. pp. 16. *Providence. John Carter, Jun'r.* 1799.

—— Reasons of the Christian Triumph. A Sermon, delivered in the Baptist Meeting House, in Providence, on Lord's Day afternoon, December 14, 1800, occasioned by the decease of Mrs. Mary, consort of Rev. Stephen Gano.
8vo. pp. *Providence. J. Carter.* [1800.]

Mrs. Gano was the daughter of Joseph Brown, one of the " Four Brothers," so called.

—— A Sermon, preached in the Baptist Meeting House, before the Female Charitable Society, September 21, 1802.
12mo. pp. 13. *Providence. Bennett Wheeler.* 1802.

Appended is an " Ode performed before the Female Charitable Society, September 20, 1802. By Paul Allen, Esq."

—— An address delivered to the graduates of R. I., College, at the Public Commencement, September 1, 1802.
8vo. pp. 14. *Wrentham. Nathaniel Heaton, Jr.* 1802.

—— Literary Remains of the Rev. Jonathan Maxcy, D. D., President of Brown University, with a memoir by Romeo Elton, D. D., Late Professor of the Latin and Greek Languages in Brown University.
8vo. pp. 452. *New York. A. V. Blake.* 1844.

Dr. Maxcy was born in Attleborough, Massachusetts, September 2, 1768, and graduated at Brown University, 1787, with the highest honors of his class. Immediately after, he was appointed tutor in the same institution. Four years later, he was chosen pastor of the First Baptist Church, in Providence. Upon the death of Dr. Manning, in 1792, when but twenty-four years of age, he was appointed President of Brown University. " The splendor of his genius, and his brilliant talents as an orator and divine," says his biographer, Dr. Blake, " had become widely known ; and under his administration the college acquired a reputation for belles lettres and eloquence, inferior to no seminary of learning in the United States." In 1802, he was induced to accept the Presidency of Union College, Schenectady, N. Y., and two years later, the Presidency of Columbia College, in South Carolina. As a scholar, Dr. Maxcy is said to have stood higher than any other President of a college in the United States, in his time. He died at Columbia, S. C., June 4, 1820, aged 52 years; thirty-eight of which he was connected with some college. His writings have been collected and published, together with a memoir of his life, by the Rev. Romeo Elton.

MAXCY, VIRGIL. A Discourse before the Phi Beta Kappa Society of Brown University. Delivered, Sept. 4, 1833. 8vo. pp. 31. *Boston. Lilly, Wait, Coleman & Holden.* 1833.

MESSER, ASA., A. M. President of Rhode Island College. An oration, delivered before the Providence Association of Mechanics and Manufacturers, at their annual election, April 11, 1803.
8vo. pp. 15. *Providence. John Carter.* 1803.

——— An oration, delivered at Providence, in the Baptist Meeting House, on the Fourth of July, 1803.
8vo. pp. 14. *Providence. John Carter.* 1803.

——— An Address, delivered to the Graduates of Rhode Island College, at the Public Commencement, September 7, 1803. Published by request.
8vo. pp. 11. *Providence. N. Heaton, Jun'r.* 1803.

MESSER, ASA., D. D. An address, delivered to the graduates of Brown University, at the Commencement, Sept. 5, 1810.
8vo. pp. 12. *Providence. Rhode Island American.* 1810.

——— A Discourse, delivered before the Warren Association, on Tuesday, September 8, 1812.
8vo. pp. 18. *Providence. D. Hawkins.* 1813.

Dr. Messer was born in Methuen, Massachusetts, May 31, 1769, and graduated at Brown University in 1790. Soon after graduating, he was appointed Tutor, afterwards Professor, and in 1802 President of the college, which office he held until the year 1826. He died on the 11th of October, 1836, in the 68th year of his age.

MEMORIAL of Dana Pond Colburn. First Principal of the R. I., State Normal School; with a sketch of the Institution. From Barnard's American Journal of Education for March, 1862. 8vo. pp. 29.

METCALF, THERON. An address to the Phi Beta Kappa Society of Brown University. Delivered, September 5, 1832.
8vo. pp. 28. *Boston. Lilly, Wait, Coleman & Holden.* 1833.

METHODISTS. See *Vindication*.

MILLS, REV. WILLIAM H. The worship of the Church. A sermon preached at the re-opening of St. Andrew's Church, Providence, R. I., July 6, 1854.
8vo. pp. 18. *Providence. Knowles, Anthony & Co.* 1854.

MINER, AMOS. Life and Confession of, who was tried and convicted before the Hon. Supreme Court of Rhode Island, at their March term, 1833, for the murder of John Smith, Esq., Town Sergeant of Foster, while in the performance of his duty in said Town on the 20th day of June, 1832. And by said Court sentenced to be hanged, July 5, 1833. Taken from his own mouth, and published by his request, and in which he has made a full and important disclosure of facts relating to the suspected murder in Connecticut, of Benjamin Berry, a pedlar, from Portland, Maine.
8vo. pp. 24. *Providence*. 1833.

MINISTRY AT LARGE. Reports of the Ministry at Large, in the city of Providence, presented and read in the First Congregational Church, from the year 1842 to 1862.— Twenty-first Report, read Sunday evening, January 25, 1863. By the Rev. Edwin M. Stone.
8vo. pp. 23. *Providence. Knowles, Anthony & Co.* 1863.

The first report of this excellent Society was made by the Rev. Henry F. Harrington in 1842, and was published in the Providence Journal. Subsequent reports to 1849 were published in the same newspaper. They first appeared in a pamphlet form in 1850, by the Rev. E M. Stone, and have been made and published by him in that form to the present time.

MITCHELL, MARY. A short account of the early part of the life of Mary Mitchell, late of Nantucket, deceased, written by herself. With some selections from some other of her writings, and two testimonies of monthly meetings of Friends on Rhode Island and Nantucket, concerning her.
12mo. pp. 74. *New Bedford. Abm. Shearman, Jr.* 1812.

MORE, CALEB. The War in New England visibly ended. King Philip, that barbarous Indian, now beheaded, and most of his bloody adherents submitted to mercy: the rest

fled far up in the country, which hath given the inhabitants encouragement to prepare for their settlement. Being a true and perfect account brought by Caleb More, master of a vessel newly arrived from Rhode Island, and published for general satisfaction.
Folio. pp. 4.
   London. Printed by J. B., for Francis Smith. 1677.

MORTON, LLOYD., M. D. Report on the physical condition of the Rhode Island Regiments, now in the field, in Virginia, and in the vicinity of Washington, D. C., also on the condition of the Hospitals in and around Washington, made to His Excellency Gov. Sprague, and by him presented to the General Assembly, January, 1863.
8vo. pp. 21.   *Providence. Alfred Anthony.* 1863.

MOUNT HOPE. Letter of the Commissioners of the United Colonies of New England, respecting Mount Hope, August 25, 1679.   *Mass. Hist. Coll.* 1st series, vol. 5.

MULCHAHEY, REV. JAMES. Minister of St. Mary's Church, Portsmouth. Review of the Rev. J. W. Cooke's pamphlet, entitled " a Statement of Facts relating to the ordination at Grace Church," in two letters addressed to the Bishop of the Diocese.
8vo. pp-   *Providence. C. Burnett, Jr.* 1847.

MUMFORD, PAUL M. An oration, delivered in the Second Baptist Meeting House, at Newport, on the 4th of July, 1801, pursuant to a vote of the Town.
12mo. pp. 23.   *Newport. O. Farnsworth.* 1801.

NARRAGANSETT. A Brief account of the several settlements and governments in and about the lands of the Narragansett Bay, in New England. By Francis Brinley.
Mass. Hist. Coll. 1st series, vol. 5.

——— A true and brief account of the just and legal righ which we, his Majesty's subjects, petitioning, have of lands in the Narragansett country, and parts adjacent, in his Majesty's Dominions, in New England. In all humility presented, 1680. (Signed by Richard Wheaton, Elisha Hutchinson, and John Saffin.)
Mass. Hist. Coll. 1st series, vol. 5.

——— Summons of the King's Commissioners to all persons claiming rights in the Narragansett country to appear. 1683.
Ibid.

——— Charles the Second's Commission to Edward Cranfield and others, to examine into the claims and titles to the Narragansett country, dated April 17, 1683. *Ibid.*

——— Report of the United Commissioners to King Charles the Second, on the Narragansett country, October 20, 1683. *Ibid.*

——— James the 2d's Commission, constituting a President and Council for Massachusetts-Bay, Narragansett country, etc. *Ibid.*

——— Order of the President and Council respecting the records of the Narragansett Country, June 17, 1686. *Ibid.*

———— Proceedings of a court held by His Majesty's Commissioners and Justices in the Narragansett Country, June 23, 1683. *Ibid.*

———— A Narrative of that part of New England called the Nanhigansett Country. *Mass. Hist. Coll. 3d series, vol.* 1.

<small>The writer of this tract is unknown. It is preserved by Trumbull in the 19th volume of his manuscripts, but evidently appears a modern copy by a hand not much skilled in orthography.</small>

NARRAGANSETT PATENT. For notice of, see *Aspinwall*.

NEW ENGLAND JUDGED, not by *Man's*, but by the *Spirit* of the Lord; and the summe sealed up of New England's Persecutions. Being a brief Relation of the sufferings of the people called *Quakers* in those parts of *America*, from the beginning of the fifth moneth, 1656, (the time of their first arrival at Boston from England,) to the latter end of the tenth moneth, 1660. Wherein the cruel whippings and scourgings, bonds and imprisonments, beatings and chainings, starvings and huntings, fines and confiscation of estates, burning in the hand and cutting off ears, orders of sale for bondmen and bond women, banishment upon pain of death, and the putting to death of those people, are shortly touched; with a relation of the manner, and some of the other most material proceedings, and a judgement thereupon. In answer to a certain Paper, intituled, A Declaration of the General Court of the Massachusetts, holden at Boston, the 18th October, 1658, apologizing for the same. By George Bishope.
Quarto. pp. 198 and 147.
London. Printed for Robert Wilson in 1661.

<small>This work contains many particulars relative to Mary Dyar, Daniel Gould, and other Rhode Island Quakers. The appendix "Contains writings of those persons which were executed, together with a short relation of the Tryal, Sentence and Execution of William Leddra, written by them in the time of their imprisonment in the *Bloody Town* of BOSTON." Among these is the statement of Mary Dyar, shortly before her execution, and another from William Coddington, of Rhode Island. The second part of this work, printed six years later, bears the following title:</small>

NEW ENGLAND JUDGED. The second part. Being a relation of the cruel and bloudy sufferings of the people called *Quakers*, in the jurisdiction of Massachusetts; beginning with the sufferings of William Ledra, whom they murthered and hung upon a tree at Boston, the 14th of the first moneth, 1660–1, barely for being such a one as is called a Quaker, and coming within their jurisdiction; and ending with the sufferings of Edward Wharton, in the 3d moneth, 1665. And the remarkable judgements of God in the death of *John Endicot*, Governor; *John Norton*, High Priest, and *Humphrey Adderton*, Major General. By George Bishope. Quarto. pp. 147.   *London. Printed in the year* 1667.

NEW ENGLAND'S ENSIGNE; it being the account of Cruelty, the Professor's Pride, and the articles of their faith; signified in characters written in blood, wickedly begun, barbarously continued, and inhumanly finished, (so far as they have gone,) by the present power of a darkness possest in the priests and rulers in *New England*, with the Dutch also, inhabiting the same land; in a bloody and cruel birth, which the husband to the Whore of Babylon hath brought forth, by ravishing and torturing the seed of the Virgin of Israel.

Happy are they who are blest out of the hands of Hypocrites, by whom my Saviour suffered, as it is said in David. Behold, and see, our hands, our sides, and our ears, if we be not the people of Christ Jesus suffers in.

This being an account of the sufferings sustained by us in New England, (with the Dutch,) the most part of it in these two last years, 1657, 1658. With a letter to John Indicot, and John Norton, Governor, and the Chief Priest of Boston, and another to the town of Boston. Also, the several late conditions of a friend upon *Road-Island*, before, in, and after distraction; With some queries unto all sorts of people, who want that which we have, &c. Written at Sea, by us whom the Wicked, in scorn, call *Quakers*, in the second month of the yeer 1659. This being a confirmation of so much as Francis Howgill truly published in his

Book titled, The Popish Inquisition newly erected in New
England, &c.
Quarto. pp. 120.
London. *Printed by T. L., for G. Calvert*. 1659.

Like George Bishope's book, this relates to the sufferings of the Quakers in
New England. Several Rhode Island Quakers are mentioned, among
them, Horred Gardner, of Newport, and Thomas Harris, of Providence,
(p. 72 and 73). At p. 110. is "A true discovery and relation of the dealings of God with Goodworth Horndall, wife of John Horndall, in Newport upon Road-Island, in New England; it being written for the information of the weak, and for the help and comfort of all such as may taste
of the like distempers; and also, a warning to all such as may strive after
salvation, and the knowledge of the things of God," etc.

NELL, WILLIAM C. Services of Colored Americans in the
wars of 1776 and 1812.
8vo. pp. 40.   *Boston. Rob't W. Wallcot.* 1852.

Contains an account of services rendered by the colored people in Rhode Isl-
and.

NEW ENGLAND'S TEARS for her present miseries; or, a late
and true relation of the calamities of New England since
April last past. With an account of the Battel between
the English and Indeans upon Seaconk Plain, and of the
Indians burning and destroying Marlbury, Rehoboth,
Chelmsford, Sudbury and Providence; with the death of
Antononies, the Grand Indian Sachem, and a relation of a
Fortification began by women on Boston Neck. Together
with an elegy on the death of John Winthrop, Esq., late
Governor of Connecticott, and Fellow of the Royal Society.
Written by an inhabitant of Boston, in New England, to
his friend in London. With allowance.
Small 4to. pp.   *London. Printed for N. S.* 1676.

NEWMAN, SYLVANUS CHACE. Rehoboth in the Past. An
Historical oration delivered on the fourth of July, 1860.
Also an account of the proceeding in Seekonk, [the ancient
Rehoboth,] at the celebration of the day completing two
hundred and sixteen years of its history.
8vo. pp. 112.   *Pawtucket. Robert Sherman.* 1860.

———— Dexter Genealogy; being a record of the families

descended from the Rev. Gregory Dexter : with notes and biographical sketches of each parent.
12mo. pp. 108.   *Providence. A. Crawford Greene.* 1859.

——— Genealogy of the READ Family, from 1598 to 1859. Printed on a large sheet.
Providence. A. Crawford Greene. 1859.

——— Numbering of the Inhabitants, together with statistical and other information relative to Woonsocket, R. I.
12mo. pp. 45.   *Woonsocket. S. S. Foss.* 1846.

NEWPORT. A hand book of Newport and Rhode Island. By the author of " Pen and Ink Sketches." [John Ross Dix,] with wood cuts.
12mo. pp. xii. and 170.   *Newport. C. E. Hammily.* 1852.

NEWPORT ILLUSTRATED, in a series of Pen and Pencil sketches. By the editor of the Newport Mercury, [George C. Mason,] with wood cuts.
12mo. pp. 110.   *New York. D. Appleton & Co.* 1854.
See also, *Cahoone, Brooks,* for other books relating to Newport.

NEWPORT ARTILLERY. The Charter and Regulations of the Artillery Company of Newport, R. I., with names of members.
18mo. pp. 24.   *New York.* 1860.

NEWPORT AND FALL RIVER RAILROAD. Argument for the extension of the Old Colony and Fall River Railroad to Newport, before a Committee of the Legislature of Massachusetts. By Hon. Josiah G. Abbott.
8vo. pp. 36.   *Boston. G. C. Rand & Avery.* 1861.

NEWPORT OLD STONE MILL. See *Lecture on Mysterious Knockings,* etc.

NEWPORT FEMALE EVANGELICAL MISCELLANY. No. 1.
8vo. pp. 16.   *Newport.* [1806.]

NEWPORT. Services at the dedication of the School House, erected by the Trustees of the Long Wharf, at Newport, Rhode Island, May 20, 1863. With an appendix.
8vo. pp. 106.   *Newport. Pratt & Messer.* 1863.

This volume contains the addresses made on the occasion by Wm. C. Cozzens, Governor of R. I.; His Honor W. H. Cranston, Mayor of Newport; A. Henry Dumont, Chairman of the Public School Committee; and Henry Rousmaniere, Public School Commissioner.

NEWPORT TAX BOOKS, from 1852 to 1863.
Various publishers.

NEWPORT ASSOCIATION OF MECHANICS AND MANUFACTURERS. The Charter, Constitution and By-laws of, with list of Officers and Committee of Correspondence.
18mo. pp. vi. and 24. *Newport. Henry Barber.* 1792.

—— Catalogue of the Library of.
8vo. pp. 43. *Newport. Cranston & Norman.* 1850.

NEWPORT—CITY DOCUMENTS.

NEWPORT. Address of George H. Calvert, Mayor of the City of Newport; and of reports of committees; comprising the Finance, Overseers of the Poor, Firewards and School Reports for the year 1853–54.
8vo. pp. 61. *Newport. Coggeshall & Pratt.* 1854.

NEWPORT. Addresses of William C. Cozzens, Mayor of the City of Newport; and reports of committees, (same as above,) for the year 1854–55.
8vo. pp. 177. *Newport. Coggeshall & Pratt.* 1855.

NEWPORT. Address of William J. Swinburne, Mayor of the City of Newport, and reports of committees, (same as above) for the year 1855–56.
8vo. pp. 64. *Newport. Coggeshall & Pratt.* 1856.

NEWPORT. Addresses of William J. Swinburne and William H. Cranston, and reports of committees, (same as above,) for the year 1856–57.
8vo. pp. 92. *Newport. Coggeshall & Pratt.* 1857.

NEWPORT. Addresses of William H. Cranston, Mayor of the City of Newport, R. I., and the reports of the various officers and committees of the government of said city, for the year 1857–58.
8vo. pp. *Newport. Fred. A. Pratt & Co.* 1858.

NEWPORT—City Documents.

Newport. Addresses of William H. Cranston, Mayor, etc., and the reports of the various officers and committees of the government of said city for the year 1858-59.
8vo. pp. 239.   *Newport. Fred. A. Pratt & Co.* 1859.

Newport. Addresses of William H. Cranston, Mayor, etc., and the reports of the various officers and committees, etc., 1859-60.
8vo. pp. 190.   *Newport. Hammond, Pratt & Co.* 1860.

Newport. Address of William H. Cranston, Mayor, etc., and the reports of the various officers and committees, etc., 1860-61.
8vo. pp. 182.   *Newport. Hammond, Pratt & Co.* 1861.

Niles, Rev. Samuel. A Summary Historical Narrative of the wars in New England with the French and Indians, in the several parts of the country.
Mass. Hist. Collections, 3d series, Vol. vi.

The author of this work was a clergyman, of Braintree, Mass. He was born at Block Island, in the State of Rhode Island, May 1, 1674, and graduated at Harvard College in 1699. He was settled at Braintree, May 23, 1711, and died May 1, 1762, aged 88 years. The original Ms. of this work was found in a box of papers, bequeathed to the Massachusetts Historical Society by the Rev. Dr. Freeman. He was, besides, the author of several Theological works. President John Adams, in a letter to the Hon. Wm. Tudor, dated Quincy, Sept. 23, 1818, thus speaks of this manuscript and its author:

"Almost sixty years ago, I was an humble acquaintance of this venerable man, then, as I believed, more than four score years of age. He asked me many questions, and informed me, in his own house, that he was endeavoring to recollect and commit to writing a History of Indian Wars in his own time and before it, as far as he could collect information. This History he completed and prepared for the press, but no printer would undertake it, or venture to propose subscription for its publication. * * * I then revered, and still revere, the honest, virtuous, and pious man; and his memorial of facts might be of great value to this country."—*Note of Publishing Com. Mass. Hist. Soc.*, preface to the work.

Niles, John M. Life of Oliver Hazard Perry; with an appendix, comprising Biographical Sketches of Captain James Lawrence, Commodores Decatur, Bainbridge, Porter, and

MacDonough, a view of the United States Navy, and a Biography of General Pike and General Harrison.
12mo. pp. 2d edition. *Hartford.* 1821.

NOYES, THOMAS., A. M. A sermon preached at Barrington, R. I., January 29, 1817, at the installation of the Rev. Luther Wright, over the church and Congregational Society in that Town.
8vo. pp. 32. *Providence. Miller & Hutchens.* 1817.

SLER, ELDER LEMUEL, Pastor. The Form of Sacred words ; or a defence of Literal Interpretation. A Discourse, delivered at the dedication of the Advent Chapel, on Broad Street, in Providence, R. I., December 23, 1857.
12mo. pp. 31.   *Boston. Kneeland Street.* 1858.

OTIS, JAMES. A Vindication of the British Colonies against the aspersions of the Halifax gentleman in his letter to a Rhode Island friend.
8vo. pp. 32.   *Boston. Edes & Gill,* 1765.

——— The rights of the British colonies asserted and proved.
8vo. pp. 120.   *London.* 1765.

" A very zealous defence of the colonies, tending to prove that every man in the British dominions is constitutionally a free man ; and that no part of His Majesty's dominions can constitutionally be taxed without their own consent, and that every part has a right to be represented in the supreme or some subordinate legislature."—*Rich's Bibliotheca Americana.*

THE OBJECTIONS to the taxation of our American Colonies, by the Legislature of Great Britain, briefly considered.
4to. pp.   *London.* 1765.

" On exactly opposite principles to the foregoing of Mr. Otis, being an attempt to prove not only the right of the Legislature of Great Britain to impose taxes on her colonies, but the expediency, and even the necessity of exercising that right in the present conjuncture."—*Rich's Bibliotheca Americana.*

THE GRIEVANCES of the American Colonies candidly examined. By Stephen Hopkins. Printed by author, at Providence, Rhode Island.
8vo. pp. 47.   London. J. Almon. 1765.

This work is noticed under the author's name. It was reprinted in London. It is placed here in connection with the celebrated work of James Otis on the same subject, and of a work published in London taking the opposite ground from that of the great Massachusetts statesman.

OLNEY, CAPT. STEPHEN. Life of, by Mrs. Catherine Williams.
12mo. pp. viii. and 312.   Providence. For the author. 1839.

OSGOOD, REV. SAMUEL., D. D. Two Sermons preached in Westminster Congregational Church, Providence, September 9, 1849, on closing his ministry there.
8vo. pp. 31.   Providence. Joseph Knowles. 1849.

These discourses contain a History of this Church and Society.

———— Sermon at the installation of. See *Peabody*.

PACIFIC CONGREGATIONAL CHURCH, in Providence, R. I. A candid statement of facts, relative to difficulties existing between this Church, and those brethren who withdrew and were formed into a separate church, with the documents which passed between the two parties, on the subject of a mutual council. Drawn up by a committee of said church.
8vo. pp. 23.   *Providence. Barnum Field.* 1823.

PAINE, EMERSON. An oration pronounced before the students of Brown University, at the First Congregational Meeting House, in Providence, July 5, 1813, in commemoration of American Independence.
8vo. pp. 30.   *Providence. H. Mann & Co.* 1813.

PARK. EDWARDS A., D. D. Memoir of the Life and Character of Samuel Hopkins, D. D. Second edition.
8vo. pp. viii. and 264.
  Boston. Doctrinal Tract and Book Society. 1854.

PARSONS, DR. USHER. Biography of Solomon Drowne, M. D. Published in the New York Lancet, and the Rhode Island Literary Journal and Weekly Register of Science and the Arts, for May 10, 1834.

——— An address, delivered before the Providence Association for the promotion of Temperance, May 27, 1831.
8vo. pp. 16. *Providence. Weeden & Knowles.* 1831.

——— Battle of Lake Erie. A Discourse delivered before the Rhode Island Historical Society, on the evening of Monday, February 16th, 1852. By Usher Parsons, M. D. Printed at the request of the Society.
8vo. pp. 36. *Providence. Benjamin T. Albro.* 1853.

Dr. Parsons was a surgeon on board of Commodore Perry's ship at the battle of Lake Erie, which event properly belongs to Rhode Island History, as its Commodore, with many of its officers and men went from Rhode Island, and built and equipped the fleet. A second reason why Dr. Parsons took this subject for his discourse, he says was, "because he could speak of it from personal knowledge," and thereby he adds, "because a very inaccurate and perverted account of it has been written and imposed upon the public by the late J. Fenimore Cooper, Esquire." The pamphlet, therefore, as it will be inferred, presents a particular account of the battle, and a defence of its gallant Commodore.

——— Sketches of Rhode Island Physicians, deceased prior to 1850. Prepared for the Rhode Island Historical Society.
8vo. pp. 64. *Providence. Knowles, Anthony & Co.* 1859.

——— Indian Names of places in Rhode Island; collected for the Rhode Island Historical Society.
8vo. pp. iv. and 32.
  Providence. Knowles, Anthony & Co. 1861.

——— Lecture on Indian Relics. 1862.

PATTEN, REV. WILLIAM., A. M. On the inhumanity of the Slave trade, and the importance of correcting it. A Sermon delivered in the 2d Congregational Church, Newport, R. I., August 12, 1792.
8vo. pp. 14. *Providence. J. Carter.* 1793.

PATTEN, REV. WILLIAM., D. D. A Discourse occasioned by the death of the Rev. President Stiles; delivered in the Second Congregational Church, at Newport.
8vo. pp. 16. *Exeter. Henry Ranlett.* 1795.

——— Reminiscences of the Rev. Samuel Hopkins, D. D., of Newport, R. I.
12mo. pp. *Warren, R. I.* 1795.

———— A discourse, delivered in the 2d Congregational Church, Newport, Dec. 29, 1799, occasioned by the death of Gen. George Washington.
8vo. pp. 19. *Newport. Henry Barber.* 1800.

———— A Discourse delivered in the 2d Congregational Church, Newport, the Sabbath succeeding the interment of Dr. Isaac Senter, who died, Dec. 20th, 1799. Aet. 45.
8vo. pp. 12. *Newport. Henry Barber.* 1800.

———— A Sermon in the 2d Congregational Church, Newport, Nov. 9, 1806, on the death of Miss Abigail Potter.
8vo. pp. 24. *Newport. Mercury Office.* 1807.

———— A Sermon delivered at the request of the African Benevolent Society, in the 2d Congregational Church, Newport, April 12, 1808.
4to. pp. 19. *Newport. Mercury Office.* [1808.]

———— Reminiscences of the late Rev. Samuel Hopkins, D. D., of Newport, R. I., illustrative of his character and doctrines, with incidental subjects; from an intimacy with him of twenty-one years, while pastor of a sister church in said town. By William Patten, D. D.
12mo. pp. xiv. and 157. *Providence. Isaac H. Cady.* 1843.

Dr. Patten's father was the Rev. William Patten, who was first settled as successor of Rev. John Cotton, first minister of Halifax, Mass.; afterwards as minister of the South Congregational Society, Hartford, Conn. His mother was Ruth, daughter of Rev. Eleazer Wheelock, D. D., founder and first President of Dartmouth College, N. H.

Dr. Patten was born in Halifax, Mass., January 10, 1763; graduated at Dartmouth College, 1780. He was settled as successor of President Stiles, over the Second Congregational Society in Newport, May 24, 1786, where he preached forty-eight years. He died in Hartford, Conn., March 9, 1839, aged 76 years. His remains, with those of the Rev. Samuel Hopkins, D. D., pastor of the first Congregational Society in Newport, cotemporaries, warmly attached, and agreeing in doctrines, rest side by side in the Church enclosure in Newport, of these two societies, now merged into "The United Congregational Society." Dr. Patten was a distinguished theologian, meek and lowly in heart, most kind and benevolent. *Sprague's Annals, Allen's Biog. Dictionary.*

His published works in addition to those mentioned, are A Sermon after his ordination, 1786. Christianity the true Theology, against Paine's age of Reason, 1792. Memoirs of Ruth Patten; and two Posthumous publications.

PEABODY, REV. EPHRAIM. The object of the Ministry. A Sermon preached at the installation of the Rev. Samuel Osgood, as pastor of the Westminster Congregational Church, in Providence, Dec. 29, 1841.
8vo. pp. 40.   *Providence. B. Cranston & Co.* 1842.

PEABODY, ANDREW P. The Immutable Right. An oration delivered before the Phi Beta Kappa Society of Brown University, Aug. 31, 1838.
8vo. pp. 25.   *Boston. Crosby, Nichols & Co.* 1838.

PEACE CONVENTION. Report made to the General Assembly of the State of Rhode Island, at their January Session, 1861, by the Commissioners on the part of the State to the Convention of Commissioners from the several States, held at the request of Virginia at Washington, on the 4th day of February, 1861.
8vo. pp. 9.   *Providence. Knowles, Anthony & Co.* 1861.
The Commissioners at this Convention were the Hon. Samuel Ames, Chief Justice of R. I. Lieut. Gov. Samuel G. Arnold, Hon. Wm. W. Hoppin, Alexander Duncan, Esq., and the Hon. George H. Browne.

PEASE, JOHN C., and John M. Niles. A Gazetteer of Connecticut and Rhode Island; with a map of each State.
8vo. pp. 390.   *Hartford. Wm. S. March.* 1819.
This work presents a geographical view of each county, with fuller details of each town in the State, embracing notices of population, business, etc.; together with biographical sketches of eminent men.

PENNY, REV. SAMUEL. Discourse in commemoration of. See *Waterman.*

PEET, REV. EDWARD W. A sermon on the occasion of Public Thanksgiving, July, 1842. See *Constitution.*

PEQUOT WAR. Leift Lion Gardeners. His Relation of the Pequott Warres, 1660.
Mass. Hist. Coll. 3d series. vol. 3.
See also, *Mason's Brief History* of the Pequot war, 8vo. 1736; *Underhill's News from America*. History of the Pequot war; *Vincent's True Relation* of the late Battell between the English and the Pequot Salvages. *Niles, Samuel.*—Summary; Historical Narrative of the wars in New England with the French and Indians. *Drake*; *Mather*; *Indian Wars.*

PEQUOT WAR. The war with the Pequots in 1637. A True relation of the late Battell fought in New England, between the English and the Pequot Salvages: in which was slaine and taken prisoners about 700 of the Salvages, and those which escaped, had their heads cut off by the Mohocks; with the present state of things there.
Small 4to. pp. 23. *London. Printed by M. P., for Nathaniel Butler and John Bellamie.* 1638.

PERRY, OLIVER HAZARD. Documents in relation to the differences which subsisted between the late Commodore O. H. Perry and Captain J. D. Elliott.
8vo. pp. 36. *Washington.* 1821. *Boston.* 1834.

"When the late Commodore Perry was about to sail on the cruise which terminated his valuable life, he requested Commodore Decatur to take charge of the following documents, to keep Capt. Elliott in check during his absence, and if any accident happened to him while on his cruise, that they might be published, as the most effectual means which would then be left, of guarding his character against the baseness and falsehoods of Captain Elliott. The original documents, of which these are copies, had all been transmitted to the Navy Department by Commodore Perry, some time before."—*Extract from the Preface.*'

———— Manifest of the charges preferred to the Navy Department and subsequently to Congress, against Jesse Duncan Elliott, Esq., a Captain in the Navy of the U. S., for unlawful conduct while Commodore of the late Mediterranean Squadron; and a refutation of the recrimination raised by that officer. By Charles Crillon Brown, U. S. Navy.
8vo. pp. 46 and xxiv. [*Washington.*] 1839.

PERRY, O. H. Battle of Lake Erie, with notices of Commodore Elliott's conduct in that engagement. By the Hon. Tristram Burges.
12mo. pp. xv. and 132. *Providence. Brown & Cady.* 1839.

———— The same.
12mo. pp. xv. and 117.
Philadelphia. W. Marshall & Co. 1839.

———— Speech of Com. Jesse Duncan Elliott, U. S. N., delivered in Hagerstown, Md., on the 14th November, 1843.

Published by the committee of arrangements of Washington County, Maryland.
8vo. pp. 55 and appendix 82.
       Philadelphia. C. B. Zieber & Co. 1844.

PERRY, O. H. Battle of Lake Erie. A discourse delivered before the R. I. Historical Society, Feb. 16, 1852. By Usher Parsons.

PERRY, O. H. Captain Heath's address relative to the Battle of Lake Erie, June 5, 1817.
12mo. pp. 24.   [*Washington.*] 1817.

PERRY, O. H. Letter from the Secretary of the Navy, transmitting, in obedience to a resolution of the House of Representatives of the 22d inst., copies of the proceedings of the Court Martial ordered by Com. Isaac Chauncey, on the Mediterranean Station, for the trial of Captain Oliver H. Perry; also, for the trial of Captain John Heath of the Marine Corps.
8vo. pp. 34.   *Washington. E. de Kraft.* 1818.

PERRY, OLIVER H. Memoir of, by James Fenimore Cooper. (In the lives of distinguished naval officers.)
2 vols. 12mo.   *Auburn, N. Y. J. C. Derby.* 1846.

——— Oration, on the occasion of celebrating the fortieth anniversary of the Battle of Lake Erie; delivered on the 10th of September, 1853, in Newport, R. I., by George H. Calvert.
8vo. pp. 40.   *Cambridge. Metcalf & Company.* 1853.

PERRY, OLIVER H. Life of, by Alexander Slidell MacKenzie.

——— Life of, by John M. Niles. See *Niles*.

——— The Heroes of the North, or the Battles of Lake Erie and Champlain. Two Poems. By Benjamin Whitman, Jr., Esq. [With two engravings of Battles.]
8vo. pp. 24.   *Boston.* 1816.

PERRY STATUE. Inauguration of the Perry Statue at Cleveland, (Ohio,) on the tenth of September, 1860; including the addresses and other proceedings, with a sketch of Wil-

liam Walcutt, the Sculptor. Published by direction of the City Council.
8vo. pp. 128. *Cleveland, O. Fairbanks, Benedict & Co.*
A large deputation from Rhode Island, numbering nearly three hundred persons, including Gov. Sprague and other State officers, the Major General of the State, and other military officers, together with the First Light Infantry Company, of Providence, were present at the ceremony referred to.

PETERSON, REV. EDWARD. Facts on Congregational intolerance and ecclesiastical despotism.
8vo. pp. 16. *Providence. B. F. Moore.* 1845.

———— History of Rhode Island.
8vo. pp. 370. *New York. John S. Taylor.* 1853.
This book abounds in errors, and is of no historical value. It is not a continuous history, but is made up of scraps without chronological arrangement.

PHILIP, (KING.) Return of loss in Scituate, in Philip's War.
Mass. Hist. Collections, 1st series, Vol. vi.

———— Answer of Sachem Philip to the letter brought to him from the Governor of New Plymouth. *Ibid.*

———— Anecdote of King Philip's Gun lock.
Ibid. 2d series, vol. iv.

———— A narrative of the causes which led to Philip's Indian Wars of 1675 and 1676. By John Easton, of Rhode Island; with other documents concerning this event in the office of the Secretary of the State of New York. Prepared from the original, with an introduction and notes. By Franklin B. Hough.
4to. pp. xxiii. and 207. *Albany, N. Y. J. Munsell.* 1858.
For other books relating to King Philip's war, see *Church, Drake, Gookin, Mather* and *More*.

PICKERING, REV. DAVID. A discourse delivered at the new Universalist Chapel, Providence, R. I., at its dedication, Dec. 29, 1825.
8vo. pp. 16. *Providence. B. Cranston.* 1825.

———— Sermon delivered at the installation of the Rev. Jacob Frieze, to the Pastoral care of the First Universalist Society, in North Providence, R. I., Dec. 24, 1828.
8vo. pp. 16. *Providence. John S. Greene.* 1829.

PINNEGER, COL. DAVID. Trial of, with the officers of the Kentish Guards, 1808. (See Trial.)

PIPON, JOHN. A discourse delivered at Newport, April 30, 1811, at the installation of Newport Royal Arch Chapter No. 2, of Newport. By John Pipon, Minister of the Gospel, in Taunton, Mass.
8vo. pp. 12.   *Newport. Rousmaniere & Barber.* 1811.

PITMAN, JOHN. Annual Address delivered before the Rhode Island Society for the Encouragement of Domestic Industry, October 21, 1828.
8vo. pp. 28.   *Providence. Carlile & Parmenter.* 1829.

PITMAN, JOHN. A Discourse delivered at Providence, August 5, 1836, in commemoration of the first settlement of Rhode Island and Providence Plantations, being the second centennial anniversary of the settlement of Providence.
8vo. pp. 72.   *Providence. B. Cranston & Co.* 1836.

———— Address to the Alumni Association of Brown University, delivered in Providence, on their first anniversary, September 5, 1843. Published by request.
8vo. pp. 64.   *Providence. B. Cranston & Co.* 1843.
This address contains a history of Brown University.

———— For an address to the General Assembly, see Constitution of 1842, art. *Suffrage*.

THE PLOUGH AND THE SICKLE; or, Rhode Island in the war of the Revolution of 1776.
8vo. pp. 28.   *Providence. B. T. Albro.* 1846.

POINDEXTER. (Mr.) Report from the Select Committee of the U. S. Senate, on the claims of Asher Robbins and Elisha R. Potter to the Rhode Island Senatorship.
8vo. pp. 17.
   Senate Doc. 23d Congress, 1st session, No. 139. 1834.

———— Minority Report of the Select Committee of the U. S. Senate, on the contested seat occupied by the Hon. Asher Robbins. By Silas Wright, Jun'r.
8vo. pp. 67.
   Senate Doc. 23d Congress, 1st session, No. 246. 1834.

POOR AND INSANE. See *Hazard*, (T. R.) Report.

POTTER, ELISHA R. Addresses from the Hon. Richard Jackson, Jun'r, and Elisha R. Potter, Representatives in Congress, from the State of Rhode Island, to their constituents, March 6, 1812.
8vo. pp. 22. [*Washington.* 1812.]

――― Address to the Freemen of the State of Rhode Island, by E. R. Potter, one of their Representatives in the Congress of the United States. (Dated) South Kingstown, R. I., August 11, 1810.
8vo. pp. 23. *Newport. Rousmaniere & Barber.* 1810.

――― An address to the Freemen of Rhode Island. By a Landholder.
8vo. pp. 16. *Providence. Herald Office.* 1831.

――― Report to the United States Senate, on the claims of Elisha R. Potter and Asher Robbins to the Rhode Island Senatorship, 1833. (See *Poindexter's Report.*)

Mr. Potter was born in Rhode Island, November 5th, 1764, and was literally a self-made man. He practiced law with great success until forty years of age, when the fascinations of political life withdrew him from the courts. He was elected to the General Assembly in 1793, of which body he was a distinguished and active member at various times for upwards of forty years, during which period, he was five times elected Speaker of the House. In 1796 and 1797, and again in 1809, he was in the Congress of the United States. Few political men in Rhode Island ever acquired or maintained a more commanding influence. This was mainly the result of his manly powers, of his rare natural endowments, and of his extensive acquaintance with the motives, principles and passions which belong to human nature, and determine the conduct of men. His speeches always produced a powerful effect. Mr. Potter died at his residence in Kingston, Sept. 26, 1835, aged 70 years. The books that follow are by his son, the Hon. Elisha R. Potter.

POTTER, HON. ELISHA R. The Early History of Narragansett; with an appendix of original documents, many of which are now for the first time published.
8vo. pp. xix. and 315.
Providence. Marshall, Brown & Co. 1835.

――― The same. Collections of the Rhode Island Historical Society, vol. 3. 1835

―――― A Brief account of the emissions of Paper Money made by the Colony of Rhode Island.
8vo. pp. 48. *Providence. John E. Brown*. 1837.

―――― Report on the affairs of the Narragansett Indian tribe, with a historical statement and a copy of the Indian Regulations of 1792.
8vo. *Printed in the Schedule for January*. 1859.

―――― Report, with abstract of Public Schools, Books used, etc. *June Schedule*. 1839.

―――― Considerations on the Rhode Island Question. (The adoption of a constitution, and extension of the right of Suffrage.)
8vo. pp. 64. *Boston. Thomas H. Webb & Co.* 1842.

―――― Speech on the memorial of the Democratic members of the Legislature of Rhode Island. Delivered in the House of Representatives, Washington, March 7, 9, and 12, 1844.
8vo. pp. 13. *Washington. Globe Office*. 1844.

―――― Annual Report, January, 1854. (Considerations on the relation of the State to Education, Religious Education, with a full catalogue of books for school libraries, etc.)
8vo. pp. 142. *Providence. Sayles, Miller & Simons*. 1854.

POTTER, HON. ELISHA R. Report to the General Assembly on the subject of religious corporations, and their right to hold property. Presented at January session, A. D. 1834. Printed in the Republican Herald, of January 25, 1834.

―――― Report to the General Assembly on the subject of Abolition petitions, January session, 1840. Printed at length in Olive Leaf, Feb. 12, 1840.

―――― Remarks on some provisions of the School Laws and the duties of officers and bodies corporate under them, with forms adapted to the law. 51 pp. 8vo. 1846.

Published by Hon. Henry Barnard, with his edition of the School Laws, and republished several times since.

—— Commissioner of Public Schools. Annual Report, January, 1850.

—— Commissioner of Public Schools. Annual Report, January 25, 1851. 8vo. pp. 6.

—— Commissioner of Public Schools. Annual Report on the condition and improvement of the Public Schools of Rhode Island, January, 1852. Published by order of the General Assembly.
8vo. pp. 78.   *Providence. Knowles, Anthony & Co.* 1852.

—— Commissioner of Public Schools. Annual Report to the General Assembly, made in 1853.
8vo. pp. 84.   *Providence. Sayles, Miller & Simons.* 1853.

—— Report on the history and character of the Registered State Debt, January, 1847.
12mo. pp. 15.   *Providence.* 1847.

—— An Address delivered before the Rhode Island Historical Society, on the evening of February 19, 1851. Published by the request of the Society.
8vo. pp. 27.   *Providence. G. H. Whitney.* 1851.

—— School Commissioners' Report on Public Schools and Education, October, 1854. (The Bible and Religion in Public Schools.)
8vo. pp. 247.   *Providence. Knowles, Anthony & Co.* 1854.

—— Address delivered at the opening of the State Normal School, at Providence, May 29, 1854, with documents.
8vo. pp. 12.   *Providence. Knowles, Anthony & Co.* 1854.

—— Commissioner of Public Schools. The Rhode Island Educational Magazine.
2 vols. 8vo.   *Providence. Sayles & Miller* 1852–53.

—— Right of a Legislature to grant a perpetual exemption from taxation. A report presented in the Rhode Island Senate, Aug. 26, 1862, recommending the Legislature to amend the Charter of Brown University, by repealing so much thereof, as exempts the professors from taxation.
8vo. pp. 16.   *Providence. Alfred Anthony.* 1862.

―――― Reports and Documents upon Public Schools and Education in the State of Rhode Island; with the school laws; forms of doing business under them; and remarks and advice relating to them.
8vo. pp. 700. *Providence. Knowles & Anthony.* 1855.

POTTER, REV. RAY. Minister of the Gospel, Pawtucket.― Memoirs of the Life and Religious Experience of, written by himself; with a letter to Lorenzo Dow, 1829.
12mo. pp. 283 and 12. *Providence. H. H. Brown.* 1829.

―――― Admonitions from "The Depths of the Earth," or the fall of Ray Potter, in twenty-four letters, written by himself to his brother Nicholas G. Potter.
12mo. pp. 192. *Pawtucket, Mass. R. Sherman.* 1838.

―――― The Poor man's Defence, exhibiting a brief account of the circumstances connected with the difficulties which of late has transpired in the village of Pawtucket, relating to the Meeting House, commonly called the Free Will Baptist Meeting House. Together with the proceedings of the Free Will Baptist Elders' conference towards Elder Ray Potter, with strictures on the same, addressed particularly to Free Will Baptists.
8vo. pp. 48. *Providence. John Miller.* 1823.

POTTER, J. B. M. Oration at Kingston, R. I., July 4, 1843.
8vo. pp. 24. *Boston. T. H. Webb & Co.* 1844.

PRESTON, REV. WILLIAM. Sermon at the installation of. See *Crane.*

PRENTISS, REV. THOMAS, A. M. A Sermon preached at the ordination of the Rev. Henry Wight, to the pastoral care of the Catholic Congregational Society, in Bristol, R. I., January 5, 1785.
8vo. pp. 26. *Providence. Bennett Wheeler.* 1785.

PROVIDENCE ATHENEUM. Charter, Constitution and By-laws of the Providence Atheneum.
8vo. pp. 14. *Providence. Cranston & Hammond.* 1831.

———— Charter, Constitution and By-laws of the Atheneum. Incorporated, January, 1836.
8vo. pp. 16. *Providence. Knowles, Vose & Co.* 1836.

———— The Same.
8vo. pp. 12. *Providence. Knowles, Anthony & Co.* 1852.

———— First Annual Report of the Directors of the Atheneum to the proprietors; submitted, February 27, 1837.
8vo. pp. 30. *Providence. Knowles & Vose.* 1842.

———— Second Annual Report submitted, Monday, September 25, 1837.
8vo. pp. 20. *Providence. Knowles & Vose.* 1842.

———— Reports presented and read at the Third Annual Meeting of the Providence Atheneum, September 24, 1838.
8vo. pp. 24. *Providence. Knowles, Vose & Co.* 1838.

———— Annual Reports from 1838 to 1863, being from the Fourth to the Twenty-eight annual meetings.

———— Catalogue of the Providence Atheneum Library.
8vo. pp. 67. *Providence. William Marshall & Co.* 1833.

———— Catalogue of the Atheneum Library; with an appendix, containing the Library regulations, and a list of the officers and proprietors.
8vo. pp. 116 and iv. *Providence. Knowles, Vose & Co.* 1837.

———— First Supplementary Catalogue of the Atheneum Library; with an appendix, containing the Library regulations, and list of the officers and proprietors.
8vo. pp. 107 and v. *Providence. Knowles & Vose.* 1839.

———— Catalogue of the Library of the Providence Atheneum, to which are prefixed the charter, constitution and by-laws, and an historical sketch of the Institution.
8vo. pp. xxxiv. and 453.
Providence. Knowles, Anthony & Co. 1853.

———— First Supplementary Catalogue of the Providence Atheneum.
8vo. pp. x. and 374.
Providence. Knowles, Anthony & Co. 1861.

PROTESTANT EPISCOPAL CHURCH. Journal of the proceedings of the Annual Convention of the Protestant Episcopal Church in the State of Rhode Island, held in St. Paul's Church, North Kingstown, Thursday, June 12, 1833.
12mo. pp. 35. *Providence. Marshall & Brown.* 1833.

―――― Journal of the proceedings of the Forty-fourth Annual Convention of the Protestant Episcopal Church in the State of Rhode Island, held in Grace Church, Providence, on Tuesday, June 10, and Wednesday, June 11, 1834.
8vo. pp. 34. *Providence. Marshall, Brown & Co.* 1834.

―――― The same. Forty-fifth, held at Zion's Church, Newport, June 10, 1835.

―――― The same. Forty-sixth, held at St. Luke's Church, East Greenwich, June 15, 1836.

―――― The Same. Forty-seventh, held at St. Mark's Church, Warren, June 14, 1837.

―――― The same, to the Seventy-third Annual Convention, held in St. Stephen's Church, Providence, June 9th, and 10th, 1863.
8vo. pp. 56. *Providence. Knowles, Anthony & Co.* 1863.

―――― A Review of the proceedings of the Protestant Episcopal Church of Rhode Island, at their conventions held June 12, and August 15, 1838; also, a review of a circular addressed to the several parishes in the State. (Signed) Washington Van Zandt.
8vo. pp. 24. *Providence. Knowles, Vose & Co.* 1838.

―――― Journals of the Conventions of the Protestant Episcopal Church in the Diocese of Rhode Island, from the year A. D., 1790, to the year A. D., 1832, inclusive.
8vo. pp. 126. *Providence. Printed by order Convention.* 1858.

See also, *Henshaw*.

―――― CLARKE, REV. J. A. A sermon preached before the Rhode Island Clerical Convention in Bristol.
8vo. pp. 32. *Providence. Marshall, Brown & Co.* 1834.

———— The Prosperity of the Church. A Discourse preached in St. Paul's Church, Pawtucket, before the Fiftieth Annual Convention of the Protestant Episcopal Church in Rhode Island, June 9, 1840. By the Rev. Henry Waterman.
8vo. pp. 53.   *Providence. B. Cranston & Co.* 1840.

PROVIDENCE ASSOCIATION OF MECHANICS AND MANUFACTURERS. Charter and By-laws, Rules and Regulations, with list of officers and members.
12mo. pp. 28.   *Providence. Bennett Wheeler.* 1789.
8vo. pp. The same.   *Providence. Bennett Wheeler.* 1798.
8vo. pp. 35. The same.   *Providence. J. Carter.* 1808.
8vo. pp. 24. The same.   *Brown & Danforth.* 1820.
———— The same.   *Cranston & Hammond.* 1826.
———— The same. Revised and corrected.
8vo. pp. 28.   *Walter R. Danforth.* 1827.
———— The same.   *Cranston & Hammond.* 1834.
———— The same.   *A. C. Greene.* 1850.
———— The same.   *Knowles, Anthony & Co.* 1857.
8vo. pp. 28. The same.   *Knowles, Anthony & Co.* 1860.

———— Addresses and Orations before the Providence Association of Mechanics and Manufacturers. For full titles, see the following authors' names.

———— Oration by the Rev. James Wilson, April 14, 1794.
———— Oration by Jonathan Maxcy, A. M., April 13, 1795.
———— Oration by George R. Burrill, A. B., April 11, 1796.
————   do.   do   do.   July 4, 1797.
———— Address by Isaac Greenwood,   July 9, 1798.
———— Lecture by John Howland,   January 14. 1799.
———— Oration by Tristam Burgess, A. M., April 14, 1800.
———— Oration by Asa Messer, A. M.,   April 11, 1803.
———— Address by John Howland, Esq., Sec., April 9, 1810.
———— Oration by John Howland, Esq.,   April 13, 1818.

———— Oration by Walter R. Danforth, Esq., April 8, 1822.
———— Address by John Howland, President, Jan. 10, 1825.
———— The same. Reprinted in 1830.
———— Oration by Josiah Lawton, April 10, 1826.
———— Mechanics' Festival. An account of the Seventy-first Anniversary of the Providence Association of Mechanics and Manufacturers, held in Howard Hall, on Monday evening, Feb. 27, 1860. Together with a sketch of the Early History of the Society, embracing its early proceedings in relation to manufactures, its action in reference to Public Schools, Savings Institutions, Temperance and Reform School, and brief notices of deceased officers. 8vo. pp. 119. *Providence. Knowles, Anthony & Co.* 1860.
The Biographical notices in this work are as follows:
Barzillai Richmond, Charles Keene, Amos Atwell, John Carlile, James Burrill, Bennett Wheeler, William Barton, William Richmond, Gershom Jones, Samuel Thurber, Richard Salisbury, Robert Newell, Sanford Newell, Isaac Greenwood, John Howland, Peter Grinnell, William Taylor, Gabrael Allen, Joseph Balch, Samuel W. Wheeler, Joel Metcalf, Joseph G. Metcalf, Henry Cushing, Thomas R. Holden, Grindall Reynolds, Benjamin Tallman, Levi Hall, John C. Jenckes, Seril Dodge, Saunders Pitman, John Cairns, Caleb Wheaton, Edward Spaulding, Payton Dana, Nehemiah Dodge, Samuel Hamlin, Peter Taylor, Ward Cowing, Jabez Gorham, James Burr, Zephaniah Andrews, John H. Greene, Stephen Wardwell and others.

———— Constitution of the subscribers to the Funeral Fund of the Association of Mechanics and Manufacturers.
12mo. pp. 4. *Providence.* 1825.

———— Catalogue of the Mechanics and Apprentices Library, established by the Providence Association of Mechanics and Manufacturers, in the year 1821.
12mo. pp. 22. *Providence. Cranston & Knowles.* 1830.
———— The same.
12mo. pp. 50. *Providence. M. B. Young.* 1847.

PROVIDENCE.—CITY OF. Books relating to.

PLAN OF CITY GOVERNMENT, reported by the committee, to be considered by the Freemen of Providence, in Town Meeting assembled, on the 1st day of October, 1828. 8vo. pp. 11. *Printed for the use of the Freemen, by order of the Town.*

PROVIDENCE—CITY OF. Books relating to.

CITY CHARTER PROPOSED for the adoption of the Freemen of Providence, at a town meeting, to be holden April 29th, 1829. Published for the use of the Freemen, by order of the town.
8vo. pp. 12. [*Providence.* 1829.]

CITY CHARTER, proposed for adoption of the Freemen of Providence, at a town meeting to be holden, October 22, 1831.
8vo. pp. 16. *Providence. Cranston & Hammond.* 1831.

CHARTER OF THE CITY OF PROVIDENCE, and the act of the General Assembly for organizing the government under the same, passed at October session, 1831. Together with a list of the city officers for the year 1832; also, the Mayor's Address to the City Council, delivered at the organization of the city government, June 4, 1832.
8vo. pp. 36. *Providence. William Marshall, & Co.* 1832.

CHARTER AND ORDINANCES, with the Acts of the General Assembly, relating to the City; published under the supervision of S. W. Bridgham, George Curtis, and Albert G. Greene.
8vo. pp. *Providence.* 1835.

——— Address of Hon. A. C. Barstow to the City Council of Providence, at his inauguration as Mayor, June 7, 1852.
8vo. pp. 12. *Providence.* 1852.

——— Addresses delivered on the 29th day of June, 1857, at the inauguration of Wm. M. Rodman, Mayor of the city of Providence, by the Hon. James Y. Smith, and others.

[PROVIDENCE GRIST MILL.] The Legal opinion of the Hon. William Hunter, on the question of the Town's interest in the Ancient Grist Mill.
8vo. pp. 15. (*Providence.*) *Patriot Office.* 1829.

——— The Legal opinion of Richard W. Greene, Esq., on the question of the Town's interest in the Ancient Grist Mill.
8vo. pp. 14. *Providence H. H. Brown.* 1830.

———— Ancient Documents relative to the Old Grist Mill, with some remarks on the opinions of Messrs. Hunter and Greene, counsel employed by the Town to examine the same. [By Benjamin Cowell.]
8vo. pp.   (*Providence.*) *Herald Office* 1832.

PROVIDENCE AID SOCIETY. Manual of. Adopted Nov. 1855.
12mo. pp.   *Providence. Knowles, Anthony & Co.* 1855.

———— Annual Reports of, 1 to 8 ; from October, 1856, to October, 1863.
8vo. pp.   *Providence. Knowles, Anthony & Co.* 1856–62.

PROVIDENCE ANTI-SLAVERY SOCIETY. The Report and proceedings of the first annual meeting of. With a brief exposition of the principles and purposes of the Abolitionists.
8vo. pp. 16.   *Providence. H. H. Brown.* 1833.

———— An appeal to the professors of Christianity in the Southern States and elsewhere, on the subject of Slavery; by the representatives of the Yearly Meeting of Friends for New England.
8vo. pp. 24.   *Providence. Knowles & Vose.* 1842.

PROVIDENCE ASSOCIATION OF THE FRIENDS OF MORAL REFORM. Address of the Executive Committee, presented at their annual meeting, held in the vestry of Richmond Street Church, Nov. 18, 1833.
12mo. pp. 12.   *Providence S. R. Weeden.* 1834.

———— The same.   Presented December 31, 1834.
12mo. pp. 23.   *Providence. Weeden & Cory.* 1835.

PROVIDENCE ASSOCIATION FOR THE BENEFIT OF COLORED ORPHANS. Annual Reports of, from May, 1841 to 1862. 1 to 22. 12mo.

PROVIDENCE ASSOCIATION FOR FRIENDLESS FEMALES. Annual Reports of, from 1852 to 1863. 12mo.

PROVIDENCE AUXILIARY UNITARIAN ASSOCIATION. First and Second series. Annual Reports of. April, 1832-33.
12mo.   *Providence. Thomas Doyle.* 1832-33.

PROVIDENCE AUXILIARY BIBLE SOCIETY. The First Annual Report of, with an appendix.
8vo. pp. 24. *Providence. Miller & Hutchens.* 1816.

PROVIDENCE YOUNG MEN'S BIBLE SOCIETY. Annual Report of, from 1828 to 18—

PROVIDENCE CHILDREN'S FRIEND SOCIETY. Annual Reports of, from October 5, 1836, to October, 1863; being 1 to 28. 12mo. and octavo. *Providence. Various years.*

―――― Purity and Charity. A discourse in behalf of the Children's Friend Society; delivered in the First Baptist Church, Providence, October 7, 1845. By Edward B. Hall, Pastor of the First Congregational Church.
8vo. pp. 16. *Providence. Charles Burnett, Jr.* 1845.

THE PROVIDENCE DIRECTORY; containing names of the inhabitants, their occupations, places of business, and dwelling houses, with lists of streets, lanes, wharves, banks, insurance offices and other public institutions, from 1824 to 1863.

From 1824, this directory was published every two years, to the year 1850, since which time it has appeared annually. Hugh H. Brown was the publisher to the year 1859 inclusive. Its form was a duodecimo, until 1860, when it was issued in octavo, under the following title, "The Providence Directory, containing a general directory of its citizens, business directory, and city record, and a variety of useful information."

PROVIDENCE DOMESTIC MISSIONARY SOCIETY. An address delivered at the First Baptist Church, in Providence, January 21, 1833, before the members of the City Mission, and of the Female Dom. Miss. Society. By the missionary of the latter Society.
8vo. pp. 17. *Providence. H. H. Brown.* 1833.

―――― Annual Report of, presented by William Douglas, at the Beneficent Congregational Meeting House, April 18, 1843.
8vo. pp. 22. *Providence. H. H. Brown.* 1843.

PROVIDENCE EMPLOYMENT SOCIETY. Annual Reports of, from May 8, 1838 to 1862. 1 to 25. 12mo.

PROVIDENCE EVANGELICAL SEAMEN'S FRIEND SOCIETY. Annual Reports of, from 1843 to 1863. 1 to 19. 12mo.

PROVIDENCE FEMALE SOCIETY. The constitution of, for the relief of indigent women and children.
8vo. pp. 12.   Providence. John Carter, Jr. 1801.

────── A sermon preached in the Baptist Meeting House in Providence, before the Female Charitable Society, September 21, 1802. By Jonathan Maxcy, D. D., President of Union College, Schenectady.
12mo. pp. 13.   Providence. B. Wheeler. 1802.

────── A discourse delivered in Providence, September 6, 1804, [before the same.] By Theodore Dehon, A. M., Rector of Trinity Church, Newport.
8vo. pp. 20.   Providence. Heaton & Williams. 1804.

PROVIDENCE FEMALE TRACT SOCIETY. Annual Reports of from 1816 to 1820. Numbers 1 to 5. 8vo.

PROVIDENCE FEMALE BENEVOLENT SOCIETY. Report and proposal from a committee of, to the public, on the subject of Female Wages.
12mo. pp. 24.   Providence. 1837.

PROVIDENCE INFANT SCHOOL SOCIETY. Report and constitution of, 1834.
8vo. pp. 8.   Providence. H. H. Brown. 1834.

PROVIDENCE LIBRARY COMPANY. Catalogue of all the books belonging to the Providence Library.
4to. pp. 24.   Providence. Waterman & Russell. 1768.
The volume also contains " Rules for governing the proprietors of, and instructions for rendering useful the books belonging to the Providence Library." The cost in sterling of each book is given.

────── Charter and By-laws of the Providence Library Company, and a catalogue of the books of the Library.
12mo. pp. 46.   Providence. Miller & Hutchens. 1818.

PROVIDENCE LADIES' BETHEL ASSOCIATION. Report of, 1841.
12mo. pp. 12.   Providence. H. H. Brown. 1841.

PROVIDENCE REFORM SCHOOL. Annual Report of, presented to the City Council of the City of Providence, from December, 1851, to December, 1863.
8vo. *Providence. Knowles, Anthony & Co.* 1852-63.

PROVIDENCE RIOTS. History of, from September 21. to September 24, 1831.
8vo. pp. 20. *Providence. H. H. Brown.* 1831.
See also, *Hardscrabble.*

PROVIDENCE SOCIETY FOR THE ENCOURAGEMENT OF FAITHFUL DOMESTIC SERVANTS. First Annual Report of, read at the annual meeting, Jan. 2, 1832.
8vo. pp. 16. *Providence. H. H. Brown.* 1832.

PROVIDENCE YOUNG MEN'S CHRISTIAN UNION. Organized, April 12, 1853.
12mo. pp. 12. *Providence. Sayles, Miller & Simons.* 1853.

—— Annual Reports of, presented to the corporation, from 1853 to 1863.

PROVIDENCE YOUNG MEN'S CHRISTIAN ASSOCIATION. Organized, September, 1853. 8vo.
12mo. pp. 16. *Providence. A. Crawford Greene.* 1854.

—— Dedication of the rooms of, Monday evening, January 30, 1854.
8vo. pp. 29. *Providence. Thompson & Crosby.* 1854.

QUAKERS. The Christian Faith of the People of God, called in Scorn, Quakers in *Rhode Island*, (who are in Unity with all the faithful Brethren of the same profession in all parts of the world,) *Vindicated* from the calumnies of *Christian Lodowick*, that formerly was of that Profession, but is lately fallen therefrom. As also, from the base Forgeries, and wicked Slanders of *Cotton Mather*, called a Minister at Boston, who hath greatly commended the said *Christian Lodowick*, and approved his false charges against us, and hath added thereunto many gross, impudent and vile calumnies against us and our brethren, in his late address, so called, in *New England*, the which in due time may receive a more full answer, to discover his Ignorance, Prejudice and Perversion against our friends in general and G. K. in particular, whom he hath most unworthily abused, etc., etc.

Small 4to. pp. 16.   *Philadelphia. Printed and sold by William Bradford.*   1692.

This tract is signed by Edward Thurston, Henry Bull, Anne Bull, Thomas Cornwall, Thomas Roadman, George Keith, Ebenezer Slocum, Joseph Nicholson, Daniel Gould, Jacob Mott, Walter Clark, Rob. Hutchins and John Easton. Most of these are Rhode Island People.

Following the above text is a collection of " Testimonies collected out of the writings of our ancient Friends, giving some account of their Faith and Belief." Faithfully collected and recommended for perusal, by *William Bradford*.

For notices of the Quakers, see *Friends' Yearly Meeting; Besse's History of the Quakers; Lowell's History of the Quakers; Burnyeatt; Fox; New England Judged, by Bishope; New England's Enigne; Edmundston.*

There was published in London a tract bearing the following title, "An examination of the Grounds or Causes, which are said to induce the Court of Boston, in New England, to make that order or law of Banishment upon pain of death against the Quakers; as also, of the grounds and considerations by them produced to manifest the warrantableness and justness both of their making and executing the same, which they now stand deeply engaged to defend, having already thereupon put two of them to death," etc. By Isaac Penington, the Younger. 4to. pp. 99. London. L. Lloyd 1660.

A number of books and tracts appeared at this time for, and against the Quakers. The controversy was carried on with the greatest violence; indeed, one can hardly believe that a religious sect of such exceeding amiability and gentleness as the Friends of our day, would have entered the arena of dispute with so much bitterness and invective as characterized the productions of their ancestors in the 17th century. Yet, they were fully justified for the severity of their remarks in self-defence, when we consider the cruelties and barbarous treatment which they were forced to undergo by the bigoted Puritans of Massachusetts. We have not space to give the titles of the books referred to, the quaintness of which is most curious to the Bibliographer. One of these against the Quakers is called "The Snake in the Grass; or, Satan transferred into an Angel of Light, discovering the deep and unsuspected subtilty which is couched under the pretended simplicity of many of the principal leaders of those people called *Quakers*." 8vo. pp. 44 and 370. London. 1698. To this, followed a reply, called "a Switch for the Snake, wherein is shown that author's injustice and falsehood, both in quotation and story, are discovered and obviated, and the truth doctrinally delivered by us stated and maintained, in opposition to his misrepresentation and perversion." By Joseph Wyeth. 8vo. London. 1699.

In the Library of the Friends' Boarding School, Providence, is a copy of the "Snake in the Grass," with the following note in the handwriting of the late venerable Moses Brown: "1831, 4th mo., 11th. Bought this book of Wm. R. Staples, as a wicked curiosity, having read several answers, had a mind to read the corruption of those times—Said to have been by John Lesley, a Scotch Churchman."

QUINCY, JOSIAH. The Memory of the late James Grahame, the Historian of the United States, vindicated from the charges of "Detraction" and "Calumny," preferred against him by Mr. George Bancroft, and the conduct of Mr. Bancroft towards that historian stated and exposed. 8vo. pp. 59. Boston. *Crosby & Nichols.* 1846.

This pamphlet relates almost exclusively to John Clarke, and his connexion with the first planting of the Colony of Rhode Island.

AILROADS. Report of the Board of Directors of Internal Improvements of the State of Massachusetts, on the practicability and expediency of a Railroad from Boston to the Hudson river, and from Boston to Providence, submitted to the General Court, January 16, 1829. To which are annexed the reports of the engineers, containing the results of the surveys.
8vo. pp. 76 and 119. Maps and plans.
Boston. Boston Daily Advertiser. 1829.

———— NEW YORK, PROVIDENCE AND BOSTON RAILROAD. Some remarks shewing the advantages of the proposed railroad from Providence to Stonington, with the acts of incorporation.
8vo. pp. 14, 12 and 9. Map. Providence. 1833.

———— Acts of the Legislatures of Rhode Island and Connecticut, relating to the New York, Providence and Boston Railroad Company, and the New York and Stonington Railroad Company.
8vo. pp.39. With map.
New York. James Van Worden. 1837.

———— BOSTON AND PROVIDENCE RAILROAD CORPORATION. Annual Reports of the Board of Directors of, from 18—

RAILROADS—Books relating to.

PROVIDENCE AND WORCESTER RAILROAD. Facts and Estimates relative to the business on the route of the contemplated railroad.
8vo. pp. 30. *Providence. Knowles & Vose.* 1844.

———— Annual Reports of the Directors of, to the stockholders, from the year 1846, to 1863.
These reports are printed annually.

———— Considerations for stockholders of the Providence and Worcester Railroad Co.
8vo. pp. 12. *Woonsocket. S. S. Foss.* 1861.

———— Further Considerations for the stockholders of the Providence and Worcester Railroad Co.
8vo. pp. 27. *Providence. Alfred Anthony.* 1863.

PROVIDENCE AND PLAINFIELD RAILROAD. Report on the Surveys of. By James Laurie.
8vo. pp. 31. *Providence. Joseph Knowles.* 1848.

PROVIDENCE, HARTFORD AND FISHKILL RAILROAD. Report on surveys for the extension of, from Waterbury to Fishkill.
8vo. pp. 62. With maps.
Hartford. Case, Tiffany & Co. 1852.

———— Annual reports of the Providence, Hartford and Fishkill Railroad Co., to the stockholders, from the year 1850, to 1863.
These reports were printed annually.

PROVIDENCE AND BRISTOL RAILROAD. Report of the committee appointed by the citizens of Providence, Warren and Bristol.
8vo. pp. 16. *Providence. Knowles, Anthony & Co.* 1852.

SEEKONK RAILROAD. Reports on the petition of Tristam Burges and others, for a branch railroad in Seekonk, with a Bill. 8vo. pp. 47 and 49.
[*Com. of Massachusetts Document.* 1836.]

———— Substance of argument of respondent's counsel on the

application of the Seekonk Branch Railroad Company to
the committee of the Legislature [of Massachusetts,] to
run locomotive engines on the Providence and Worcester
Railroad, and through the Worcester merchandize depot.
8vo. pp. 46. *Boston. John H. Eastburn.* 1838.

——— Report and Bill on the petition of the Seekonk
Branch Railroad Company.
8vo. pp. 64. *Mass. Senate Doc. No.* 98. 1838.

RAMUSIO, (G. B.) Navigationi et Viaggi raccolto da Ramusio,
et con molti vaghi discorso, da lui in molti luoghi dichiarato,
et illustrato.
3 vols. folio. *Venetia.* 1554-59-56.

The third volume of this valuable collection relates almost entirely to America,
containing translations into the Italian, of most of the works which had
been previously published in Spanish, French and Latin on the subject,
and some from manuscript works which had never been published.

"Collection precieuse, elle est estime par les savants, et regardee encore
aujourd hui parles Geographes, comme un des recueils les plus impor-
tants."—*Camus.*

The reference to Rhode Island in this collection is in the narrative of
the voyage of Verrazzano to the coast of North America, in the year 1524,
when he entered Newport Harbor, and traversed Narragansett Bay. His
ship remained about two weeks in the bay. He is therefore the earliest
European who visited our waters, and his account of the Indian tribes at
that day is very interesting. For translations of the voyage, see Hakluyt,
and New York Historical Soc. Collections, Vols.

RANDALL, DEXTER. Democracy vindicated, and Dorrism unveiled.
8vo. pp. 100. *Providence. H. H. Brown.* 1846.

RANDOLPH, EDWARD. Instructions from the Commissioners to
Edward Randolph, Esq., Collector, Surveyor and Search-
er of his Majesty's Customs in New England, July 9,
1678. *Mass. Hist. Coll.* 3d *series, vol.* VII.

Randolph made himself particularly obnoxious to Rhode Island as well as to
Massachusetts, from powers assumed under subsequent instructions. He
let no opportunity escape of demonstrating his resolution to have his instructions executed to the very letter. "The authorities of Massachusetts
were far from wishing him success in carrying his purpose into all the
effect which he desired and sought. They looked on the instructions as
trenching too much on their Charter privileges." *Note. Mass. Hist. Coll.
Ibid.* Randolph, some years after, sent a petition to James the Second,

accompanied by serious charges against Rhode Island, (see Colonial Records, vol. 3, p. 175,) asking for writs of *quo-warranto* against Connecticut and Rhode Island, which were granted accordingly. See also, address from the Governor and Company of Rhode Island, in relation to the quo-warranto. Ibid. p. 193.

READ. Genealogy of the Read Family, from 1598, to 1859. Compiled by S. C. Newman. Printed on a very large sheet. *Providence. A. Crawford Greene.* 1859.

REASONS why the Hon. Elisha R. Potter should not be a Senator in Congress. By one of the People.
8vo. pp. 12. [1834.]

REDWOOD, LIBRARY. The Laws of the Redwood Library Company, and a Catalogue of the Books bought in London, by John Thomlinson, Esq., with the Five Hundred Pounds Sterling, given by Abraham Redwood, Esq., to the Company of the Redwood Library. Also a list of Books given by several gentlemen.
8vo. pp. 28. *Newport. Samuel Hall.* 1664.
The Preface to this Catalogue was written by Rev. Ezra Stiles.

—— Charter of the Redwood Library Company, granted, 1747. Newport, 1816, and Catalogue of the Books belonging to the Redwood Library Co.
8vo. pp. 39. *Newport. Rousmaniere & Barber.* 1816.

—— Laws and Regulations of the Redwood Library Company, as revised and adopted, September 26, 1810.
8vo. pp. 25. *Newport. Rousmaniere & Barber.* 1816.

—— Appendix to the Catalogue of Books belonging to the Redwood Library Company, Newport, R. I., September, 1829.
8vo. pp. 14. *Newport. W. & J. H. Barber.* 1829.

—— A catalogue of the books belonging to the company of the Redwood Library and Atheneum, in Newport, R. I., to which is prefixed a short account of the institution, with the charter, laws and regulations.
8vo. pp. xix. and 95. *Providence. Knowles & Vose.* 1843.

——— A catalogue of the Redwood Library and Atheneum, in Newport, R. I., together with a supplement, addenda, and index of subjects and titles, shewing all the books belonging to the company on the first of June, 1860. To which is prefixed a short account of the Institution; with the Charter, Laws and Regulations.
8vo. pp. LIII. and 383.   *Boston. John Wilson & Sons.* 1860.

——— Annual Report of the Directors of the Redwood Library and Atheneum, to the proprietors. Submitted, Wednesday, September 26, 1860.
8vo. pp. 23.   *Boston. John Wilson & Sons.* 1860.

——— An Historical Sketch of the Redwood Library and Atheneum, in Newport, R. I., from its origin, in 1747, to 1860. By David King, M. D.
8vo. pp. 53.   *Boston. John Wilson & Sons.* 1860.
Contains a list of officers, members, donors, and catalogue of pictures and busts.

——— Annual Report. September 25, 1861.
8vo. pp. 20.   *Boston. John Wilson & Sons.* 1861.

——— Annual Report. Submitted, September 24, 1862.
8vo. pp. 61.   *Newport. James Atkinson.* 1862.

REFORM SCHOOL, Providence. Report on the subject of a House of Reformation, made to the City Council of Providence, February 14, 1848.
8vo. pp. 15.   *Providence. Joseph Knowles.* 1848.

——— Annual Reports of, presented to the City Council of the City of Providence, from December, 1851, to December 31, 1863.
8vo.   *Providence. Knowles, Anthony & Co.* 1852-62.

REGISTERED STATE DEBT. For publications relating to, see *State Debt of Rhode Island.*

REGISTRATION REPORTS. First Report to the General Assembly of Rhode Island, relative to the Registry and Returns of Births, Marriages and Deaths, in the State. For the

year ending May 31st, 1853. Prepared under the direction of Asa Potter, Secretary of State. By Thomas H. Webb.
8vo. pp. vi. and 188.
Providence. Sayles, Miller & Simons. 1854.

———— Second Report. From June 1, 1853, to December 31, 1854. Prepared under the direction of John R. Bartlett, Secretary of State. By Charles W. Parsons, M. D.
8vo. pp. vii. 80 and 84.
Providence. A. Crawford Greene & Brother. 1856.

———— Third Report, for the year ending December 31, 1855. Prepared under the direction of John R. Bartlett, Secretary of State. By Charles W. Parsons, M. D.
8vo. pp. vii. and 83.
Providence. A. Crawford Greene & Bro. 1857.

———— Fourth Report, for the year ending December 31, 1856. Prepared under the direction of John R. Bartlett, Secretary of State. By Charles W. Parsons, M. D.
8vo. pp. vii. and 84.
Providence. Knowles, Anthony & Co. 1857.

———— Fifth Report, for the year ending December 31, 1857. By Charles W. Parsons, M. D.
8vo. pp. vii. and 96.
Providence. Knowles, Anthony & Co. 1858.

———— Sixth Report, for the year ending December 31, 1858. Prepared under the direction of John R. Bartlett, Secretary of State. By Charles W. Parsons, M. D.
8vo. pp. vii. and 96. *Providence. Knowles, Anthony & Co.* 1859.

———— Seventh Report, for the year ending December 31, 1859. Prepared under the direction of John R. Bartlett, Secretary of State. By Edward A. Crane, M. D.
8vo. pp. iv. and 96. *Providence. A. Crawford Greene.* 1860.

———— Eighth Report, for the year ending December 31, 1860. Prepared under the direction of John R. Bartlett, Secretary of State. By Edward A. Crane, M. D.
8vo. pp. vii. and 93. *Providence. Cooke & Danielson.* 1862.

────── Ninth Report, for the year ending December 31, 1861. Prepared under the direction of John R. Bartlett, Secretary of State. By Charles W. Parsons, M. D.
8vo. pp. vii. and 75. *Providence.. Alfred Anthony.* 1862.

────── Tenth Report, for the year ending December 31, 1862. Prepared under the direction of John R. Bartlett, Secretary of State. By Edwin M. Snow, M. D.
8vo. pp. vii. and 80. *Providence. Alfred Anthony.* 1864.

REGISTRATION REPORTS, CITY OF PROVIDENCE, by Edwin M. Snow, M. D., City Registrar.

CITY REGISTRAR'S REPORT on the Births, Marriages and Deaths, in the City of Providence, during the year ending December 31, 1855; with an Appendix, showing the mortality of Providence, during fifteen years, from 1840, to 1854 inclusive.

Providence. Knowles, Anthony & Co. 1856.

SECOND ANNUAL REPORT on the Births, Marriages, and Deaths, in the City of Providence, for the year ending December 31, 1856. By Edwin M. Snow, M. D., City Registrar. *Providence.* 1857.

────── Third Annual Report, &c., for 1857.
Providence. Knowles, Anthony & Co. 1858.

────── Fourth Annual Report, &c., for 1858.
Providence. Knowles, Anthony & Co. 1859.

────── Fifth Annual Report, &c., for 1859.
Providence. Knowles, Anthony & Co. 1860.

────── Sixth Annual Report, &c., for the year 1860, with a recapitulation of the Vital Statistics of the City, for the last five years, and an abstract of the census of Providence in 1860; by Edwin M. Snow, M. D., Sup't of Health and City Registrar. *Providence. Printed.* 1861.

────── Seventh Annual Report, &c., for 1861.
Printed. 1862.

────── Eighth Annual Report, &c., for 1862.
Printed. 1863.

THE REMEMBRANCER; or Impartial Repository of Public Events.
19 vols. 8vo. *London. Almon.* 1775-84.

The publication of this important collection of papers and documents, to which the American War gave rise, and to which it wholly relates, was commenced in the year 1775, and was continued down to the year 1784; making seventeen volumes. "Every authentic paper relative to the war, as also, with England and Spain, whether published in England or America, by the British Ministry, or the American Congress, are all carefully inserted in this work. The letters of the several commanding officers, addresses, resolutions of the various committees, conventions, etc. To these have been prefixed, at the desire of many persons, a collection of authentic papers on the various subjects of dispute, from the resolutions which gave rise to the Stamp Act in 1764, to the battle of Lexington in 1775. This volume should accompany the Remembrancer, and is called, "Prior Documents, or a Collection of interesting Authentic Papers, relative to the dispute between Great Britain and America; shewing the causes and progress of that misunderstanding, from 1764 to 1775." *Almon's Catalogue*, 1786. Mr. Almon was assisted by Governor Pownall, in the compilation of this work.

THE RESULT of an ex-parte council, convened in Providence, June 19, 1832, by letters missive from aggrieved members of the Richmond Street Church; with a brief history of the origin and progess of the difficulties which led to the convocation of said conucil.
8vo. pp. 24. *Providence. H. H. Brown.* 1832.

RHODE ISLAND ART ASSOCIATION. Circular and Constitution of, with officers for 1854.
8vo. pp. 29. *Providence. Knowles, Anthony & Co.* 1854.

——— School of Design, proposed to be established by.
8vo. pp. 13. *Providence.* 1858.

——— Catalogue of the First Exhibition of Paintings, Statuary and other works of art, at Westminster Hall, Providence, September, 1854.
8vo. pp. 16. *Providence. Knowles, Anthony & Co.* 1854.

RHODE ISLAND BOOK. Selections in Prose and Verse, from the Writings of Rhode Island Citizens. By Anne C. Lynch. (1st and 2d editions.)
12mo. pp. v. and 351.
Providence. Henry C. Whitaker. 1845.

THE RHODE ISLAND BAPTIST. By Allen Brown, Preacher of the Gospel.
Vol. 1. 8vo. *Providence. John Miller.* 1823.
The second volume of this periodical was never finished.

RHODE ISLAND BRIGADE. Report of Tristam Burges, of the select committee of the House of Representatives, of the U. S., to which was referred the Memorial of the Officers and Soldiers of the Rhode Island Brigade, their heirs and representatives, February 25, 1835. (23d Congress, 2d session. Report No. 128.)
8vo. pp. 40. (*Washington.*)

———— Memorial of the Officers and Soldiers of the Rhode Island Brigade.
8vo. pp. 5. (22d *Cong.* 1st *Sess. Doc. No.* 77.) Jan. 9, 1832.
This memorial presents a history of the claims of the Brigade for depreciation of pay for Revolutionary services, sometimes called the "Crary Balances."

———— Memorial to Congress from Archibald C. Crary, of Utica, New York, relative to the Rhode Island Brigade. Presented at the 2d Session of the 37th Congress, 1862-63.
Folio. pp. 5. *No Place or date.*
This memorial makes a claim for depreciation of the pay of Colonel Archibald Crary, father of the memorialist, who was Colonel of a regiment in the Rhode Island Brigade. The General Assembly of Rhode Island passed a Resolution at their January session, 1863, instructing their Senators and Representatives in Congress to lend their aid in obtaining relief for Mr. Crary, and for the claims of the regiment under him.

RHODE ISLAND HOMŒPATHIC SOCIETY. An address delivered before, by A. Howard Okie, M. D., President of the Society.
8vo. pp. 28. *Providence. George H. Whitney.*

———— An address delivered before, November 3, 1852, by Henry C. Preston, M. D., President of the Society.
8vo. pp. 44. *Providence. Sayles & Miller.* 1852.

RHODE ISLAND LITERARY REPOSITORY. A Monthly Magazine, containing Biographical Sketches, Reviews, Dissertations, Poetry, Anecdotes, etc. From April, 1814, to April, 1815.
8vo. pp. 672. *Providence. Robinson & Howland.*

Conducted by Isaac Bailey. Contains biographies of Captain W. H. Allen; the Rev. Enos Hitchcock; Dr. Benjamin West, and the Rev. Dr. Manning, with portraits.

RHODE ISLAND MEDICAL SOCIETY. A Discourse read before, on their anniversary, September, 1813. By Henry E. Turner.
8vo. pp. 9.   *Newport. Mercury Office.* 1813.

RHODE ISLAND PENSION ROLL. Shewing the names, rank, &c., of the Invalid Pensioners in Rhode Island. Congressional Document. (No. 514, 23d Cong. 2d Sess. House of Representatives.) 1835.
8vo. pp. 46.   *Washington.* 1835.

RHODE ISLAND PEACE SOCIETY. Annual Reports of. Published at various times from the year 1819, in which year it was established.

THE RHODE ISLAND REGISTER for the year 1795. 12mo. pp. 12. Annexed to the New England Almanac, by Elijah Fenton.

RHODE ISLAND REGISTER, and United States Calendar, for the year 1820.
12mo. pp. 108.   *Providence. Hugh H. Brown.* 1820.

This series was continued annually to the year 1832 inclusive, and issued from the same press.

RHODE ISLAND REGISTER, for the year 1853; containing a Business Directory of the State, with a variety of useful information. By George Adams.
12mo. pp. 180. vol. 1.
   Providence. Gladding & Brother. 1853.
—— The same. Vol. 2. pp. 184.
   Providence. Gladding & Brother. 1856.

THE RHODE ISLAND SCHOOLMASTER. A monthly magazine, established and edited by Robert Allyn, School Commissioner, in 1856; edited by William A. Mowry in 1858-59– and 60; by a Board of Editors in 1861; and by a similar Board in 1862-63, the principal managers now being Messrs. J. J. Ladd and N. W. De Munn.

An ably edited work devoted to the cause of education, literature, science, moral culture, languages, history, etc., etc.

RHODE ISLAND SUNDAY SCHOOL UNION. Annual Reports
of, read at their annual meetings, from 1826, to 18—

RHODE ISLAND SOCIETY FOR THE ENCOURAGEMENT OF DO-
MESTIC INDUSTRY. Transactions of, in the year 1850, with
an appendix.
8vo. pp. 124.   *Providence. Joseph Knowles.* 1851.

——— The same. Continued annually to the year 1862.

——— The following addresses were delivered before the
Society:

——— Tristam Burges.   Delivered   October 17, 1821.
——— Asher Robbins.   do.   do.   16, 1822.
——— Solomon Drown, M. D.   do.   do.   15, 1823.
——— William Hunter.   do.   do.   20, 1824.
——— William E. Richmond.   do.   do.   19, 1825.
——— John Pitman.   do.   do.   21, 1828.
——— Francis Wayland.   do.   do.   6, 1841.
——— Francis Wayland.   do.   September 12, 1851.
——— George R. Russell,   do.   do.   17, 1852.

THE RHODE ISLAND UNION CONFERENCE MAGAZINE. Edited by the Rev. Ray Potter, of Pawtucket.
8vo.   *Providence H. H. Brown.* 1829.

RHODES, N. C. An address before the Society of Moral Phil-
anthropists of the City of Providence, Jan. 29, 1834, at
the celebration of the 97th anniversary of the birth day of
Thomas Paine, Esq. With an account of the Proceedings
of the Festival.
8vo. pp. 15.   *Providence.* 1834.

RHODOMANTHUS; and the Tunnel Pump and Measure Guard.
12mo. pp. 23. [*Providence.*] *Published for the author.* 1858.

A Drama. Persons represented. Rhodamanthus,—*Judge Barstow*-dikos,
Bradles-thenes, *Sanford*-ion. Aspiring Politicians—*Slack*-bonion, *Crans-
ton*-ion and *Cobb*-os. *The Nuisance Guard,* etc.
This squib relates to the attempts of Mayor Rodman to enforce the nui-
sance act against the rum sellers. Rhodomanthus is meant for the Mayor.
The others may be recognized by the portion of the names in Italics.

RICHMOND, REV. JAMES COOK. Metacomet; A Poem of the North American Indians.
12mo. pp. 47.   *Providence. John F. Moore.* 1851.
RICHMOND, WM. E.   Mount Hope; an Evening Excursion.
12mo. pp. 69.   *Providence. Miller & Hutchens.* 1819.
This poem was read before the Federal Adelphi of Brown University, September, 1816. Nearly one-half the work consists of historical notes.

———— Annual Address delivered before the Rhode Island Society for the Encouragement of Domestic Industry, October 19, 1825.
8vo. pp. 24.   *Providence. Carlile & Brown.* 1826.

RICHMOND, JOHN W.   History of the Registered State Debt of Rhode Island, in three chapters.
12mo. pp. 106.   *Providence. John F. Moore.*

———— Personal. [Relative to the State Debt.]
12mo. pp. 12.   *December 5,* 1849.

———— Rhode Island Repudiation of her Registered State Debt. (By John W. Richmond, agent for creditors.)
12mo. pp. 16.   *No date.* [1853.]
For various publications relative to the State Debt of Rhode Island, see *State Debt.*

ROBBINS, ASHER. An Address to the Society for the promotion of Agriculture and other useful Arts, in the State of Rhode Island and Providence Plantations, at their annual meeting, holden in Providence, on the 2d day of September, A. D. 1802. Printed for, and at the request of the Society.
8vo. pp. 16.   *Newport. Mercury Office.* (1802.)

———— An Address to the Rhode Island Society for the Encouragement of Dometic Industry, delivered at Pawtucket, October 16, 1822.
8vo. pp. 54.   *Providence. Miller & Hutchens.* 1822.

———— Oration, delivered on the 4th of July, 1827, at Newport, R. I.
8vo. pp. 27.   *Providence. Miller & Hammond.* 1827.

———— A Statement of some leading principles and measures adopted by General Jackson, in his administration of the

national government; and the effects of those principles and measures on the union, prosperity and constitution of the American People. Addressed to the citizens of Rhode Island, in answer to their call on the delagation of this State in Congress.
8vo. pp. 12.   *Providence. Wm. Marshall & Co.* 1832.

——— Report to the U. S. Senate, 1834, on the contested seat occupied by.
8vo. pp. 67.   *Senate Doc. 23d Cong. 1st Sess. No.* 246. 1834.

——— Silas Wight's minority report on ditto, April 4, 1834.
8vo. pp. 34.

See also, *Pindexter's Report* on the same subject.

——— A Discourse before the Phi Beta Kappa Society of Brown University. Delivered September 3, 1834.
8vo. pp. 28.   *Boston. Lilly, Wait, Colman & Holden.* 1834.

——— Report of the Committee on Commerce, in the Senate of the United States, to whom was referred the memorial of David Melville, of Newport, R. I.
8vo. pp. 35.   [*Washington.*] 1836.

Mr. Robbins was born in Connecticut, and graduated at Yale College in 1782, soon after which, he was elected a tutor in Brown University, which office he held for six years. On leaving the College, he studied law in Newport, where he established himself in practice, and where he resided during the remainder of his life. From 1825 to 1839, he was a member of the Senate of the United States. He was much attached to the ancient classics, especially the Greek, which he cultivated with the greatest delight. In 1835, Brown University conferred on him the degree of Doctor of Laws. He died in 1845, aged about 82 years, respected and lamented by all who knew him.

RODMAN, THOMAS P. A discourse on Liberty, delivered before an assembly of the Friends of Emancipation, in the Christian Chapel, in Providence, July 4, 1840.
8vo. pp. 15.   *Providence. B. T. Albro.* 1840.

RODMAN, WM. M. A Poem delivered at the Anniversary of American Independence, in Providence, July 4, 1856. (With Mr. Kimball's Oration.)
8vo. pp. 52.   *Providence. Knowles, Anthony & Co.* 1852.

ROSS, ARTHUR A. A Discourse embracing the Civil and

Religious History of Rhode Island, delivered in Newport, April 4, 1838.
12mo. pp. 161. *Providence. H. H. Brown.* 1838.

Mr. Ross was pastor of the First Baptist Church in Newport. His work is quite full upon the history of Newport from its first settlement in 1638.

ROUSMANIERE, H., of Warwick. Letters from the Pawtuxet. A series of Letters on the History of the Valley of the Pawtuxet river. Published in the Providence Journal during the years 1859 and 60.

These letters cover the history of an important district, in which facts are brought to light which illustrate the progress of the mechanic arts. As early as the year 1732, Joseph Bucklin established a machine shop five miles north of the village of Washington, now in the town of Coventry. In 1740, the six sons of Jabez Greene, of Warwick, established a forge and anchor shop in the same town. They were also the owners of the ancient anchor mill at Potowomut. Nathanael, one of the brothers, was the father of Gen. Nath. Greene. The latter was managing the concern in Coventry, when he was summoned to the war. The progress of manufactures on the Pawtuxet River are narrated in detail, and with great accuracy in these letters. They also contain notices of the prominent men, with histories of their families.

——— Biography of Christopher Greene, the hero of Red Bank. Published in the " Kent County Atlas," during the year 1852.

——— Annual Reports, as Commissioner of Public Schools, for the years 1861 and 62.

RUM. At a Court held at Punch Hall in the Colony of Bacchus. The indictment and trial of Sir *Richard Rum*, a person of noble birth and extraction, well known both to rich and poor throughout all America ; who was accused for several misdemeanors against his majesty's liege people, viz : killing some, wounding others, bringing thousands to poverty, and many good families to utter ruin.

It is not the USE but the ABUSE of any good thing that makes it hurtful.

The ninth edition, with a preface and a song, composed by Sir Richard immediately after his discharge.

12mo. pp. 19. *Providence. Prin ted and sld by John Waterman.* 1774.

RUSSELL, JONATHAN. Oration pronounced in the Baptist Meeting House, in Providence, on the anniversary of American Independence, July 4, 1800.
8vo. pp. 23.   *Providence. Bennett Wheeler.* 1800.
―――― The same.
12mo. pp. 38.   *Warren. Nathaniel Phillips.* 1800.
―――― The same. 14th edition.
8vo. pp. 26.   *Providence. Robinson & Howland.* 1814.
―――― The same.
8vo. pp. 20.   *Watertown, N. Y. Woodward.* 1830.
―――― To the Freemen of Rhode Island, &c. By a Republican. (attributed to Mr. Russell.)
8vo. pp. 16.   *No date.*

Jonathan Russell, son of Thomas Russell, was born in Providence, in 1771, and graduated at Brown University in 1791, with the highest honors of his class. He was a versatile, forcible and elegant writer, and well versed in political science. He filled several high and responsible diplomatic stations, and performed their duties with marked ability. For several years he was Minister Plenipotentiary of the United States at Stockholm, and one of the Commissioners who negotiated the Treaty of Peace with Great Britain, at Ghent, in 1814. On his return, he settled at Mendon, Mass., and was soon after elected a Representative to Congress. With the exception of the Fourth of July Oration, above mentioned, which passed through more than twenty editions, and his diplomatic correspondence while in Paris, London and Stockholm, Mr. Russell has left few records of his varied intellectual gifts. He died at Milton, Massachusetts, in 1832, aged 61 years. George R. Russell, of Roxbury, Mass, distinguished also for his talents, is the son of Jonathan Russell.

RUSSELL, GEORGE R. Address before the R. I. Society for the Encouragement of Domestic Industry, and the R. I. Horticultural Society, Sept. 17, 1852.
8vo. pp. 28.   *Providence. Knowles, Anthony & Co.* 1852.

SCHOOLS. Report to the General Assembly, June Session, 1799, on the expediency of making provisions by law for the support of Free Schools. With "An Act to establish Free Schools." 12mo. pp. 12. *Newport. Oliver Farnsworth.* 1799.
This Report is signed by Moses Lippitt, Richard Jackson, Jr. and James Burrill, Jr., Committee.

—— Report of the Committee on Public Schools. (F. Wayland, Wm. T. Grinnell, and Thomas T. Waterman, Committee.)
8vo. pp. 11.   *April* 22. 1828.

—— Debate on the Bill establishing Free Schools, at the January Session of the Rhode Island Legislature, 1828.
8vo. pp. 24.   *Providence. F. Y. Carlile.* 1828.

—— The Report of a Committee on the subject of Schools, with a Table, showing the number of Schools in Rhode Island, the sums expended for their support, and the number of scholars taught in them. Submitted May 17, 1832.
8vo. pp. 12.   *Providence. J. Knowles.* 1832.

—— Acts relating to the Public Schools of Rhode Island. Published by order of the General Assembly, January Session, 1839.
8vo. pp. 34.   *Providence.* 1839.

—— By-laws of the School Committee, and Regulations of the Public Schools in the City of Providence.
8vo. pp. 32.   *Providence. B. Cranston & Co.* 1840.

Schools. Books relating to.

——— Address delivered before the Washington County Association, for the Improvement of Public Schools, at Wickford, January 3d, 1845. By Rowland G. Hazard.
8vo. pp. 42.   *Providence. Benjamin F. Moore.* 1845.

——— Act relating to the Public Schools of Rhode Island.
8vo. pp. 16   *Providence. B. Cranston & Co.* 1846.

——— Report to the City Council of Providence, presented June 1, 1846; by their committee appointed Sept. 3, 1838, to superintend the erection of School Houses, on the reorganization of Public Schools.
8vo. pp. 16.   *Providence. Knowles & Vose.* 1846.

For other books relating to Public Schools, see *Colored Schools, Factories, Twaney, Barnard, E. R. Potter.*

——— Acts relating to the Public Schools of Rhode Island, with remarks and forms. Published by order of the General Assembly.
8vo. pp. 79.   *Providence. Charles Burnett, Jr.* 1847.

——— The same. Consolidated and Revised, June, 1851.
8vo. pp. 124.   *Providence. Sayles & Miller.* 1851.

——— Journal of the Rhode Island Institute of Instruction, from 1845 to 1848. Edited by Henry Barnard, Commissioner of Public Schools.
3 vols. 8vo.   *Providence.* 1846–48.

——— Report of the Commissioner of Public Schools. By E. R. Potter, January 25, 1851. 8vo. pp. 8.

——— Report of the Committee on Finance, in relation to the School Fund, made to the Senate, October, 1851.
8vo. pp. 14.   *Providence. Sayles & Miller.* 1851.

——— Report on the condition and improvement of the Public Schools of Rhode Island, January, 1852. By Elisha R. Potter, Commissioner.
8vo. pp. 78.   *Providence. Knowles, Anthony & Co.* 1852.

——— Report on ditto. January, 1853. By Elisha R. Potter, Commissioner.
8vo. pp. 77.   *Providence. Sayles, Miller & Simons.* 1853.

Schools. Books relating to.

——— Address at the opening of the Rhode Island State Normal School, at Providence, May 29, 1854. By E. R. Potter, Commissioner of Public Schools.
8vo. pp. 12.   *Providence. Knowles, Anthony & Co.* 1854.

——— Report of the Commissioner [W. B. Sayles] appointed to ascertain the number, ages, hours of labor, and opportunities for the education of children employed in the manufacturing establishments of Rhode Island; made to the General Assembly, at its January session, 1853.
8vo. pp.   *Providence. Sayles, Miller & Simons.* 1853.

——— Report on the Condition and Improvement of the Public Schools of Rhode Island, Nov. 1, 1845. By Henry Barnard, Commissioner.
8vo. pp. 255.   *Providence.* 1854.

——— Report upon Public Schools and Education in Rhode Island, October, 1854. (Bible and Prayer in Schools.) By E. R. Potter, Commissioner.
8vo. pp. 248.   *Providence. Knowles, Anthony & Co.* 1854.

——— Reports and Documents upon Public Schools and Education in the State of Rhode Island. By E. R. Potter, late Commissioner of Public Schools; with the School Laws; forms for doing business under them, and remarks and advice relating to them.
8vo. pp. 700.   *Providence. Knowles, Anthony & Co.* 1855.

——— Acts and Amendments relating to the Public Schools of Rhode Island; with remarks, forms and decisions. Published by order of the General Assembly.
8vo. pp. 166.   *Providence. A. Crawford Greene.* 1856.

——— Acts relating to the Public Schools of Rhode Island; with remarks and forms. Printed by order of the General Assembly.
8vo. pp. 188.   *Providence. Sayles, Miller & Simons.* 1857.

——— Will the General Assembly put down Caste Schools? Signed by George T. Downing and others.
8vo. pp. 15.   *Dated, Providence, December,* 15. 1857.

SCHOOLS. Books relating to.

———— Minority Report of the Committee on Education, of the General Assembly of Rhode Island, on the abolition of Caste Schools. January session, 1858.
12mo. pp. 10.   *Providence. J. Flagg, Carr & Co.* 1858.

———— To the Friends of Equal Rights in Rhode Island. Signed by George T. Downing and others.
8vo. pp. 8.   *Dated, Providence, April.* 1859.

———— Report of the Minority of the Committee upon the Memorial of Samuel T. Hopkins, against the validity of the election of the Fourth Representative from the City of Newport, the Hon. Charles C. Van Zandt.
8vo. pp. 14.   *Providence. H. L. Tillinghast.* 1859.

———— Minority Report of the Committee on Education, upon the petition of Isaac Rice and others.
8vo. pp. 5.   *Providence. Knowles, Anthony & Co.* 1859.

———— We would ask, why deny us our School Rights? Broadside.   *Dated, Rhode Island, Jan.* 1859.
Signed by Downing and others.

THE RHODE ISLAND SCHOOLMASTER. A monthly magazine, established and edited by Robert Allyn, School Commissioner, in 1856; edited by William A. Mowry in 1858-59- and 60; by a Board of Editors in 1861; and by a similar Board in 1862-63; the principal managers now being Messrs. J. J. Ladd and N. W. DeMunn.   *Providence.*

RHODE ISLAND EDUCATIONAL MAGAZINE. Edited by E. R. Potter, Commissioner of Public Schools.
2 vols. 8vo.   *Providence.* 1852-1854.

SCITUATE, RHODE ISLAND. Valuation of Property in the Town of, October, 1863.
12mo. pp. 27.   *Providence. Alfred Anthony.* 1864.

SCOTT, JOB. Journal of the Life, Travels and Gospel Labours of that faithful servant and minister of Christ, Job Scott.
12mo. pp. xii. and 360.   *New York. Isaac Collins.* 1797.

——— The same. With a supplement. "The Baptism of Christ."
12mo. pp. 281. *Warrington. W. Leicester.* 1798.

SARGENT, L. M. Address delivered at the Beneficent Congregational Meeting House, July 4, 1838; being the first Temperance Celebration of American Independence in Providence.
8vo. pp. 32. *Providence. B. Cranston & Co.* 1838.

SEARS, BARNAS. A Memoir of the Rev. Bela Jacobs, A. M. Compiled chiefly from his Letters and Journals, by his daughter; with a sketch of his character.
12mo. pp. vii. and 305.
Boston. Gould, Lincoln & Edmands. 1837.

SEWEL, WILLIAM. The History of the Rise, Increase, and Progress of the Christian People, called Quakers; intermixed with several remarkable occurrences. Written originally in Low Dutch, and also translated into English. The second edition corrected.
Folio. pp. xii. and 699. *London. J. Sowle.* 1725.

——— The same.
2 vols. 8vo. *Philadelphia.* 1823.

SHARP, REV. DANIEL. A Discourse delivered in the First Baptist Meeting House, in Providence, August 20, 1828, at the interment of the Rev. Stephen Gano, A. M., late Pastor of that Church.
8vo. pp. 20. *Boston. Lincoln & Edmands.* 1828.

SHEFFIELD, WILLIAM P. The substance of a paper read before the Rhode Island Historical Society, upon the early history of Block Island.
Published in the Providence Journal. 1859.

——— A Speech in opposition to the Personal Liberty Bill, delivered in the House of Representatives of Rhode Island, February 12, 1858.
Published in the Providence Journal, February. 1858.

―――― Speech delivered in the House of Representatives of R. I., upon the repeal of the Personal Liberty Bill, January 22, 1861.
Published in the Providence Journal. 1861.

SHEPARD, REV. THOMAS, D. D. An Historical Discourse from Psalm XLVIII. 12, 13, delivered in Bristol, November 25, 1856, on the occasion of taking leave of the old house of worship, reviewing the chief incidents in the history of the Church and Society since their formation; the latter, in 1680, and the former in 1687.
8vo. pp. 26. *Providence. Sayles, Miller & Simons.* 1857.

―――― A Discourse preached at the Dedication of the new Congregational Church, Nov. 25, 1856; Psalm LXXVII. 13.
8vo. pp. 29. *Providence. Sayles, Miller & Simons.* 1857.
These discourses are historical, and contain notices of the early settlers of Bristol.

―――― "A Ministry of fourteen years." A Discourse preached from Psalm XC. 12, at Ashfield, Mass., June 16, 1859, it being the 40th anniversary of his settlement in that town.
8vo. pp. 24. *Providence. Knowles, Anthony & Co.* 1859.

―――― "A Memorial of a Ministry of 25 years." Psalm LXXXVII. 7, in which a concise history of his pastorate of a quarter of a century was given; issued on the morning of Jan. 1, 1860.
8vo. pp. 9. *Providence. Knowles, Anthony & Co.* 1860.

―――― Annual Reports on the state of the Public Schools, in Bristol, from about the year 1848 to 1862.

SHERMAN, SYLVESTER G. Address before the North Kingstown Temperance Society, Nov. 4, 1832.
8vo. pp. 16. *Providence. Wm. Simons, Jr.* 1832.

―――― Report on the petition of Henry J. Duff and others, for alteration of the State Constitution, to admit naturalized citizens to vote, January session, 1847.
8vo. pp. 16. *Providence. M. B. Young.* 1847.

SHERMAN, ELDER ELEAZER. Trial of, before an Ecclesiastical Council, held at the Meeting House of the Christian Society, in Providence, July 21, 1835.
8vo. pp. 16. Providence. H. H. Brown. 1835.

SIMONS, BENJAMIN B. Funeral Oration, delivered in the Chapel of Rhode Island College, on Friday, the 13th November, 1795, occasioned by the death of Mr. Thomas Edwards, classmate of the deceased.
8vo. pp. 10. Providence. B. Wheeler. [1795.]

SIMMS, WM. GILMORE. The Life of Nathanael Greene, Major General in the Army of the Revolution.
12mo. pp. 395. New York. G. F. Coolidge & Bro. 1849.

SLATER, SAMUEL. Memoir of, see *White*.

SLANDERS REFUTED. Being a reply to the foul and abusive attacks made on Dutee J. Pearce and Tristam Burges.
8vo. pp. 18. [Subsequent to 1826.] *No date*.

SLAVE-TRADE. Constitution of a Society for abolishing the Slave-Trade; with several acts of the Legislatures of the States of Massachusetts, Connecticut and Rhode Island, for that purpose.
8vo. pp. 19. Providence. John Carter. 1789.

See Mr. Patten's Sermon on the Slave-trade.

SMITH, HON. C. B., of Indiana. Speech on the Rhode Island Controversy, 1844. (See *Constitution*.)

SMITH, REV. FRANCIS. A Discourse delivered in the Fourth Baptist Meeting House, Providence, on the re-opening of the House, after its enlargement, October 20, 1850.
8vo. pp. 22. Providence. John F. Moore. 1851.

SMITH, REV. WM., A. M. Rector of Trinity Church, Newport. A Discourse at the opening of the Convention of Clerical and Lay Delegates of the Church in the State of Rhode Island. Delivered in Trinity Church, Newport, Thursday, the 18th of November, 1790.
8vo. pp. 19. with an appendix. xii.
 Providence. J. Carter. [1790.]

Smith. Rev. Wm. A Discourse delivered before the Grand Lodge of the most ancient and honorable fraternity of Free and Accepted Masons of the State of R. Island, June 29, 1791.
Small 4to. pp.   *Providence. Bennett Wheeler.* 1791.

——— A Discourse delivered in St. John's Church, Providence, before the Rt. Rev. Samuel, Bishop of Connecticut and Rhode Island, and the Clerical and Lay Delegates of the Protestant Episcopal Courch, in the State of Rhode Island, July 31, 1793; at the ordination of the Rev. John Usher, of Bristol.
8vo. pp. 16,   *Providence. J. Carter.* 1793.

Dr. Smith was born in Scotland about the year 1752; was educated at one of its universities, and came to America as an ordained minister in 1785. He was, at various times, settled in Maryland, Rhode Island, Connecticut, New York, and other places, never remaining long in one place. He had the reputation of being an excellent scholar. For a while he taught school in some of these places. The latter part of his life was spent in the city of New York, in writing for the press. "His colloquial powers," says Dr. Blake, in his Biog. Dictionary, "were extraordinary, rendering him an agreeable companion; and he frequently preached extemporaneously—being always interesting, and sometimes eloquent." He died in New York, April 26, 1821.

Snow, Edwin M., M. D., Superintendent of Health, and City Registrar. Report on the Births, Marriages and Deaths in the City of Providence, during the year ending December 31, 1855; with an Appendix, showing the mortality of Providence, during fifteen years, from 1840 to 1854, inclusive.
8vo.   *Providence. Knowles, Anthony & Co.* 1856.

The publication of these reports, which commenced in the year 1856, have been continued to the present time by Dr. Snow, and have been pronounced the most thorough and complete of their kind, of any published in the United States.

——— Census of the City of Providence, taken in July, 1855, with a brief account of the Manufactures, Trade, Commerce, and other Statistics of the city; and an Appendix, giving an account of previous enumerations of the population of Providence. By Edwin M. Snow, M. D. First and Second Editions, Providence, 1856. Pages 82.

―――― Statistics and Causes of Asiatic Cholera, as it prevailed in Providence, in the Summer of 1854; being a letter addressed to the Mayor of Providence, by Edwin M. Snow, M. D., Providence, 1855.

―――― First Annual Report of the Superintendent of Health of the City of Providence. Year ending July 1, 1857.
Providence.. 1857.

―――― History of the Asiatic Cholera, in Providence, R. I. Printed from the Providence Journal of December 31, 1857. *Providence.* 1857.

―――― Report on the Small Pox in the City of Providence, from January to June, 1859. *Providence.* 1859.

―――― Address on the Epizooty, lately prevalent among swine; with the results of post-mortem examinations. By G. L. Collins, M. D., of Providence. Read before the Rhode Island Medical Society, at their annual meeting, June 19, 1861.
8vo. pp. 22. *Providence.* 1861.

SNOW, REV. JOSEPH. Funeral Sermon on, see *Gano.*

SPEAR. Proceedings in the Supreme Court of Rhode Island; March Term, 1825, in relation to two indictments against William S. Spear, for an alleged libel on Edward Dexter and Sarah Mumford.
8vo. pp. 20. *Providence. William S. Spear.* 1825.

SPRAGUE, WILLIAM, JUN'R. An Official Report of one of the committee of the House of Representatives of Rhode Island, on the subject of Masonry.
8vo. pp. 23. *Providence. Daily Advertiser.* 1832.

SPRAGUE, WILLIAM, Governor of Rhode Island. Memoir of, in "Heroes and Martyrs: Notable Men of the Time."
4to. vol. 1. *New York. G. P. Putnam.* 1862.

STAPLES, WILLIAM R. Annals of the Town of Providence, from its first settlement to the organization of the City Government, in June, 1832.
8vo. pp. vi. and 670. *Providence. Knowles & Vose.* 1843.

―― The same. Collections of the Rhode Island Historical Society, Vol. v.

―― The Documentary History of the Destruction of the Gaspee. Compiled for the Providence Journal. Royal 8vo. pp. 56. *Providence. Knowles, Vose & Co.* 1845.

―― The Proceedings of the First General Assembly of " The Incorporation of Providence Plantations," and the Code of Laws adopted by that Assembly, in 1647. With notes Historical and Explanatory.
8vo. pp. 63. *Providence. Charles Burnett, Jr.* 1847.

―― History of the Criminal Law of Rhode Island. Charge delivered to the Grand Jury of the Court of Common Pleas in Newport and Providence. Published by order of the General Assembly.
8vo. pp. 29. *Providence. No date.*

―― See also, *Gorton's Simplicities Defence*, printed in the R. I. Historical Collections, Vol. 2.

STATE PAPERS included in the Public Archives of the State: The following is a list of the several manuscript volumes in the office of the Secretary of State, and known as the *State Archives*. The various papers are all chronologically arranged and bound in volumes, and classified according to their several subjects.

THE CHARTER of the governor and company of the English Colony of Rhode Island and Providence Plantations, in New England, in America, granted by King Charles the Second, in 1663.
The original Charter, beautifully written on three large sheets of parchment, mounted on linen and framed.

RECORDS of the Colony of Rhode Island, from the year 1638 to 1696. Folio.
This volume contains a record of the transactions of the first settlers, at Portsmouth and Newport, with records of Deeds of lands from the Indians, and conveyances from the early colonists to each other, lists of freemen, etc. It also contains the agreement of the first settlers of the Island of Rhode Island, with their autograph signatures.

STATE PAPERS.

RECORDS of the Colony of Rhode Island from 1646 to 1699—one large folio volume.

This volume embraces the official journals of the General Assembly, proceedings of the Governor and Council; some records of the Court of Trials, with a number of Indian Deeds and other land evidences.

RECORDS of the Colony of Rhode Island from 1671 to 1686, one folio vol.

——— The same. from 1686 to 1715, one vol., folio.
——— The same. do. 1715 to 1745, one vol., folio.
——— The same. do. 1745 to 1841, 21 vols., folio.

These are all originals, with the exception of the volume containing the records from 1686 to 1715, which is a copy made by order of the General Assembly, in 1827. The copy of the Journals of the General Assembly, in the Secretary's Office, during this period, were quite imperfect, some sessions being wanting, while others were so defaced as to be scarcely legible. To make them complete, and in a condition for reference, the transcript referred to, was made.

ANCIENT RECORDS of the Colony of Rhode Island, from 1638 1679; also, the Court Records during the Administration of Sir Edmund Andros, 1685 to 1688. 1 volume, folio.

This is a copy of the early records transcribed by Mr. Charles Gyles, of Newport, under the direction of Chris. E. Robbins and Henry Bull, by Resolution of the General Assembly, in 1821, and is the only record that can be used, owing to the illegible condition of the originals.

RECORDS OF INDIAN DEEDS, conveyances, and other land evidences, chiefly before the year 1700. 4 volumes, folio.

BODYE OF LAWS of the Colony of Rhode Island, from 1663, to 1705, being the first known digest, a manuscript volume.

BOOK OF RECORDS, containing the acts and orders of the Governor and Council, both general and particular, since May 1, 1667. 1 volume, folio.

This volume contains chiefly the proceedings of the Governor and Council during the war of Great Britain with Holland, France and Spain, and extends to the year 1753. Their meetings were between the sessions of the General Assembly.

PROCEEDINGS of the Colonies of the English Colonies in North America, held at Albany, 1756, for the purpose of making a Treaty with the Six Nations of Indians. 1 volume folio.

STATE PAPERS.

JOURNAL OF THE COUNCIL OF WAR, from 1776 to 1781 inclusive. 4 volumes, folio.

PROCEEDINGS of the General Council and of the Council of War, from 1755 to 1772. 1 volume, folio.

PROCEEDINGS in the Court of Equity, from 1741 to December, 1743. 1 volume, folio.

CENSUS of the Inhabitants of the Colony of Rhode Island, taken in 1774. 1 volume, folio.

MARINE PROTESTS, from 1721 to 1795. 5 volumes, folio.

ORIGINAL MANUSCRIPT SCHEDULES, or acts and proceedings of the General Assembly, from 1649 to 1710. 4 vols. folio.

JOURNALS of the Senate from 1740 to 1792, in 7 port-folios.

JOURNALS of the House of Representatives, from 1728 to 1782, in 13 port-folios.

MISCELLANEOUS PAPERS from 1780 to 1783, in two port-folios.

ACTS AND RESOLUTIONS of the General Assembly, from the year 1728 to 1860, in 52 folio volumes.

RHODE ISLAND LAW CASES; appeals to the General Assembly, from the year 1725 to 1740, nine volumes, folio.

——— From the year 1780 to 1799, four volumes, folio.

RHODE ISLAND CASES IN EQUITY, 1741 to 1743, six volumes.

PETITIONS to the General Assembly, with accompanying acts and charters, 1725 to 1860, seventy-two volumes, folio.

CHARTERS, 1780 to 1863, twenty-two volumes, folio.

REPORTS of the Committees to the General Assembly, 1728 to 1860, 14 volumes, and one vol. of index.

MISCELLANEOUS PAPERS relating to the Old French War, 1755 to 1761, one volume, folio.

ADMIRALTY PAPERS, 1726 to 1750, two volumes, folio.

MILITARY RETURNS, Revolutionary War, 1776 to 1782, two volumes.

STATE PAPERS.

MILITARY ROLLS of 1778, one volume, folio.

CERTIFICATES of the Rhode Island Line, 1784, one vol. folio.

CENSUS of the inhabitants of the Colony of Rhode Island, taken in 1774 and 1776, two volumes, folio.

DOCUMENTS relating to the destruction of the British schooner Gaspee, in Narragansett Bay, 1772 to 1773, one volume.

PETITIONS with Letters of Marque, 1776 to 1780, one volume.

ORDERS of the King in Council, relating to Rhode Island, 1734 to 1783, one volume.

LETTERS RECEIVED, 1731 to 1800. 21 volumes, folio.

MASSACHUSETTS AND CONNECTICUT BOUNDARY; papers, letters and reports relating to, 1690 to 1842, two volumes.

RECORDS of the Rhode Island and Massachusetts Boundary Commission, 1741, one volume.

PAPERS relating to the Easterly Boundary of Rhode Island— case of Rhode Island vs. Massachusetts Bay, two volumes.

NARRAGANSETT INDIANS; papers and reports relating to, 1755 to 1842, one volume.

DIVISION of Towns, 1725 to 1842, one volume.

MASONRY and Anti-Masonry, 1833 and 1834, one volume.

CONSTITUTION of 1841–'42, petitions, reports, etc., one volume.

REGISTERED STATE DEBT; report made in 1849, with certificates and other papers, one volume.

PROCEEDINGS and Acts of the General Assembly, from 1649 to 1721, four volumes.

SURVEYS of Turnpikes, in an atlas.

MINUTES of the Convention for the adoption of the Constitution of the United States in 1790. Instructions to the members of the Convention, and the votes of the towns on the adoption of the Constitution. 1 folio volume.

STATE PAPERS.

STATE PAPERS. Letters, Reports, etc., relating to Rhode Island; copied from the originals in Her Majesty's State Paper Office, London. From 1636 to 1769, manuscript. Bound in 10 vols. Royal folio.

The State papers in this collection, were carefully selected from the originals in the British State Paper Office, by our townsman, the Hon. Samuel G. Arnold, during his stay in London, and copies made therefrom for Mr. John Carter Brown, of Providence, in whose possession they remain. They extend from 1636 to 1769, and embrace a vast number of letters and papers of interest, connected with the early history of the Colony. A large number of the letters are printed in the Rhode Island Colonial Record, having been kindly loaned to the Secretary of State for this purpose.

——— Letters and various papers in the Trumbull Collection relating to Rhode Island, from 1660 to 1680, manuscript, six vols. 4to.

This collection of State Papers, consisting chiefly of letters, was also copied for Mr. John Carter Brown, from the originals in the library of the Massachusetts Historical Society.

STATE PAPERS OF RHODE ISLAND. Transmitted by Samuel Eddy, from the records of the State, and printed in the *Massachusetts Historical Collections*, 2d series, vol. vii. viz:

Deposition of Roger Williams,	1682.
Deposition of William Coddington,	1677.
Form of Government agreed on by the first settlers on the Island of Rhode Island, 7th day, 1st mo.,	1638.
Laws of Rhode Island,	1647.
Letter from Oliver Cromwell to Rhode Island Colony, 29 March,	1655.
Letter of Commissioners to Captain Dennison, 4th July,	1677.
Letter from the General Assembly to the Commissioners of the United Colonies, March 13,	1657–58.
Letter of the Commissioners to John Clarke,	Nov. 5, 1658.
Letter from the Colony of Rhode Island to Richard Cromwell,	May, 1659.
Commission to John Clarke,	Oct. 18, 1660.
Decision of Robert Carr, and others, Commissioners, relative to Misquamacock,	April 4, 1665.
Commission from Robert Carr, Geo. Cartwright and Samuel Maverick, appointing Justices of the Peace for King's Province,	April 8, 1665.
Proposition of ditto to the General Assembly,	May 13, 1665.
Addresses to the King and Earl of Clarendon, respecting Charter Rights,	May 3, 1665.
The General Assembly of Rhode Island to the Governor of Plymouth,	Nov. 2, 1671.
do. do. to the General Assembly of Connecticut,	Oct. 25, 1676.

STATE DEBT OF RHODE ISLAND. History of the Registered State Debt of Rhode Island, in three chapters. By John W. Richmond.
12mo. pp. 106. *Providence. John F. Moore.*

―――― Rhode Island Repudiation, or the History of the Revolutionary Debt of Rhode Island, in three chapters.
8vo. pp. 208. 2d edition.
Providence. Sayles, Miller & Simons. 1855.

―――― A Petition in relation to the State Debt. Presented to the General Assembly at its May session.
12mo. pp. 12. *Providence. No date.*

―――― History of the Alleged State Debt of Rhode Island. By Wilkins Updike, Esq., December 16, 1846.
8vo. pp. 12. Double columns. [*Providence.*] 1846

―――― Report of the Commissioners. [By E. R. Potter,] appointed at the January session of the General Assembly, A. D., 1846, " to enquire into and report upon the history and character of the registered debt," [of Rhode Island,] etc.
12mo. pp. 15. *January.* 1847.

―――― Personal. By John W. Richmond.
12mo. pp. 12. *Providence. Dec. 5.* 1849.

" This article is intended solely as an exposition of the personal imputations which have passed during the last six years, arising out of claims of individuals against the State."—*Extract from the work.*

―――― Report of George Turner, Amherst Everett and J. Russell Bullock, a Committee on the Registered State Debt of Rhode Island, appointed by the Governor, Lieutenant Governor, and Secretary of State; Reported at the October session, 1849.
12mo. pp. 75. *Providence. John F. Moore.* [1849.]

―――― Appendix to the Report on State Certificates of the Registered State Debt, made October, 1849. By order of the General Assembly.
8vo. pp. 126. *Providence. Sayles & Miller.* 1852.

This appendix consists of sixty papers.

STATE DEBT OF RHODE ISLAND.

——— The Plough and the Sickle : or Rhode Island in the War of the Revolution of 1776. 8vo. pp. 28. Double columns. *Providence. B. T. Albro.* 1846.
Relates to the State Debt.

——— Rhode Island Repudiation of her Registered State Debt. " By John W. Richmond, Agent for Creditors." 12mo. pp. 16. [*No date.* 1853.]

STATE PRISON. Annual Reports of the Board of Inspectors, Warden and Physician of the State Prison of Rhode Island, made to the General Assembly at their October Session, 1844.
8vo. pp. 38 *Providence. Knowles & Vose.* 1844.

——— The same. Annual Reports to 1863.
Previous to the year 1844, the annual reports were brief and incoporated in the schedules of the General Assembly. Since that time they have been enlarged, and printed in separate pamphlets.

STILLMAN, SAMUEL, M. A. Death, The Last Enemy, Destroyed by Christ. A Sermon, preached March 27, 1776, before the Honorable Continental Congress; on the death of the Honorable Samuel Ward, Esq., one of the delegates from the Colony of Rhode Island, who died of the smallpox, in this city, (Philadelphia.) March 26, Act. 52. Published at the desire of many who heard it.
8vo. pp. iv. and 28. *Philadelphia. Joseph Crukshank.* 1776.

STILLMAN, SAMUEL, D. D. A Sermon, preached May 31, 1791, in Providence, R. I., on the death of Nicholas Brown, Esq., who died May 29th, Aetat 62.
8vo. pp. 24 and iv. *Providence. J. Carter.* [1791.]

STETSON, Mr., of New York. Speech on the Rhode Island Controversy, 1844. (See *Constitution*.)

STONE, JOHN S. Life of Bishop Griswold. See *Griswold*.

STONE, T. B. P. Biography of Mrs. Rebecca Gain Webster. 12mo. pp. 412. *Boston. Crocker & Brewster.* 1848.

STONE, EDWIN M. The Life and Recollections of John How-

land, late President of the Rhode Island Historical Society. By Edwin M. Stone.
12mo. pp. 348.   *Providence. George H. Whitney.* 1857.

―――― Annual Reports of the *Ministry at Large,* which, see.

STONE, EDWIN W.   Rhode Island in the Rebellion.
12mo. pp. 398.   *Providence. George H. Whitney.* 1864.
Fifty copies of this work were printed in 8vo. on *large paper.*

STOWE, MRS. HARRIET BEECHER.   The Minister's Wooing.
12mo. pp. 578.   *New York. Derby & Jackson.* 18―
The scene of this novel is laid in Newport, and portrays the manners of the people in the middle of the last century.

STILES, EZRA., D. D.   Pastor of the 2d Congregational Church, in Newport. A discourse on Sacred Worship, delivered at the instalment of the Rev. Samuel Hopkins, A. M., into the pastoral charge of the First Congregational Church, in Newport, R. I., Wednesday, April 11, 1770.
8vo. pp. 48.   *Newport. Printed and sold by Solomon Southwick, in Queen street.*   1779.

―――― Discourse on the Christian Union, delivered before the Convention of Congregational Ministers of Rhode Island, at Bristol, April 23, 1760.
8vo. pp.   *Boston.* 1791.
This sermon, with the appendix, contains valuable historical and statistical information respecting the churches of New England.

―――― A History of the Judges of King Charles I. Major General Whalley, Major General Goffe, and Colonel Dixwell, who, at the restoration, 1660, fled to America, and were secreted and concealed in Massachusetts and Connecticut for near thirty years. With an account of Mr. Theophilus Whale, of Narragansett, supposed to have been one of the Judges.
12mo. pp. 357.   Portrait of the author.
   Hartford. Elisha Babcock. 1794.

―――― Address to the public, [concerning the sending of Black Freemen to the coast of Africa,] signed by Ezra Stiles and Samuel Hopkins.
8vo. pp. 8.   *Newport. April* 10. 1776.

This rare pamphlet has no title page. The little above given in brackets, is in the handwriting of William Ellery.

Dr. Stiles was born in North Haven, Connecticut, in 1727. In 1746, he graduated at Yale College, and was tutor there during six years. On the 18th October, 1755, he was ordained minister over the Second Congregational Church, in Newport, where he remained until his people were dispersed by the Revolutionary war, in 1776. He then preached at Portsmouth, R. I. In 1777, he was chosen President of Yale College, which station he held until his death in May, 1795. Dr. Stiles was one of the most learned men of his time. He possessed a critical knowledge of Hebrew, Greek and Latin, and was more or less familiar with the Samaritan, Chaldee, Syriac, Arabic, Persian and Coptic languages. He was well versed in mathematics, and, as a theologian, ranked second to none in the country.

THE SWAN POINT CEMETERY; its Charter, Rules and Regulations, List of lot owners, and first annual report of the Actuary.
12mo. pp. 36.   *Providence. Joseph Knowles.* 1848.

——— A Report of the committee on the present position of Swan Point Cemetery, made at an adjourned meeting of lot owners, held in Westminster Hall, March 30, 1857.
8vo. pp. 8.   *Providence. Knowles, Anthony & Co.* 1857.

SUPREME COURT. Report of cases, argued and determined in the Supreme Court of Rhode Island.
6 vols. 8vo.   *Boston and Providence.* 1847 to 1862.

Vol. 1. pp. 531. By Joseph K. Angell.   *Boston. Little & Brown.* 1847.
Vol. 2. pp. 570. By Thomas Durfee.
   Providence. Knowles, Anthony & Co. 1854.
Vol. 3. pp. 311. By John P. Knowles.   do.   do.   do.   1856.
Vol. 4. pp. 651. By Samuel Ames, Chief Justice.
   Boston. Little, Brown & Co. 1858.
Vol. 5. pp. 671. By Samuel Ames,   do.   do.   do.   do.   1859.
Vol. 6. pp. 636. By Samuel Ames,   do.   do.   do.   do.   1862.
Vol. 7. pp. ——— By Samuel Ames, Chief Justice.
   Providence. Knowles, Anthony & Co. 1864.

The 7th volume of these Reports is in the hands of the printers, while the present work is going through the press.

STONINGTON RAILROAD. Some remarks shewing the advantages of the proposed Railroad from Providence to Stonington. With a map.
8vo. pp. 6.   *No date.*

——— Report on the surveys for a railroad from Stonington,

Connecticut, to Providence. R. I., with an approximate estimate of its cost, March, 1832.
8vo. pp. 14. *March*. 1833.

────── An Act to Incorporate the New York, Providence and Boston Railroad Company, passed at June session, 1832. (Charter of Rhode Island.)
8vo. pp. 10. *Providence. B. Cranston & Co*. 1832.

────── An Act to Incorporate the New York and Stonington Railroad Company, passed, May, 1832. (Charter of Connecticut.)
8vo. pp. 9. (*New York*. 1832.)

────── Report of the Directors of the New York, Providence and Boston Railroad Company, to the Stockholders, at their annual meeting, Providence, Sept. 24, 1844.
8vo. pp. 8. *New York. Francis Hart*. 1844.

────── Remarks of Mr. R. G. Hazard, * * * relative to the charges for carrying freight over the Stonington Railroad, 1851. (See *Hazard*.)

STORY, MR. JUSTICE. Charge on the Law of Treason, delivered to the Grand Jury of the Circuit Court of the U. S., at Newport, R. I., June 15, 1842.
8vo. pp. 48. *Providence. H. H. Brown*. 1842.

[SUMNER, CHARLES.] The Outrage in the Senate upon. Proceedings of a Public Meeting of the citizens of Providence, held in Howard Hall, on the evening of June 7th, 1856.
8vo. pp. 12. *Providence. Knowles, Anthony & Co*. 1856.

The object of this meeting was to consider the assault upon the Hon. Charles Sumner, in the Senate Chamber at Washington, by Brooks. Alexander Duncan presided on the occasion, and speeches were made by Professor Gammell, the Hon. Charles S. Bradley, Rev. Dr. Hedge, and the Rev. Dr. Wayland.

TAYLOR, MRS. JEANNETTE H. Startling Incidents in the life of a lady! The eventful autobiography of Mrs. Jeannette H. Taylor, née Hoppin, [formerly of Providence.] Comprising a thrilling romance in real life. Embodying in its melodramatic and mysterious developement the most flagrant and diabolical plots ever concocted by human fiends and carried out by persevering villainy, claiming as *dramatis personae* in these scenes of dark endeavors, (to ruin the domestic peace of a defenceless woman,) the *soi disant* and pretended *distingues* of the United States. Moreover, a very concise, but graphic delineation of the morals, manners, official delinquency and mysterious *modus operandi* of New York officials.
8vo. pp. 24.   *New York.* 1856.
Many Providence people figure in this scandalous pamphlet.

TAYLOR VS. PLACE. Report of the Case G. & D. Taylor & Company vs. R. G. & J. T. Place. Decided by the Supreme Court of Rhode Island, September Term, County of Providence, 1856. Printed by order of the House of Representatives, 1858.
8vo. pp. 34.   *Providence. Knowles, Anthony & Co.* 1858.

TALBOT, SILAS. A Commodore in the Navy of the United States. By Henry T. Tuckerman.
18mo. pp. vii. and 137.   *J. C. Riker. New York.* 1850.

TAPPAN, DAVID., D. D.. of Harvard College. A Funeral Discourse, delivered to the Congregational Society, in Providence, R. I., on the Lord's Day, after the interment of Enos Hitchcock, D. D., delivered February 27, 1803.
8vo. pp. 24.   *Cambrige University Press.* 1803.

TEMPERANCE.

ALLEN, REV. JOSEPH W. Address before the North Kingstown Temperance Society, May 25, 1831.
8vo. pp. 16.   *Wickford. J. J. Brenton.* 1854.

BRANCH, STEPHEN. Address before the Providence Union Temperance Society, June 17, 1835.
8vo. pp. 18.   *Providence. H. H. Brown.* 1835.

BROOKS, CHARLES T. Think Soberly. A Sermon on Temperance, delivered in the Unitarian Church, Newport, R. I., Sunday evening, February 6, 1842.
8vo. pp. 18.   *Newport. James Atkinson.* 1842.

CONSTITUTION of the Providence County Temperance Society, together with an address of the Board of Officers, to all the local societies with in the county.
8vo. pp. 12.   *Providence. H. H. Brown.* 1838.

CONSTITUTION and List of Members of the Providence Young Men's Temperance Society.
12mo. pp. 12.   *Providence.* 1832.

CONSTITUTION and By-laws of Washington Section No. 2. Cadets of Temperance, Providence, Rhode Island. Instituted, July, 1848.
12mo. pp. 16.   *Providence. M. B. Young.* 1848.

CONSTITUTION and By-laws of Franklin Section, No. 3. Cadets of Temperance, Pawtucket, R. I. Instituted Aug. 1848.
12mo. pp. 16.   *Providence. M. B. Young.* 1848.

CONSTITUTION and By-laws of Channing Division No. 5, of the Sons of Temperance of the State of Rhode Island. Instituted, Providence, September 13, 1847.
12mo. pp. 20.   *Providence. M. B. Young.* 1848.

TEMPERANCE.

CONSTITUTION and By-laws of William Penn Division, No. 8, of the Sons of Temperance, of the State of R. I. Instituted at Pawtucket, June 29, 1848.
12mo. pp. *Providence. M. B. Young.* 1848.

CONSTITUTION and By-laws of the May Queen Union, No. 2, Daughters of Temperance, Natick, R. I. Instituted May 10, 1851.
12mo. pp. 24. *Providence. A. C. Greene.* 1852.

CONSTITUTION and By-laws of Olneyville Division, No. 10, of the Sons of Temperance, of the State of Rhode Island. Instituted September, 1848.
12mo. pp. 16. *Providence. M. B. Young.* 1848.

CONSTITUTION, By-laws and Rules of Narragansett Division, No. 3, of the Sons of Temperance, of Warren, R. I. Instituted December 14, 1846.
12mo. pp. 24. *Providence. J. Amsbury, Jr.* 1850.

CONSTITUTION and By-laws of Providence Division, No. 2, of the Sons of Temperance, of Providence, State of Rhode Island. Instituted July 31, 1846.
12mo. pp. 16. *Providence. Amsbury & Lincoln.* 1847.

DOW, DANIEL, of Thompson, Conn. A Discourse delivered in Chepachet, R. I., December 5, 1830. Before the Glocester Temperance Association.
12mo. pp. 24. *Providence. H. H. Brown.* 1831.

DRURY, LUKE. Address before the Bristol Association for the promotion of Temperance, March, 23, 1832.
8vo. pp. 28. *Providence. Weeden & Knowles.* 1832.

EXTRACTS from the proceedings and reports of the R. I. State Total Abstinence Society from its organization, January, 1841 to January, 1846; with the constitution of the Society, and the Licence Law of 1846.
12mo. pp. 36. *Providence, B. T. Albro.* 1846.

FOLSOM, REV. NATHANIEL S. Discourse before the R. I. State

TEMPERANCE.
―― Temperance Society, delivered in Providence, January 11, 1839.
12mo. pp. 35.   *Providence. Knowles, Vose & Co.* 1839.
GARDNER, MALBONE. Address on Temperance, South Kingstown, June, 1856.
8vo. pp. 20.   *Providence. Knowles & Anthony.* 1856.
HAZARD, ROWLAND G. Address before the Pawcatuck Temperance Society at Westerly, July 4, 1843.
12mo. pp. 30.   *Providence. B. F. Moore.* 1843.
HISTORY OF TEMPERANCE and Temperance Societies in Rhode Island, in a series of articles published in the Providence Daily Post, 1861.
LAWRENCE, WM. B. Speech of Lieut. Gov. Lawrence in the Senate of Rhode Island, Feb. 10, 1852, on the Maine Law Bill.
8vo. pp. 16.   *Providence.* 1852.
LICENSES. License Law passed, January session, 1844.
8vo. pp. 8.   *January.* 1844.
―― Considerations on the present state of the License Question.
8vo. pp. 8.   [*Providence.* 1844.]
―― Acts in relation to Licenses, for retailing Strong Liquors, [1844 to 1848.]
8vo. pp. 14.   *Providence.* 1848.]
―― An Act for the suppression of Drinking Houses and Tippling Shops, passed at the May session, 1852.
8vo. pp. 16.   *Providence. Sayles & Miller.* 1852.
―― An Act for the more effectual suppression of Drinking Houses and Tippling Shops, passed at the January session, 1853.
8vo. pp. 12.   *Providence. A. H. Stillwell.* 1853.
PARSONS. USHER. An Address delivered before the Providence Association for the promotion of Temperance, May 27, 1831.
8vo. pp. 16.   *Providence.* 1831.

TEMPERANCE.

PETERSON, REV. EDWARD. The Bible Temperance Review.
8vo. pp. 76.   *Providence. Printed for the publisher.* 1848.

PICKERING, DAVID. The Evils of Intemperance. A Discourse delivered on Sabbath evening, January 14, 1827, at the Universalist Church.
8vo. pp. 22.   *Providence. Miller & Grattan.* 1827.

——— The same. Second edition.
12mo. pp. 22.   *Taunton. S. W. Mortimer.* 1827.

PITMAN, HON. JOHN. An Address delivered before the Providence Union Temperance Society, February 24, 1835.
12mo. pp. 24.   *Providence. Knowles & Burroughs.* 1835.

PROCEEDINGS of the Rhode Island State Temperance Society at its Second Annual Meeting, held in the city of Providence, Monday, October 22, 1832.
12mo. pp. 24.   *Providence. Wm. Marshall & Co.* 1832.

PROCEEDINGS of the Rhode Island State Total Abstinence Society, at their annual meeting in Providence, January 25, 1854, with the report of the corresponding Secretary, and the speech of J. P. Knowles, Esq.
8vo. pp. 23.   *Providence. Albert Crawford Greene.* 1854.

PROVIDENCE WASHINGTON TOTAL ABSTINENCE SOCIETY.—
First Quarterly Report of, made October 8, 1841.
12mo. pp. 12.   *Providence. S. M. Millard & Co.* 1841.

REPORT of a committee of a meeting of the citizens of Providence, friendly to the promotion of Temperance, 1828.
12mo. pp. 16.   *Providence. F. Y. Carlile & Co.* 1828.

REPORT (Quarterly) of the committee of the Providence Association for the promotion of Temperance, July, 1830.
8vo. pp. 22 and vii.   *Providence. Hutchins & Weeden.* 1830.

REPORT of the Managers of the Providence Association for the promotion of Temperance, presented and read at their quarterly meeting, Jan. 27, 1834.
12mo. pp. 14.   *Providence. W. Marshall & Co.* 1834.

TEMPERANCE.

REPORT. The Seventh Annual Report of the Rhode Island State Temperance Society, January 11, 1838, together with the correspondence of the local societies.
8vo. pp. 26.　　　*Providence. H. H. Brown.* 1838.

REPORT. First Quarterly Report of the Providence Washington Total Abstinence Society, made Oct. 8, 1841.
12mo. pp. 12.　　*Providence. S. M. Millard & Co.* 1841.

REPORT of the Rhode Island State Temperance Society for 1843.
12mo. pp. 24.　　　*Providence. B. T. Albro.* 1844.

SHERMAN, SYLVESTER G. Address before North Kingstown Temperance Society, Nov. 4, 1832.
8vo. pp. 16.　　　*Providence. Wm. Simons, Jr.* 1832.

SLACK, DR. D. B. Lecture on Drunkenness, delivered before the Temperance Society in Providence, Feb., 1827.
12mo. pp. 22.　　　*Providence. B. T. Albro.* 1838.

TENNEY, CALEB J. The Intemperate use of Ardent Spirits. Two discourses, preached at the First Congregational Church in Newport, R. I., July 24, 1814. By its Pastor.
8vo. pp. 23.　　　*Newport. Mercury Office.* 1815.

WAYLAND, FRANCIS, D.D. An Address delivered before the Providence Association for the promotion of Temperance, October 20, 1831; also the first report of the State Temperance Society.
8vo. pp. 20 and iv.　*Providence. Weeden & Knowles.* 1831.

WELLS, THOMAS R. Address on Temperance before the South Kingstown Temperance Society.
12mo. pp. 16.　　　　　　　*Newport.* 1830.

TENNEY, REV. CALEB J., of Newport. Sermon at the ordination of. See *Asa Burton.*

THORNTON, ELDER ABEL., late of Johnston, R. I. The Life of. A Preacher in the Free-Will Baptist Connexion, and

a member of the R. I. Q. Meeting. Wrttten by himself.
Published by the R. I. Quarterly Meeting.
12mo. pp.   *Providence. Office of the Investigator.* 1828.

TILLINGHAST, JOSEPH L. An Oration pronounced at the First Congregational Meeting House, in Providence, before the Greene Association, on their anniversary, August 7, 1813. Being the birth-day of their Patron, General Nathanael Greene.
8vo. pp. 31.   *Providence. H. Mann & Co.* 1813.

TOBEY, REV. ZALMON. For Funeral Discourse on, see *Henry Jackson*.

TRIVETT vs. WEEDEN, Case of, see *Varnum*.

TRIAL of Col. David Pinneger, Lieut. Col. Wm. P. Maxwell, Maj. Nathan Whiting, and Captain Allen Tillinghast, of the Kentish Guards, before a General Court Martial, holden at the Court House, in Providence, April 27, 1808, for a disobedience of orders and a neglect of duty.
12mo. pp. 46.   *Warren. N. & J. F. Phillips.* 1808.

TRINITY CHURCH, Newport, Rhode Island. The Charter of, with the Constitution of the Protestant Episcopal Church in the State of Rhode Island.
8vo. pp. 8.   *Newport. Wm. & J. H. Barber.* 1823.

——— First Annual Report of the Board of Managers of the Society of Trinity Church, Newport, for the promotion of Christianity.
8vo. pp. 11.   *Boston. James B. Dow.* 1842.

——— Appeal to the Public from. See *Bours*.

TRUMAN, THOMAS, M. D. An Oration delivered in Public, at the State House, in Providence, (*Rhode Island,*) before the most Ancient and Honorable Fraternity of Free and Accepted Masons, on the Anniversary Festival of St. John the Evangelist, December 27, 1781. Published at the request of the Brethren. Let Brotherly Love continue: *Heb.* xiii. 1.
Small quarto. pp. 14.   *Providence. John Carter.* 1782.

TUCKER, MARK, D. D. Thanksgiving Discourse, July 21, 1842. (See *Constitution*.)

——— The Centennial Sermon preached before the Beneficent Congregational Church and Society, in Providence, R. I., March 19, 1843, together with the Articles of Faith, Covenant, etc., and a list of members of said Church.
12mo. pp. 84.   *Providence. Knowles & Vose.* 1845.

TUCKERMAN, HENRY T. The Life of Silas Talbot, a Commodore in the Navy of the United States.
18mo. pp. vii. and 137.   *New York. J. Riker.* 1850.

TURNER, HENRY E. An Oration delivered at East Greenwich, July 4, 1809, at the request of the Kentish Guards. By Dr. Henry E. Turner. Published by the author's friends.
12mo. pp, 12.   *Providence. J. Carter.* [1809.]

TURNER, GEORGE. An Official Report by William Sprague, Junior, one of the committee of the House of Representatives of Rhode Island, upon the subject of Masonry.
8vo. pp. 23.   *Providence. Daily Advertiser Office.* 1832.

Written by Geo. Turner, of Newport, and presented by Governor Sprague as a minority report.

TUSTIN, REV. JOSIAH P. A Discourse delivered at the dedication of the new church edifice of the Baptist Church and Society, in Warren, R. I., May 8, 1845.
18mo. pp. viii, and 146.   *Providence. H. H. Brown.* 1845,

An appendix extends from p. 125 to p. 193, and contains notes A to R. Among these are Biographical notices of Captain T. Willett, Rev. Charles Thompson and the Rev. John Pitman.

PDIKE, WILKINS. History of the Episcopal Church in Narragansett, Rhode Island, including a history of other Episcopal Churches in the State; with an appendix, containing a reprint of a work now extremely rare, entitled "America Dissected." By the Rev. J. MacSparran, D. D. With notes containing Genealogical and Biographical accounts of Distinguished Men, Families, etc.
8vo. pp. xxiii. and 533.
New York. Henry M. Onderdonk. 1847.

―――― Memoirs of the Rhode Island Bar.
8vo. pp. xii. and 311. *Boston. Thomas H. Webb & Co.* 1842.

This volume contains memoirs of Henry Bull, James Honeyman, Daniel Updike, Augustus Johnson, Oliver Arnold, Henry Marchant, William Channing, Henry Goodwin, Rouse J. Helme, John Cole, Archibald Campbell, Jacob Campbell, James M. Varnum, Mathew Robinson and Robert Lightfoot.

―――― History of the alleged State Debt of Rhode Island.
8vo. pp. 12. *Providence. December.* 1846.

―――― Facts relative to the political and moral claims of, for the support of the Whig electors, etc., in the Western District.
8vo. pp. 16. *Providence* 1847.

―――― See "An Address to the People of R. I., upon the claims of," for ditto.

UNDERHILL, CAPTAIN JOHN. Newes from America; or, a

new and experimental discoverie of New England; containing a Trve Relation of their warlike proceedings these two yeares last past, with a figure of the Indian Fort, or Palizado. Also a discoverie of these places, that as yet have very few or no inhabitants, which would yeeld speciall accommodation to such as will plant there, viz: Qeenapoick, Aguwom, Hudson's river, Long Island, Nabanticut, Martin's Vineyard, Pequot, Narragansett Bay, Elizabeth Island, Puscataway, Casko, with about a hundred islands neere to Casko. By Captain Iohn Underhill, a Commander in the Warres there.

4to pp. *London Printed for J. D., for Peter Cole, and are to be sold at the signe of the Glove in Cornhill, neere the Royal Exchange.* 1638.

———— The same.

Massachusetts Hist. Soc. 3d series, *Vol.* VI.

Captain Underhill was one of the first planters of Massachusetts, and one of the three first deputies from Boston to the General Court.

UNITED BRETHREN, Newport. Ode in commemoration of the first settlement of a Congregation of the United Brethren at Newport, Rhode Island, November 10, 1758, for the Jubilee in 1808. The Chapel was dedicated, June 26th, 1768.

8vo. pp. 10. *Newport.* 1808.

USHER, REV. JOHN, of Bristol. Sermon at the ordination of. See *Wm. Smith.*

ARNUM, JAMES M. The Case of Trevett against Weeden; On information and complaint, for refusing Paper Bills in payment for Butcher's meat in Market, at par with specie. Tried before the Honorable Superior Court, in the County of Newport, September Term, 1786. Also, The Case of the Judges of said Court, before the Honorable General Assembly at Providence, October Session, 1786, on citation, for dismissing said complaint. Wherein the Rights of the People to Trial by Jury, etc., are stated and maintained, and the Legislative, Judiciary and Executive Powers of Government examined and defined. By James M. Varnum, Esq., Major General of the State of Rhode Island, etc., Counsellor at Law, and member of Congress for said State. 4to. pp. iv. and 60. *Providence. John Carter.* 1787.

—— Discourse on the death of, see *Browne.*

VAIL, REV. THOMAS H. Catalogue of the Pawcatuck Library, with forms of regulations, hints on reading, etc.
8vo. pp. 120. 1848.
Prepared at the request of Mr. H. Barnard, intended as a model catalogue and the evident result of labor and research.

VINTON, REV. FRANCIS. Loyalty and Piety. A Thanksgiving Discourse. (See *Constitution.*)

—— A Remembrance of Former days; being a farewell

discourse to Trinity Church, Newport, R. I., preached on the Fifth Sunday after Trinity, July 7, 1844.
8vo. pp. 33.   Providence. Samuel C. Blodgett. 1844.

VINTON, REV. FRANCIS, D. D. An Oration on the Annals of Rhode Island and Providence Plantations; and a Rhyme of Rhode Island and the Times, by William George Curtis, Esq. Delivered before the Sons of Rhode Island in New York, May 29, 1863.
8vo. pp. 80.   New York. Printed for the Association. 1863.

This oration was also delivered in Providence and Newport. It abounds in historical facts, and is copiously illustrated with notes of great interest and value.

VINCENT, P. A True Relation of the late Battell fought in New England, between the English and the Pequot Salvages. In which were slaine and taken prisoners about 700 of the Salvages, and those which escaped, had their heads cutt off by the Mohocks: With the present state of things there.
4to. pp.   London. Printed by Thomas Harper, for Nathaniel Butler and John Bellamie. 1638.

——— The Same.
Massachusetts Historical Collections, 3d series, vol. VI.

A VINDICATION of Public Justice and of Private Character, against the attacks of a "Council of Ministers," of the "Methodist Episcopal Church."
8vo. pp. 51.   Providence John Miller. 1823.

ALMSLEY, AMASA E. Life and Confession of, who was tried and convicted of the murder of John Burke and Hannah Frank, in Burrillville, (R. I.) Sept. 11, 1831, and sentenced to be hanged on Friday, June 1, 1832. Taken from his own mouth in the presence of Stephen Wilmarth, Jailor.
8vo. pp. 16.   *Providence*, 1832.

WALKER, vs. MARTIN. Succinct account of the Case Sarah Walker vs. John Martin, in which a system of Spunging and Fraud is exposed. With an appendix by John Martin, Broker.
8vo. pp. 36.   *Printed for the author*, 1827.

WAITE, DANIEL. An Address delivered before the Mutual Humane Working Class Association, March 15, 1830.
8vo. pp. 8.   *Providence. Marshall & Hammond.* 1830.

WARD, HENRY. A Letter to the Freemen of the State of Rhode Island, dated Providence, April 11, 1789.
A broad side asking the votes of the Freemen for the office of Secretary of State.

WARD, SAMUEL. Life of, by William Gammell. (Spark's American Biography, vol. 19.)

——— Memoir of. By Charles H. Dennison. Printed in the Narragansett News, Westerly, R. I., 1859.

———— [A Letter addressed to the Hon. Stephen Hopkins, Esq., in reply to his letter to the People of Rhode Island, dated March 31, 1757.] Without title page.
Folio. pp. 4. *Dated Newport, April* 12. 1757.
For notice of the controversy between Ward and Hopkins. See *Hopkins*.

———— Sermon on the death of, March 27, 1776. See *Stillman*.

WARE, HARRIET. Memoir of. First Superintendent of the Children's Home, in the city of Providence.
12mo. pp. v. and 151. *Providence. G. H. Whitney.* 1850.

WATERMAN, HENRY. A discourse preached in St. Paul's Church, Pawtucket, before the 50th annual convention of the Protestant Episcopal Church, in Rhode Island, June 9, 1840.
8vo pp. 24. *Providence. B. Cranston & Co.* 1840.

———— An Address delivered in St. Stephen's Church, Providence, R. I., on Wednesday, Sept. 1, 1853, at services held in commemoration of the late Rev. Samuel Penny, Rector of Emanuel Church, Manville, R. I.
8vo. pp. 27. *Providence.* 1853.

WATERMAN STREET BAPTIST CHURCH, Providence. A Brief History of; with articles of Faith, Church Covenant, Rules and Regulations, and List of Members.
12mo. pp. 34. *Providence. Knowles, Anthony & Co.* 1857.

THE WATER PROJECT. A few plain suggestions to the Taxpayers of Providence. By an old inhabitant.
12mo. pp. 10. *Providence. H. H. Brown.* 1853.

WATERS OF THE STATE. Report of the Special Committee of the General Assembly relative to the deleterious substances deposited in the public waters of the State. By Prof. Geo. I. Chase.
8vo. pp. 8. *May.* 1860.

———— See, also, Examination by chemical analysis, &c.

WAYLAND, FRANCIS, D. D., President of Brown University.

Address delivered before the Providence Association for the promotion of Temperance, October 20, 1831. Also the First Report of the State Temperance Society.
8vo. pp. 20 and 4. *Providence. Weeden & Knowles*. 1831.

―――― A Discourse delivered at the dedication of Manning Hall, the Chapel and Library of Brown University, Feb. 4, 1835.
8vo. pp. 40. *Providence. Marshall & Brown*. 1835
To this Discourse are appended historical notes.

―――― A Discourse delivered at the opening of the Providence Atheneum, July 11, 1838.
8vo. pp. 57. *Providence. Knowles, Vose & Co*. 1838.

―――― An Address before the Rhode Island Society for the Encouragement of Domestic Industry, October 6, 1841.
8vo. pp. 33. *Providence. B. Cranston & Co*. [1841.]

―――― The Affairs of Rhode Island. A Discourse delivered in the Meeting House of the First Baptist Church, in Providence, May 22, 1842. 1st and 2d editions.
8vo. pp. 32. *Providence. B. Cranston & Co*. 1842.

―――― A Discourse delivered at the First Baptist Church, Providence, R. I., on the day of Public Thanksgiving, July 21, 1842.
8vo. pp. 31. *Providence. H. H. Brown*. 1842.

―――― A Discourse in commemoration of the Life and Character of the Hon. Nicholas Brown, delivered in the Chapel of Brown University, Nov. 3, 1841.
8vo. pp. 30. *Boston. Gould, Kendall & Lincoln*. 1841.

―――― The Death of the Believer. A Sermon preached in the Chapel of Brown University, June 30, 1850, the Sabbath after the decease of Mrs. Ester Lois Caswell, wife of Professor Alexis Caswell. (Private printed.)
8vo. pp. 29. *Providence. Joseph Knowles*. 1850.

―――― A Discourse in Commemoration of the Life and Services of William G. Goddard, L. L. D. Delivered at the request of the Faculty, in the Chapel of Brown University, March 12, 1846.
8vo. pp. 31. *Providence. B. Cranston & Co*. 1846.

—— Address delivered at the dedication of the new School House in District No. 1, North Providence, October 31, 1846, and the Remarks of the Rev. Mr. Osgood and Mr. Bishop on the same occasion.
8vo. pp. 16.   *Pawtucket. Gazette & Chronicle Press.* 1846.

—— Report to the Corporation of Brown University, on the changes in the System of Collegiate Education, read March 28, 1850.
8vo. pp. 76.   *Providence. George H. Whitney.* 1850.

—— Address before the R. I., Society for the Encouragement of Domestic Industry, and the R. I., Horticultural Society, at their Second Annual Exhibition in Providence, September 12, 1851.
8vo. pp. 27.   *Providence. Knowles, Anthony & Co.* 1852.

—— The Introductory Discourse delivered before the American Institute of Instruction, at their twenty-fifth annual meeting in Providence, R. I., Aug. 8, 1854.
12mo. pp. 35.   *Boston. Ticknor & Fields.* 1855.
Pertains to Rhode Island History.

—— A Discourse in commemoration of the Life and Character of Moses Brown Ives.
8vo. pp. 25.   *Providence. Knowles, Anthony & Co.* 1857.

—— A Discourse in commemoration of the Character and Services of the Rev. James Nathaniel Granger, D. D., Pastor of the First Baptist Church in Providence, Sunday, January 18, 1857. Also an Address delivered at the Funeral of Dr. Granger, January 8, 1857. By the Rev. Alexis Caswell, D. D.
8vo. pp. 48.   *Providence. George H. Whitney.* 1857.

WEBSTER, DANIEL. The Rhode Island Question. Arguments of Messrs. Whipple and Webster, in the Case of Martin Luther, Plaintiff in error, versus Luther M. Borden and others, in the Supreme Court of the United States, January Term, 1848.
8vo. pp. 56.   *Providence. Charles Burnett, Jr.* 1848.

—— The Rhode Island Question. Argument in the Su-

preme Court of the United States, in the Case of Martin
Luther vs. Luther M. Borden and others, Jan. 27, 1848.
8vo. pp. 20.   *Washington. J. & G. S. Gideon.*

WEBSTER, MRS. REBECCA GAIR. Biography of. See *Stone*.

WEIGHTS AND MEASURES. Report of the Special Committee
[of the General Assembly of R. I.] in relation to Weights
and Measures.
8vo. pp. 7.   *Providence. Knowles, Anthony & Co.* 1860.

WEST, BENJAMIN. An Account of the Observation of Venus
upon the Sun, the third day of June, 1769, at Providence,
in New England. With some Account of the Use of those
Observations. "The Course of Nature is the Art of God."
8vo. pp. vi. and 22. *Providence. Printed by John Carter,*
            at Shakspeare's Head.   1769.

The expence of the instruments to make these observations was borne by
Joseph Brown, a very respectable merchant of Providence, "says Mr.
West:" "a gentleman of a solid, active genius, strongly turned to the
study of Mechanics and Natural Philosophy, which has induced him to
construct and furnish himself with as curious and complete an apparatus
for electrical experiments as any perhaps in America, and of which he well
knows the use."

WHALLEY AND GOFFE. The Regicide Judges. Papers relating to. (Mass. Hist. Coll. 3d series, vol. VII.) See also,
Stiles' History of the Regicide Judges.

WHAT A PLOUGHMAN said about the "Hints to Farmers,"
made last April by the Men of "Trade."
8vo. pp. 33.   *Kingston.* 1829.

WHEATON, HENRY. An Oration delivered before the Tam-
many Society, or Columbian Order, and the Republican
Citizens of Providence and its vicinity, at the Town House,
on the Anniversary of American Independence, July 4th,
1810.
8vo. pp. 20.   *Providence. From the Phenix Press,*
                  (Jones & Wheeler Printers.)

——— Discourse before the Phi Beta Kappa Society of
Brown University, September 10, 1847.
8vo. pp. 54.   *Boston. Little & Brown.* 1847.

WHEATON, HON. HENRY. The Value of a Man. A Discourse occasioned by the death of, delivered Sunday evening, March, 19, 1848, in the First Congregational Church, Providence, R. I. By the Rev. Edward B. Hall, Pastor of the Church.
8vo. pp. 23. *Providence. Charles Burnett, Jr.* 1848.

―――― Notice of Mr. Wheaton's diplomatic career, and of the antecedents of his life. By Wm. Beach Lawrence. (See Introduction to Wheaton's International Law.)
8vo. *Boston.* 1855.

Henry Wheaton, son of Seth Wheaton, was born in Providence, Nov. 27, 1785, and graduated at Brown University in 1802. After being admitted to the bar, he visited Europe, and attended a Law School at Poiters, in France. On his return he commenced the practice of law in Providence, but finding the field too limited, he removed to New York. Here he published "a Digest of the Law of Maritime Captures or Prizes," and "An Essay on the means of maintaining the Commercial and Naval Interests of the U. S." In 1816, he became Reporter of the decisions of the Supreme Court of the U. S., which office he held eleven years, and published 12 vols. of Reports. His other writings are, a "History of the Law of Nations, in Europe and America;" "History of the Northmen;" "History of Scandinavia;" "Life of William Pinckney;" and an "Essay on the Progress and Prospects of Germany." But the most important of Mr. Wheaton's writings is his "Elements of International Law," which has passed through seven editions, the last two, since his death, were edited and enlarged by Wm. Beach Lawrence. Mr. Wheaton received the degree of L. L. D., from Brown University, Hamilton College, N. Y. and Harvard College, Mass. He died in Dorchester, Mass., March 11, 1848·

WHEATON, ROBERT. Memoir of, with Selections from his Writings.
12mo. pp. 385. *Boston. Ticknor, Reed & Fields.* 1854.

WHIPPLE, JOHN. Report [to the Rhode Island Legislature,] touching certain Resolutions passed by the House of Representatives of the U. S., Dec. 12, 1838, relative to petitions for the abolition of Slavery. With a letter from the Hon. Harrison Gray Otis, to John Whipple, dated Boston, March 1, 1839.
8vo. pp. 30. *Boston. Cassady & Marsh.* 1839.

―――― Speech delivered at the Whig Meeting, held in the Town House, Providence, R. I., August 28, 1837.
8vo. pp. 16. *Providence.* 1837.

────── The Rhode Island Question ; Arguments of Messrs. Whipple and Webster, in the case of Martin Luther, Plaintiff in error vs. Luther M. Borden and others, in the Supreme Court of the United States, January Term, 1848.
8vo. pp. 56. *Providence. Charles Burnett, Jr.* 1848.

────── Address to the People of Rhode Island, on the approaching Election.
8vo. pp. 16. *Providence. Knowles & Vose.* 1843.

────── A Discourse delivered before the Municipal Authorities and Citizens of Providence, July 4, 1838.
8vo. pp. 30. *Providence. Knowles, Vose & Co.* 1838.

WHITAKER, HENRY C. Poem by, at the Dedication of Lyceum Hall. Oration by Francis E. Hoppin.
8vo. pp. *Providence. Knowles, Anthony & Co.* 1859.

WHITE, GEORGE S. Memoir of Samuel Slater, [of Rhode Island,] the father of American Manufactures, with a History of the rise and progress of the Cotton Manufacture in England and America. (Portrait of S. Slater.)
8vo. pp. 448. *Philadelphia. 46 Carpenter Street.* 1836.

WHITMAN, BENJAMIN, JUN'R. The Heroes of the North, or the Battles of Lake Erie and Champlain. Two Poems. With two engravings of Battles.
8vo. pp. 24. *Boston.* 1816.

WHITMAN, SARAH HELEN. Poem, recited before the Rhode Island Historical Society, on the evening of January 13, 1847 ; previous to the delivery of Judge Durfee's Discourse.
8vo. pp. 6. *Providence. C. Burnett, Jr.*

WHITTINGHAM. Our need of more Faith. A Sermon preached at St. John's Church, Providence, August 11, 1843, at the consecration of J. P. K. Henshaw, D. D., as Bishop of Rhode Island. By the Rt. Rev. Wm. R. Whitingham, D. D., Bishop of Maryland.
8vo. pp. 32. *Providence. Burnett & Blodgett.* 1843.

WHOLESOME SEVERITY reconciled with Christian Liberty, or A True Resolution of a present Controversie concerning *Liberty of Conscience*. Here you have the question stated, the middle way betwixt Popish Tyrannie and Schismatizing Liberty approved, and also confirmed from scripture, and the testimonies of Divines, yea of whole churches. The chiefe arguments and exceptions used in the *Bloudy Tenent*. *The Compassionate Samaritaine*, M. S. to A. S. &c., examined. Eight distinctions used for qualifying and clearing the whole matter. And, in conclusion, a Parœnetick to the five apologists for choosing accommodation rather than Toleration. Imprimatur. Ia. Crawford, Decemb. 16, 1644.
Small 4to. pp. vi. and 40.   *London. Printed for Christopher Meredith, signe of the Crane, in Paul's Churchyard.*   1645.

WIGHT, REV. HENRY, of Bristol. Sermon at the Ordination of, see *Prentiss*.

WILBUR, JOHN. A Narrative and Exposition of the late proceedings of the New England Yearly Meeting, with some of its subordinate meetings and their committees, in relation to the doctrinal controversy now existing in the Society of Friends, etc. With an appendix edited from records kept, from time to time, of these proceedings, and interspersed with occasional remarks and observations. Addressed to the members of the said Yearly Meeting.
12mo. pp. 352.   *New York. Piercy & Read.* 1845.

WILKINSON, JEMIMA. History of, containing an authentic narrative of her life and character, and the rise, progress and conclusion of her ministry. By David Hudson.
12mo. pp. 208. and 20.   *Geneva, N. Y. S. P. Hull.* 1821.
Relates chiefly to the proceedings of the Friends in Rhode Island.

Jemima Wilkinson was born in Cumberland, R. I, about the year 1753, and was educated as a Quaker. She became a religious fanatic, and claimed to be invested with divine attributes. She professed to work miracles, and induced many to become her followers. In 1787-89, she and her followers removed to, and founded a colony in what is now Yates County, in the State of New York. She exacted from her followers the most complete submission and the most menial services, and exerted a powerful influence over them. She insisted on the Shaker doctrine of celibacy, and the exercises of their religious meetings resembled those of that sect. After her death, which took place on the 1st of July, 1819, at Jerusalem, Yates County, N. Y., her followers were scattered and broken up.

WILLIAMS, MRS. CATHERINE R. Biography of Revolutionary Heroes; containing the Life of Brigadier General Wm. Barton; and also, of Captain Stephen Olney.
12mo. pp. viii. and 312.
Providence. Published for the Author. 1839.

———— Fall River. An Authentic Narrative.
18mo. pp. 193.   <i>Providence. Marshall, Brown & Co.</i> 1833.

———— Tales. National and Revolutionary.
2 vols. 18mo. Vol. 2. pp. 269.
Providence. Cranston & Hammond. 1835.

———— Annals of the Aristocracy; being a Series of Anecdotes of some of the Principal Families of Rhode Island. Numbers 1 and 2.
8vo. pp. 80 and 80.   <i>Providencee. B. T. Albro.</i> 1845.

WILLIAMS. ROGER. A Key into the Language of America, or an Help to the Language of the Natives in that Part of America called New England; together with briefe Observations of the Customes, Manners and Worships, &c. of the aforesaid Natives, in Peace and Warre, in Life and Death. On all which are added spirituall Observations, generall and particular, by the Authour, of chiefe and speciall use (upon all occasions) to all the English inhabiting those Parts; yet pleasant and profitable to the View of all Men. By Roger Williams, of Providence, in New England.
18mo. pp. 216.   <i>London. Printed by Gregory Dexter.</i> 1643.

———— The same work.
Mass. Hist. Soc. Coll. 1st series, vols. 3 and 5.

———— The same work.
Rhode Island Hist. Soc. Coll. Vol. 1.

This is the earliest printed book of Roger Williams. In the Preface he says, "I drew the materialls in a rude lumpe at sea, as a private helpe to my

owne memory, that I might not by my present absence lightly lose what
I had so dearely bought in some few yeares hardship and charges among
the barbarians; yet being reminded by some, what pitie it were to bury
those materialls in my grave at land or sea."

The nation who spoke this language has long since disappeared, and
the only monuments that remain, besides this "Key" of Roger Williams,
are the translation of the Bible, by John Eliot, and the Indian Grammar, by
the same indefatigable missionary and student.

——— Mr. Cotton's Letter lately printed, examined and
answered. By Roger Williams, of Providence, in New
England.
Small 4to. pp. 47. Dedicatory 2 pages.
London. Imprinted in the yeere 1644.

In his dedicatory address the author thus gives his reasons for publishing this
"Letter:" This Letter I acknowledge to have received from Mr. Cotton
(whom for his personall excellencies I truly honour and love.) Yet at
such a time of my distressed wanderings amongst the Barbarians, that
being destitute of food, of cloths, of time, I reserved it (though hardly,
amidst so many barbarous distractions) and afterward prepared an answer
to be returned."

"In the interim, some friends being much grieved, that one publikely
acknowledged to be godly and dearly beloved, should yet be so exposed to
the mercy of an howling wildernesse in frost and snow, &c., Mr. Cotton
to take off the edg of Censure from himself, profest both in speech and
writing, that he was no procurer of my sorrows.'

"Some letters then passed between us, in which I proved and exprest,
that if I had perished in that sorrowfull Winter's flight; only the blood of
Jesus Christ could have washed him from the guilt of mine."

"His finall answer was, had you perished, your blood had beene on your
owne head; it was your sinne to procure it, and your sorrow to suffer it."

"Here I confesse I stopt, and ever since supprest mine answer; waiting
if it might please the father of mercies, more to molifie and soften, and
render more humane and mercifull, the care and heart of that (otherwise)
excellent and worthy man."

"It cannot now, be justly offensive, that finding this letter publike (by
whose procurement I know not) I also present to the same publike view,
my formerly intended answer."

The following is the title of the letter to which it is a reply:
"A Letter of Mr. John Cottons, Teacher of the Church in Boston, in New
England, to Mr. Williams, a Preacher there; wherein is shewed, that
those onght to be received into the Church who are godly, though they
doe not see, nor expressly bewaile all the pollutions in Church-fellowship,
Ministry, Worship, Government. Small 4to. pp. 13. Printed at London
for Benjamin Allen. 1643."

This work was re-published in London in 1818, by the "Hanserd Knollys Society," in connection with William's Bloudy Tenent. In it the author

vindicates the act of the Magistrates in banishing Roger Williams from Massachusetts, though he denied that he had any agency in it.

———— The Bloudy Tenent of Persecution, for cause of Conscience, discussed in a Conference betweene Truth and Peace, who, in all tender Affection, present to the High Court of Parliament, (as the Result of their Discourse,) these, (amongst other Passages) of the highest Consideration.

Small 4to. pp. 24 of preliminary matter and 247.

Printed in the year 1644.

Upon a close comparison of the two copies of this work in the Library of Brown University, printed in the same year, it is evident from differences in the type and orthography of their title pages, as well as from the headings of the chapters, that there were two editions of it. One contains a list of *errata* at the end, which is corrected in the other.

This work owes its origin to a very interesting circumstance. In the first volume of the publications of the Hanserd Knolly's Society, may be found a piece entitled, "An Humble Supplication to the King's Majesty, as it was presented, 1620." "This," says Mr. Underhill, was a Baptist production." It was a well arranged, clear and concise argument against persecution, and for liberty of conscience. It was written by one imprisoned in Newgate for conscience' sake. So rigid was his confinement that paper, pens, and ink were denied him. He had recourse, therefore, to sheets of paper sent by a friend in London, as stoppers to the bottle containing his daily allowance of milk. He wrote his thoughts in milk, on the paper thus provided, and retured them to his friend in the same way. It is well known that writing of this kind becomes legible by holding it to the fire.

From this treatise were taken those arguments against persecution, which, being replied to by Mr. Cotton, gave rise to the work of Mr. Williams, and which he has so significantly called, in reference to Cotton's views as opposed to the mild doctrines of toleration, " The Bloudy Tenent of Persecution Discussed." It was written while he was occupied in obtaining the Charter for Rhode Island. In many parts it bears evident tokens of haste, and occasional obscurities show that he had no time to amend his work. Indeed, he tells us that these discussions were prepared in London, "for publike view, in change of roomes and corners, yea, sometimes in variety of strange houses, sometimes in the fields, in the midst of travel ; where he hath been forced to gather and scatter his loose thoughts and papers." It is nevertheless considered to be the best written of all his works. The doctrines of religious freedom are fully set forth, the style is throughout animated, and the page is adorned with frequent images of great beauty. *Guild's Account of the writings of Roger Williams.*

In 1617, John Cotton published a reply to Williams' " Bloudy Tenent," entitled "The Bloudy Tenent washed and made white in the Bloud of the Lambe"; for the full title of which, see *Cotton*. To this Mr. Williams made a rejoinder, bearing the following title:

——— The Bloody Tenent yet more Bloody, by Mr. Cotton's Endevour to wash it white in the Blood of the Lambe; of whose precious Blood spilt in the Blood of his Servants, and of the Blood of Millions spilt in former and later Wars for Conscience Sake, that most Bloody Tenent of Persecution for Cause of Conscience, upon a Second Tryal, is found now more apparently and more notoriously guilty. In this Rejoinder to Mr. Cotton are principally,
1. The Nature of Persecution,
2. The Power of the Civill Sword in Spirituals,—examined.
3. The Parliaments Permission of Dissenting Consciences justified. Also (as a Testimony to Mr. Clark's Narrative) is added a Letter to Mr. Endicot, Governor of the Massasetts in N. E. By R. Williams, of Providence, in New England.

Small 4to. pp. Dedication to the High Court of Parliament, 18 pages. Ded. to the General Courts, especially that of Massachusetts, in N. England, 7 pages. To the merciful and compassionate reader, 12 pages. Table of contents, 16 pages. Text, 320. *London. Printed by Giles Calvert, and are to be sold at the Black-Spread-Eagle, at the West-End of Pauls.* 1652.

This work discusses the same great questions as the preceding, and maintains the same views, with additional arguments. "Both," says Prof. Gammell, "are pervaded with a mildness quite unusual in the controversial writings of that day, and are enriched with an amount of learning that does credit to the varied scholarship of their author.

——— The Hireling Ministry None of Christ's, or a Discourse touching the Propagating the Gospel of Christ Jesus. Humbly presented to such pious and honourable Hands, whom the present Debate thereof concerns. By Roger Williams, of Providence, in New England.

Small 4to. pp. viii. and 36.
London. Printed in the Second Moneth. 1652.

This pamphlet is extremely valuable, because it contains a clearer exposition of Mr. Williams' views respecting the ministry, than any other of his works. It begins with an "Epistle Dedicatory, to all such honorable and pious hands, whom the present debate touching the propagating of Christ's Gospel concerns; and to all such gentle Bereans, who, with ingenious civility, desire to search, what's presented concerning Jesus Christ be so or not." In this the author says of himself, " I have not been altogether a stranger to the learning of the Egyptians, and have trod the hopefullest paths to worldy preferment, which for Christ's sake I have forsaken. I know what it is to study, to preach, to be an elder, to be applauded; and yet also what it is to tug at the oar, to dig with the spade and plow, and to labor, and to travel day and night amongst English, amongst barbarians! Why should I not be humbly bold to give my witness faithfully, to give my counsel effectually, and to persuade with some truly pious and conscientious spirits, rather to turn to law, to physick, to soldiery, to educating of children, to digging, (and yet not cease from prophesying) rather than to live under the slavery, yea under the censure (from Christ Jesus and his saints and others also) of a mercenary and hireling ministry."

The purpose of the work appears to be, to oppose a legal establishment of religion and the compulsory support of the clergy. The principal points maintained are: 1. Neither the "begetting ministry" of the Apostles to the nations, nor the "feeding and nourishing ministry" of pastors and teachers, according to the first institutions of the Lord Jesus is now extant. 2. There ought to be a perfect liberty to all men to maintain such worship and ministry as they please. 3. Ministers ought to be supported by voluntary donations, and not by legal provisions.

——— Experiments of Spiritual Life and Health and their Preservatives, in which the weakest Child of God may get Assurance of his Spirituall Life and Blessednesse, and the strongest may finde proportionable Discoveries of his Christian Growth and the Means of it. By Roger Williams, of Providence, in New England. Small 4to. pp. 50.

London. Printed in the Second month. 1652.

The Epistle dedicatory to the Hon. the Lady Vane the younger, fills 4 pages, and that to the Christian reader, 4 pages. The work is in the form of a letter from Williams to his wife upon her recovery from a dangerous illness, beginning with "My dearest love and companion in this vale of tears."

An exact reprint of this exceedingly rare work was made in Providence, in 1862, with an Introduction by the Rev. Francis Wayland, D. D., at the expense of Samuel Randall, Esq., a descendant of Roger Williams.

——— George Fox digg'd out of his Burrowes, or an Offer of Disputation on fourteen Proposalls, made this last Summer, 1672, (so call'd) unto G. Fox, then present on R. Island, in New England, by R. W. As also how

(G. Fox slily departing) the Disputation went on, being managed three dayes at Newport on R. Island, and one day at Providence, between John Stubs, John Burnet, and William Edmundson, on the one Part, and R. W. on the other. In which many Quotations of G. Fox and Ed. Burrowe's Book in Folio are alleadged. With an Appendix, of some Scores of G. F., his simple lame answers to his Opposites in that Book quoted and replyed to. By R. W., of Providence, in N. E.

Small 4to. pp. 327. *Boston. Printed by John Foster.* 1676.

Mr. Williams, in writing this book, used a style of contemptuous bitterness which seems not to have been natural to him. Mr. Fox and Mr. Burnyeat replied in the same strain, though with more coarseness. Their Book is a quarto of four hundred and eighty-nine pages, entitled, "A New England Firebrand Quenched," &c. It would be well, says Prof. Knowles, for the reputation of all parties, if both of these works could be forgotten. In referring to this controversy, we must avoid confounding the fanatical extravagances of some of the adherents of George Fox, at that period, in New England, which were generally regarded as injurious to the morals and order of society, with the principles of the large and influential denomination of Friends, so called, at the present day. *Guild's Writings of R. Williams.*

ROGER WILLIAMS. Letter to Major Mason, dated Providence, June 20, 1670.

Massachusetts Hist. Coll. 1st series, *Vol.* I. *p.* 275.

This letter gives an account of Williams' being driven away from Massachusetts, of his settlement in Providence, and of subsequent occurrences.

—— The settlement of the first churches in Massachusetts. Account of ministers who were fixed in Salem, Charlestown, Dorchester and Boston, Watertown and Roxbury. Controversy with *Roger Williams* and Mrs. Hutchinson. Synod in 1637; and state of religion to the year 1647.

Mass. Hist. Coll. 1st series, *Vol.* IX.

—— Deposition of 1682. *Ibid.* 2d series, *Vol.* VII.

—— Letter to Governor Bradstreet, dated May 6, 1682.

Ibid. 2d series, *Vol.* VIII.

—— Letter to Governor Leverett, dated 16th, 8th mo., 1676. *Ibid.* 3d series, *Vol.* I.

—— Seven Letters of, to Governor Hutchinson, of Massachusetts, 1636 to 1638. *Ibid.*

From the Hutchinson Papers. The note which precedes them says: "The first of these letters of Roger Williams, was probably written either in August, 1636, before Endecott's Expedition, or in October after it; the second, 20th August, 1637; the third, October 28, 1637; the fourth, probably in June, 1638; the fifth, about August, 1638; the sixth, about September, 1638; all addressed to Gov. Winthrop; the seventh, to his eldest son has a full date."

———— Letters from, to Governor Winthrop, of Connecticut. (See Winthrop Papers in *Mass. Hist. Coll. 3d series, vol.* IX.)

There are twenty-four letters in this collection, written between the years 1645 and 1651.

———— Letters from, to John Winthrop, Jr., Governor of Connecticut. (*Ibid. vol.* X.)

The letters included here are from 1654 to 1660.

———— Letters from, to John Winthrop and John Winthrop, Jun'r. *Mass. Hist. Coll. vol.* 6, *4th series.*
8vo. pp. 127. *Boston. Printed for the Society.* 1863.

The earliest of these letters was written in the year 1636, from which period they extend to the year 1675. They are sixty-five in number.

———— Memoir of, the Founder of the State of Rhode Island. By James D. Knowles, Professor of Pastoral Duties in the Newton Theological Institution; with a fac simile of R. Williams' handwriting.
12mo. pp. xvi. and 437. *Boston. Lincoln, Edmands & Co.*

———— Life of, the earliest Legislator and True Champion for full and absolute Liberty of Conscience. By Romeo Elton, D. D., F. R. P. S.
12mo. pp. viii. and 173. *Providence. G. H. Whitney.* 1853.

———— An Account of the Writings of. By R. A. Guild.
8vo. pp. 11.

This pamphlet contains a full account of the published works of Williams, and has been of much service to me in preparing this bibliography.

———— Life of. By Wm. Gammell, A. M.
16mo. pp. ix. and 221. *Boston, Little, Brown & Co.* 1854.

———— Whatcheer; or Roger Williams in Banishment. See *Durfee.*

———— Account of the writings of. see *Guild.*

———— Spirit of Roger Williams. See *Johnson*.

Roger Williams was born in Wales in 1599, and was educated at Oxford. He arrived in America in 1631, and was settled at Salem, Massachusetts. In 1635, on being banished from that colony, he came to Rhode Island, where he arrived the following spring, and founded the Colony of Providence Plantations. In 1643, he was sent to England, and in the following year returned with a patent for the territory and permission to form a government. In 1651, he was again sent to England, as an agent of the colony. Returning three years after, he was chosen President of the government. He died in April, 1683, aged 84 years. Mr. Williams was the great originator of the doctrine of Liberty of Conscience in religious matters, and was a bright example of the toleration which he demanded from others. His mind was strong and well cultivated. His several works, all of which are very rare, and the titles of which are above given, are in the Library of Brown University, and also in that of Mr. John Carter Brown, of Providence.

See the anonymous work, entitled "Wholesome Severity Reconciled with Christian Liberty," which is mentioned on page 274.

WILLIAMS, THOS. A Sermon on the Conclusion of the Second Century, from the settlement of the State of Rhode Island and Providence Plantations. By Thomas Williams, Pastor of the Church, Barrington, R. I.

8vo. pp. 32. *Providence. Knowles, Vose & Co.* 1837.

———— A Discourse on the Life and Death of Oliver Shaw. 12mo. pp. 39. *Boston. C. P. Moody.* 1851.

WILSON, JAMES. An Oration, delivered before the Providence Association of Mechanics and Manufacturers, at their Annual Election, April 14, 1794. By James Wilson, Co-Pastor of the Congregational Society on the West Side of the River.

8vo. pp. 27. *Providence. Bennett Wheeler.* 1795.

WINSLOW, EDWARD. Hypocrisie Unmasked: A True Relation of the Proceedings of the Governour and Company of the *Massachusetts* against Samvel Gorton (and his Accomplices) a notorious disturber of the Peace and quiet of the severall Governments wherein he lived; With the grounds and reasons thereof, examined and allowed by their Generall Court holden at *Boston in New England* in *November* last, 1646.

Together with a particular Answer to the manifold slanders, and abominable falsehoods which are contained in a Book written by the said Gorton, and entituled, *Simplicities defence against Seven-headed Policy, &c.*
Discovering to the view of all whose eyes are open, his manifold Blasphemies; As also the dangerous agreement which he and his Accomplices made with ambitious and treacherous *Indians*, who at the same time were deeply engaged in a desperate Conspiracy to cut off all the rest of the *English* in the other Plantations.
Whereunto is added a briefe Narration (occasioned by certain aspersions) of the true grounds or cause of the first Planting of *New England*; the President of their Churches in the Way and Worship of God; their Communion with the *Reformed Churches;* and their practice towards those that dissent from them in matters of Religion and Church-Government. Psal. 120. 3. What shall be given unto thee, or what shall be done unto thee thou false tongue? Vers. 4. Sharpe arrows of the Mighty, with coales of Juniper.
Small 4to. pp. 103. *London. Printed by Rich. Cotes for John Bellamy at the three Golden Lions in Cornhill, neare the Royall Exchange.* 1646.

The volume begins with an apology for his book in a dedication to the " Rt. Hon. Robert Earl of Warwick, Governor-in-Chief and Lord High Admiral of all those island and other plantations of the English in America," as follows:

" Were not your wisdome and experience in the great and weighty affaires of State so well known, and were yee not so much accustomed to the unjust complaints of clamorous persons, I might be discouraged to appeare in the righteous cause of the United Colonies of New England, and more especially in the behalf of the Governour and Company of the Massachusetts, to render a reason for their just and righteous proceedings against Samuel Gorton and his companions, who however, (where they are unknown) they goe here under the garb of peaceable people; yet if your Honours, and the rest of the Honourable committee shall be pleased (when more weighty employments shall give way) to peruse our last defence against the clamorous complaints, and scandalous Treatise, called, *Simplicitis defence against Seven-headed Policy, &c.*, I make no question but yee will receive full satisfaction in what we have done, and be ready to justifie our proceedings against them as godly and righteous."

Following the dedication which extends to six pages, is the "True Relation of the Proceedings of the Governor and Company of the Massachusetts" against Gorton, examined and allowed by their General Court holden at Boston in November, 1646.

——— The Danger of tolerating Levellers in a Civill State; or an Historicall Narration of the dangerous, pernicious practices and opinions, wherewith Samuel Gorton and his levelling accomplices so much disturbed and molested the severall Plantations in New England; (Parallel to the positions and Proceedings of the present Levellers in Old England,) Wherein their severall errors dangerous and very destructive to the peace both of Church and State, their carriage and reviling language against Magistracy and all Civill Power, and their blasphemous speeches against the holy things of God; together with the course that was there taken for suppressing them, are fully set forth; with a satisfactory answer to their complaints made to the *Parliament.* By Edw. Winslow of Plymouth in New England.
Small 4to. pp. 103. *London. Printed by Richard Cotes, for John Bellamy, at the three Golden Lions in Cornhill neare the Royall Exchange.* 1649.

This work is the same as the "Hypocricie Unmasked," with a different title. The Dedication to the Earl of Warwick is omitted, and in its place is a table of contents filling the two pages.

——— New England's Salamander, discovered by an irreligious and scornful pamphlet, called New England's Jonas cast up at London, &c., owned by Major John Childe, but not probable to be written by him. Or, a satisfactory Answer to many aspersions cast upon New England therein. Wherein our Government there is shewed to bee legall and not arbitrary, being as neere the Law of England as our condition will permit. Together with a briefe Reply to what is written in answer to certaine Passages in a late Booke called Hypocracie Unmasked.
Small 4to. pp. *London. Printed by Ric. Cotes, for John Bellamy, and are to bee sold at his shop at the signe of the three Golden Lions in Cornehill, neere the Royall Exchange.* 1647.

―――― The same Reprinted in
                    Mass. Hist. Coll. 3d series, vol. 2.
WOODBURY, REV. AUGUSTUS, Chaplain of the Regiment. A Narrative of the Campaign of the First Rhode Island Regiment, in the Spring and Summer of 1861. Illustrated with a portrait [of Gen. Burnside,] and a map.
12mo. pp. 260.   *Providence. Sidney S. Rider.* 1862.

―――― The same work on large paper, 50 copies printed.

―――― Oration delivered before the M. W. Grand Lodge of Rhode Island, at Newport, June 25, A. L. 5860.
8vo. pp. 12.   *Providence. Cooke & Danielson.* 1860.

―――― The Preservation of the Republic. An Oration delivered before the Municipal Authorities and Citizens of Providence, July 4, 1862.
8vo. pp. 23.   *Providence. Knowles, Anthony & Co.*

WRIGHT, REV. LUTHER. Sermon at the installation of. See *Noyes.*

OUNG MEN'S CHRISTIAN UNION. Annual Reports of the President and Directors of the Young Men's Christian Union, presented to the Corporation, from 1854 to 1859.

YOUNG LADIES' HIGH SCHOOL. Exercises at the Reunion of, in Providence, R. I., February 5. 1858; with a brief notice of its founder. [John Kingsbury.]
8vo. pp. 36. Portrait of Mr. Kingsbury.
Providence. George H. Whitney. 1858.

YOUNG MEN'S CHRISTIAN ASSOCIATION, BRISTOL. Constitution and List of Officers of. Organized December, 1863.
Small 12mo. pp. 14. *Providence. Alfred Anthony.* 1863.

OMITTED IN ITS PROPER PLACE.

BROWNE, ANSEL. Wonderful Works of God. A Narrative of the wonderful facts in the case of Ansel Browne, of Westerly, Rhode Island, who, in the midst of opposition to the Christian religion, was suddenly struck blind, dumb, and deaf; and after 18 days was suddenly and comparatively restored, in the presence of hundreds of persons, in the Christian Chapel, at Westerly, on the 15th Nov. 1857. Written under his direction.
18mo. pp. 47. and portrait. *Irvinton, N. J.* 1858.

COLBURN, DANA POND. First Principal of the Rhode Island State Normal School. With a sketch of the Institution. From Barnard's American Journal of Education for March, 1862.
8vo. pp. 29.

EASTBURN, JAMES WALLIS. Yamoyden; A Tale of the Wars of King Philip, in Six Cantos; by the late Rev. James Wallis Eastburn and his Friend. Published by James Eastburn.
12mo. pp. xii. and 339. *New York*. 1820.

_{This work was written by Eastburn, in connection with the late Robert C. Sands of New York, during his residence at Bristol, as a student of divinity, with Rt. Rev. A. V. Griswold, Bishop of the Eastern Diocese, and was left in an unfinished state, at his death, December 2d, 1819. It was finished and prepared for publication by Sands immediately afterwards.}

www.ingramcontent.com/pod-product-compliance
Lightning Source LLC
Chambersburg PA
CBHW031340230426
43670CB00006B/389